AN

INSIDER'S GUIDE

TO

MAINE POLITICS

1946–1996

AN

INSIDER'S GUIDE

TO

MAINE POLITICS

1946–1996

Christian P. Potholm

MADISON BOOKS

Lanham ♦ *New York* ♦ *Oxford*

Published by Madison Books
4720 Boston Way
Lanham, Maryland 20706

12 Hid's Copse Road
Cumnor Hill, Oxford OX2 9JJ, England

Distributed by National Book Network

Library of Congress Cataloging-in-Publication Data

Potholm, Christian P., 1940–
    The insider's guide to Maine politics, 1946–1996 / Christian P.
Potholm.
        p.   cm.
    Includes index.
    ISBN 1-56833-105-3 (cloth : alk. paper).—ISBN 1-56833-106-1
(pbk. : alk. paper)
        1. Maine—Politics and government.   2. Political culture—Maine.
3. Political participation—Maine.   4. Politics, Practical—Maine.
I. Title.
JK2889.P67   1998
324.7'09741'09045—dc21   97-51622
                                                                                              CIP

ISBN 1-56833-105-3 (cloth : alk. paper)
ISBN 1-56833-106-1 (pbk. : alk. paper)

To

all those who took

the time and effort

to make Maine a better place

and especially

to Billy and Angus,

the best of the best

CONTENTS

INTRODUCTION

After having participated in Maine politics for over 25 years, I decided to teach a course on that subject at Bowdoin. As I was putting together the materials for "Understanding Maine Politics," I discovered how little had been written about the course of Maine politics since World War II.

In an effort to fill that gap, I began writing what I hope will be a scholarly book about the course of politics in Maine from 1946 to the year 2000. I hope that *Maine Politics Since World War II* will bring together the various historical strands of Maine politics in a coherent and overarching way. I want it to be very balanced, very objective, capturing the realities of this important period in an academically satisfying way. Like most of my previous dozen books, it is hard work, slow going and often difficult to write.

This is not that book.

An Insider's Guide to Maine Politics flowed rapidly and almost irresistibly into my head as I tried to write the other book. In attempting to do a scholarly, objective overview with grand themes and the limitations of focus, a writer is by necessity forced to overlook many of the minor actors and forces at work in the political arena. Indeed, the very nature of a scholarly work mandates many omissions. These omissions change the tone because one is forced to eliminate phrases and political utterances and blend trends into a more homogenized form of historical analysis.

But as I worked my way through the academic exercise, phrases, foibles, incidents, slogans, ironic utterings, sayings, obscure and not so obscure players came to mind—like corks bobbing up to the surface. They all insisted on being described. The political landscape of Maine since World War II came alive in front of me, with real people, speaking in the idiom of their subculture, appearing and demanding to be a part of the description. The result was another book altogether.

An Insider's Guide to Maine Politics is that work.

As *An Insider's Guide* developed, I did find myself coming back to a number of fundamental assumptions which provide the thematic consistency and intent of the work, a way to put the corks into patterns which make sense if you are trying to understand the sweep of politics in Maine since World War II.

First, I felt that all political participants in the Maine political process since World War II should have at least one mention—unedited and without comment—of their accomplishments. (See "The Warriors.")

I believe the political history of Maine is not just the story of the Cohens and the Muskies, the Margaret Chase Smiths and the Mitchells. It is the story of all who took time out of their daily lives to contribute to the political process. I wanted those who gave of their time and energy to seek higher office in Maine, to get some well-deserved recognition.

Many of these only ran in a single primary for Congress or governor or participated in a campaign for a cycle or two, but they were a part of that political process which is so important to the fabric of this nation and this state. The citizen-politician still epitomizes what is the very best America has to offer in terms of political participation.

I also wanted to highlight the political activists, people who may not have run for office but who, in the aggregate, made a great deal of difference in the political process and whose activities help explain why a particular candidate won an election or lost. Far too often the candidates alone get the media attention. And in terms of ballot measures—referenda and bond issues—it had been these activists more than candidates or office holders who have made major policy initiatives into law, changing in profound ways the political culture of the state of Maine.

With thousands of people involved in these aspects, it was not possible to include them all, so I ended up highlighting those who seemed to have a pattern of important participation. I chose the designation "player" for those participants who have influenced the course of both candidate and ballot measure candidates in the Maine political arena for at least five election cycles (a decade to "civilians"). I have tried not to leave anyone out, but obviously material and memory are more readily available for the 1970's, 80's and 90's than for the 50's and 60's. But if readers think I have left out any players or activists who should be included in the next edition, they should let me know.

Second, I also thought that true students of Maine politics would like to have something of the flavor of partisanship and subculture which goes on behind the newspaper articles and television coverage, and especially an appreciation of the language, word pictures and mind-sets of various interest groups.

As a professor of government at Bowdoin College for the last 25 years (and before that at Dartmouth and Vassar), I have always tried to make history and politics come alive by using real incidents, real vocabulary and real world views which help explain the course of politics.

As Ralph Waldo Emerson wrote, "The language of the street is always strong." Nowhere is this seen more keenly than in the real language of politics. Much of the insider terminology is not seen on the 6 o'clock news. I hope by giving the interested reader the terminology and especially the word play which various subcultures in Maine contribute to the political process, they will develop a deeper appreciation of the diversity of world views we have in Maine.

I believe that the language used by various subgroups in Maine reflects more than just a surface difference in speech; that language often illustrates underlying political realities which much be addressed if one is to be successful long term in Maine politics.

Third, I wanted students of Maine politics to have some understanding of how the media, field work, polling and other aspects of campaign situations come together to influence the way candidates look at their situations and react to them.

For the past 25 years, I have been very fortunate to have participated in a great many candidate and ballot measure efforts, and I believe that the internal dynamics of those efforts is often at variance with the public and commentator views of those realities. Campaigns are not just as they are presented in the newspapers and on TV.

Even the best reporters simply do not have the inside information to capture all the nuances of campaign dynamics. Many of them are very good at anticipating outcomes and interactions, but few have been on the inside of enough campaigns to discern internal processes. How campaigns really work is often reflected in the assumptions and internal world views of the participants. Why candidates join one party or another, why one interest group supports one particular candidate and opposes another, often has more to do with these dynamics than with rational choice and cerebral activity. Even the ways in which those who participate in politics view themselves become very important in grasping the reality of electoral politics.

Fourth, I have long believed that the most fundamental distinction in politics today is—and has been for a long time—between participant and non-participant, between activist and civilian.

Republicans, Democrats, Greens and Reform party activists actually have much more in common with one another than they do with the "civilians" in that in the very act of going through a campaign they acquire insights and psychic rewards denied even the most conscientious voter or reporter.

This is true even though many partisan Democrats or Republicans or Greens or Reformers deny it with a vehemence that is truly astounding. I have listened to Republican ministers pray for the defeat of any and all Democrats! I have listened to otherwise rational people, even (or perhaps, especially) college professors, say that any Democrat candidate is preferable to any Republican. But then in the often Alice-in-Wonderland world of campus political correctness, I have also witnessed the head of the Bowdoin *Diversity Committee* stating that he could not understand how *any* 18-year-old could even be a Republican let alone believe in what Republicans believe!

But it is precisely that group of Democratic, Republican and Green activists which in fact makes the subculture of politics so dynamic, interesting and important. Because of their activism, they have much more in common with one another than they do with the rest of the population that sits and watches a lot of television and complains about the American political system but does not participate actively.

This interaction of doers is a vital part of what makes our political system work. The Maine political scene is a better place for the actions of the doers. Even if they do not always appreciate or understand their common bonds, the mutual interaction of relatively small numbers of people has greatly influenced the course of politics in Maine. *An Insider's Guide* tries especially to capture this dynamic.

Fifth, and this may be seen as a major failing for a professor of government, I am not much interested in how the government of Maine runs. This lack of interest contrasts with the point of view of most articles and books about politics that tend to focus on the personalities of public figures or on the way in which government is supposed to or actually does work. My interests have always been in the electoral process. Who gets elected and why? Why does one candidate win and another lose? Why does one interest group elect its candidates and another fail? Why do some causes succeed at the ballot box and others go down to defeat? What role do personality, ethnicity, and various coalitions play in getting someone elected? What are the dynamics that puts one person or group in the winner's circle and another waiting for the next election?

This book tries to capture some of the interplay of personality, advertising, polling and time which help the interested reader know more about what actually happened and why. I am not much interested in what happens after people get elected or their causes are enshrined in law. I am not interested in the lawmakers and the elected officials as elected officials. I *am* very interested in the complicated and fascinating process by which they get elected or their causes triumph.

Sixth, understanding this dynamic has always made me more aware of the malleability of the political process.

This malleability is very important because I am always struck with how easily the public and press accept what happens in politics *as something which had to happen.* Once an election is over, most people and most reporters accept these *fait accompli* as givens. With self-fulfilling hindsight, most people conclude that what happened was going to happen no matter what the other candidate or interest group did. This bias of inevitability runs very counter to my sense of historical malleability.

I know of many situations in Maine politics in which one candidate won because of things he or she did while the campaign was in process— perhaps more often what they did early in the campaign rather than later, but what they did nevertheless. I know of many ballot measures which passed because of what their campaigns did or which failed because of what they didn't do.

There is nowhere near as much "inevitability" in Maine politics as the pundits, historians and even many pollsters would have you believe. What happened did not necessarily have to happen. What did occur was the result of many interactions, often over a considerable period of time, many of which could have gone another way (or two).

Seventh, I have always found politics to be humorous.

Some of the funniest things imaginable occur when otherwise sane men and women decide they want to run for public office. Some of the truly ironic and humorous things happen behind the scenes in politics. Without straining too much, I therefore wanted this account to be humorous. Politics is fun and often hilarious. It should be fun. Politics mirrors the human condition and there is plenty of humor in that. Nearly everybody who participates does humorous things. Even the most serious cause or campaign does silly things. Nicknames help us appreciate the way in which we look at others and others look at us. Nicknames also help us to see ourselves.

Few articles or books capture this sense of play and fun which is so much a part of Maine politics. In this study, I've tried to poke as much fun at myself as at others, and I've tried to portray the amusing aspects and foibles of others in a way which avoids meanness. At the same time, there are some very pompous people in Maine politics. Many commentators know very little about what they pontificate upon and I have tried to capture some of their absurdity as well.

To paraphrase General Leonard Wood, "Public people must expect public abuse." This should apply to commentators, pundits and talking heads on television as much as to the candidates and their supporters. There is much humor in Maine politics and I have tried to capture some of it as I have listened to the unfolding of politics over the last 25 years and have studied the course of Maine politics since World War II. I have left out the crueler and more obscene of the nicknames but I have included those which I have heard and which make a political point by their utterance. Insiders, including candidates, do talk differently when the cameras are not rolling and the microphones are not on. To capture the flavor of the insider's game, I have sacrificed some political correctness on the altar of reality.

When I was a junior in high school, I had a truly outstanding history teacher who taught Modern European History by using key terms. Maura G. Sullivan insisted we learn the terms and be able to "identify, explain and apply" them. I found it a method to be of lifelong value and have used it here, taking political terms, identifying where they came from and explaining them and applying them by using short "quotations." Unless noted otherwise, these quotations are for illustrative purposes only and obviously are not to be considered as historical utterances. If any seem to have the ring of authenticity about them, that authenticity is not found in time or space but in the mind and heart and eye of the beholder! But boy they were fun to write and I learned a lot writing them.

Eighth, speaking of abuse (deserved and otherwise) and humor, I must confess, I have no real interest in the Maine Legislature and no room in this already long book to tackle that subject.

This lack of interest quite naturally rules out many opportunities to have fun at the expense of the political process, but one human can only do so much. Although a lack of interest and experience do not normally deter determined writers, I have stayed away from the Legislature *qua* Legislature. This took a lot of self-control.

In 30 years of consulting, I have been fond of saying, "I don't do the Legislature" and "I don't do fund-raising." However, I have not avoided the Legislature altogether. Occasionally driven by the need for college tuition payments, or having children in college who wanted to do something with their friends on a Tuesday morning, I have packed a few hearing rooms (or even the Augusta Civic Center) in conjunction with Edie "Wonder Woman" Smith, Lillian "Diamond Lil" Caron and George "SAM I AM" Smith. But that was just for a change of pace. Generally speaking, certainly in recent times, legislators aren't terribly important to the course of Senate or Congressional or gubernatorial elections and of even less consequence when it comes to ballot measure campaigns. Few of them believe this observation but it is true nevertheless. At the same time, the Legislature as an incubator of talent for the worlds of Congress, governor and U.S. Senate is important.

In this work, I have tried to capture the importance of those political figures who come out of the Legislature into the arena which does interest me: namely the races for Congress, U.S. Senate and governor. Every once in a while, I had to bring in some Maine legislative background to make sense of subsequent events in the other races.

For example, without knowing the legislative background, the inside baseball if you will, how could anyone understand how liberal state Senator Ben Katz could support conservative Jim Erwin in the 1974 gubernatorial primary and not the moderate/liberal Harry Richardson? Because Jim Erwin was nicer to him than "Snort" or "Fat Albert" is probably the simplest and least ideological explanation.

Ninth, I really wanted readers to capture a bit of the spirit and agendas of the "scorps," the men and women who report on Maine politics, and especially to give readers a sense of what the reporters look like from the inside of a campaign.

I guess most Maine readers of daily and weekly newspapers would, if pressed, indicate that this reporter or that one "liked" or "disliked" a particular candidate, philosophy, even a party. I doubt, however, that most would have a systematic list of those reporters in their heads and the extent to which many do have biases which influence the way they report "the news" and the extent to which they are "receptive" to "news" from one camp or the other.

Yet most political insiders carry such a list in their heads, and rightly or wrongly, campaign judgments are made precisely because of those perceptions. I have known of a number of press secretaries who got their jobs in large part because they could "deliver" a particular reporter to their campaign. Reporters may think they are regarded as completely "neutral" or "objective." Few are and fewer still are regarded as such by political operatives.

I do believe that many—even most—political reporters in Maine do a good job in trying to be balanced in their reporting but not all accomplish this goal. To political insiders, the reporters often are seen as simply reflecting the editorial biases of their newspapers. Whether they are told to favor a particular candidate or cause or not, they often appear to do so.

For example, the 1996 campaign for U.S. Senate provided a very clear instance of this. Two major campaigns based their strategies on their perceptions that the two largest daily newspapers in the state were backing two different candidates for the U.S. Senate. One campaign struggled for ten days to right itself after it got the worst of the press exchanges of charges and counter-charges.

During the fall of 1996, the Democratic Senatorial Committee in Washington hired a person to look into the background of Susan Collins, the Republican candidate for Senate. On that, the two largest newspapers of the state, the *Bangor Daily News* and the *Portland Press Herald*, and their chief political reporters agreed.

But beyond this, the papers differed widely. The *Bangor Daily News* (BDN)—which had endorsed Collins in the Republican primary and would endorse her in the general election—carried a number of stories indicating that the Democrats had hired a "private eye" to "dig up dirt" on Collins. The *Bangor Daily News* political reporter John Day, receiving a good bit of information from the Collins camp, wrote a very strong piece about the worst case assumption of Democratic skullduggery, and that piece, labeled "analysis," appeared on the front page with blaring headlines.

If you read the BDN, you might assume that this courageous young woman was being stalked by an unscrupulous dirt digger and you could not help but feel sympathy with her and question the motives of her Democratic opponent, Joe Brennan. Brennan, the story suggested, either knew about the effort and gave it his blessings, didn't know about the effort and was thus something of a pawn to political forces beyond Maine borders, or did know about it, tried to stop it and was ineffective. With any of these three assumptions, Joe Brennan looked bad.

But in an almost mirror image, the *Portland Press Herald* (PPH), which had supported Joe Brennan in the primary (having previously compared him favorably to FDR!), and would vigorously endorse him in the general election, had its political reporter, Steve Campbell, do the story from a different angle. Campbell talked extensively with the Brennan campaign and ended up with a story which not only totally exonerated Joe Brennan, it made Collins look like a crybaby, someone not up to the task of running for major office. It also made the BDN reporter look like a not-so-closet supporter of Collins (in contrast to the "objective" *Portland Press Herald* reporting team).

Indeed, if you read the *Portland Press Herald*, you would have thought that the Democratic Senatorial Committee, itself a paragon of virtue, had paid some chap good hard cash to fly up to Maine and spend time in the local library doing research of the most benign and scholarly nature! In the process, Steve Campbell took an unusual and powerful shot at his counterpart at the BDN, John Day. The shot was so hard that I have always thought it was lucky for Day's continuing career at the "Bangor Deadly" that Collins won the election.

Now, if you were already a supporter of Collins as you read about the story, you probably tended to believe the BDN. If you were already a supporter of Brennan, you tended to believe the PPH. If you had been undecided, depending on the paper you read, you may have been more inclined to believe the story you read rather than the story you did not.

But to political insiders, there was a definite and longstanding pattern here. The BDN usually favors Republicans (and an occasional conservative Democrat such as John Baldacci or an independent such as James Longley, Sr.). On the other hand, the PPH now usually favors Democrats (and an occasional moderate Republican). The editorial page editor of the BDN, Mark Woodward, and the editorial page editor of the PPH, George Neavoll, have definite points of view, the former tending to be conservative and Republican in nature, the latter tending to be more liberal and Democratic in nature.

To insiders, the fact that their two top political reporters come at political "reality" from different points of view as well is not surprising. Even when trying to be "objective" and "balanced," political reporters tend to favor one candidate or cause over another. Political insiders were not surprised when both papers subsequently endorsed the candidates they had presented in the best light. Interestingly enough, in 1997, Mark Woodward, managing editor of the BDN, became communications director for Senator Collins!

Now it is very true that in the newspaper subculture, editorial pages and news stories are supposed to be separate. There are undoubtedly editors who keep them separate. Certainly, there are also independent reporters who would rebel at the notion of doing a story with a slant they got from their editor. But to insiders, it is very hard to believe. In any case, enormous amounts of campaign time—not just on candidate but on ballot measures—are spent on the assumption that there is a connection between coverage and editorial position. Rightly or wrongly, campaign operatives are delegated to try to put pressure on either editor or reporter in order to "to work the refs."

Over the years, print reporting has diminished somewhat in terms of importance due to the rising impact of TV and radio. Radio especially is often overlooked as a medium where many people listen as they are in their cars every day. Thus radio stories which may lead or drive print stories can have considerable import for campaigns. But to most political insiders, it is the print piece which hangs around the campaign headquarters and calls out for action more often than not.

What I have tried to do in this book is to include the major political reporters and commentators who deal with political campaigns and to indicate not only what I think their point of view is, but how easy they are to spin, that is, give information to the reporters about a given campaign which is favorable to one's cause or candidate.

But a word of caution. *"Spinnable" is not necessarily a negative adjective.* A reporter who cannot be spun usually has such a definite personal or ideological point of view that he or she will not take in countervailing information or opposing interpretations. As a campaign operative, you should be able to spin or influence a reporter toward your point of view *if* you have strong, factual or fast-breaking new evidence. You should be able to spin a reporter if that reporter does not have a closed mind—or if he or she has not already written the story when they call you. Many consultants believe, quite rightly I think, that many times political reporters have "a story" already in mind or actually down on paper when they call you, and they are just looking for confirming evidence or quotes which can be made to seem to support their existing reportage.

I would argue that a reporter who can be spun is probably a better reporter than one who can't or won't be spun. A reporter who is "unspinnable" is simply not as good a reporter as one who can be spun with facts and solid analysis. Many times in my career, I have been called by reporters who already had their story written and who not only didn't want new information, they didn't want any information which did not fit the thrust of their story. In fact, they refused to accept new information which ran counter to the prevailing thrust of their piece! Really good and accurate stuff was deliberately left out of the story because the new material did not support the reporter's existing central conclusions.

Also, it has been my overall experience that most Maine reporters, whatever their personal beliefs and biases, generally tend to do a pretty good job. Take Nancy Perry of the Portland papers. I have always found Nancy to be a fair reporter when dealing with me and she generally writes a pretty balanced account of what is going on in a campaign. But in the 1994 gubernatorial contest, Nancy got it into her head early that Angus King could not be governor—or should not be governor—I was never sure of which.

Before and since, Nancy has been far more balanced in her political coverage and I have a high regard for her overall reporting objectivity and ability. But for the 1994 campaign at least, her point of view transcended the realities on the ground and therefore, I believe she missed much of the surge for King, especially that in the Lewiston-Auburn area, an area which eventually turned out to be one of the differences which gave the hotly contested election of 1994 to Angus King.

Again it should be noted that the *Portland Press Herald* endorsed Joe Brennan for governor in the primary and would again in the general election. There was probably absolutely no connection between the endorsements and the reporting but in the hothouse atmosphere of a campaign, it was more than possible to believe there was.

All I know is, I was never able to "spin" Nancy Perry toward the reality that King *could* eventually become competitive and that there was no *a priori* reason why an independent *could not* win in 1994. I never asked her to believe that King *was* going to win, only that he *could* win.

So in this book, I have tried to have a little fun with reporters (see "Scorps") in Maine and I have high hopes that most of them will be as good at taking any little humorous jabs as they are at giving them out. Most reporters I have met in Maine tend to be pretty good about taking what you dish out verbally. Many in fact take abuse as a compliment as long as it is delivered verbally and in private. Since they always have the last word in print, they may have a relaxed view of such criticism. Then again, they may not. We'll have to wait for the reviews, for once again they'll have the last word!

I believe that as a class, in public, reporters do get something of a free ride from other reporters and the general range of pundits, so there will be more than a few references to reporters who have tried to give the appearance of objectivity but in fact who had—and have—an agenda. So I've tried to give reporters a view of how at least one observer and consultant looks at them and their methods of operation.

Tenth, this book is also somewhat different in that it tries to capture the various subcultures of Maine which interact on various political planes.

I am a great believer in the interaction of the various demographic and psychographic groups of Maine. Many popular and scholarly accounts of what happens in Maine politics miss this interplay. That is why I have included so many words and phrases from the various subcultures, believing that even if you find someone's point of view—or assumptions— insupportable, you must accept that the subcultures themselves have a life of their own.

Politics is not just about Republicans, Democrats, Reformers, Independents and Greens. It is not just about northern Maine and southern Maine. It is not just about rich and poor. It is about the way ordinary men and women look at political events through the eyes of their socio-economic, demographic and especially psychographic subcultures.

Maine society has a number of powerful subcultures which shape and provide world views for their members. These subcultures need care and feeding if you are going to be successful in Maine politics over a long period of time. There are not two Maines but a dozen or so.

Some that we have tried to highlight in this work include the "Ma Mères," the middle-aged and elderly Franco-American women who are such an important swing vote; the "GOBs," the good old boys for whom hunting and fishing and SAM provide symbolic references of note; and the "Cruel Yuppies," who, whether they are Republicans, Democrats or Independents, want "cutters" of government rather than "protectors" of government programs in their candidates and vote accordingly.

There are also the "Style Yuppies" who vote their class in terms of political style, choosing Jock McKernan over Joe Brennan and Tom Andrews over Dave Emery (but Olympia Snowe over Tom Andrews). The urban blue-collar subculture too is important, providing bedrock support for Joe Brennan and Dave Emery over a long period of time. The farming and small-town communities with their Grange referents continue to play important roles in close elections, choosing candidates such as Jim Longley over Duke Dutremble, and Susan Collins over Joe Brennan.

Maine politics really has a great deal of point-of-view diversity if you only know where to look for it. I hope we have included enough material to make these subcultures come alive for the reader in the way they are so very real to anybody who wishes to master the operative political culture of Maine. Their language of political expression is important; their political idiom is about more than words, it is about attitudes and expectations.

Eleventh, there is also the question of the hubris of the title of this book.

I really had to deal with that question myself as I conceived of and then wrote this book. How can any person claim to write an "insider's" guide? Can anyone really be an "insider" in Maine politics and still write convincingly about it? All I can say is that in putting myself in that position, I have tried to avoid the "Bishop Homer Tomlinson" syndrome and I have asked for, and received, a lot of help on getting the inside stuff right.

Who is Bishop Tomlinson and why is he such a good measuring stick?

When I was a young lad, Bowdoin College was not coed and the Maine winters were both long and dull. Most of us did not have cars in those days so that even skiing expeditions were rare. In that context it was necessary to bring in outside entertainment. My senior year, we heard about, and invited, Bishop Homer Tomlinson, self-proclaimed "King of the World" and a regular candidate for President on the Theocratic Party ticket to our dull midwinter campus. Tomlinson actually ran for President of the United States in 1952 after a 21-day fast, but we didn't know that at the time.

The bishop was a very kindly gentleman in his late 70's who traveled around the world by bus and boat, carrying with him a small aluminum collapsible seat which he called his "throne" and a silver paper crown. He had proclaimed himself King of Russia in Red Square much to the bemusement of Soviet authorities in 1958 and puzzled others in Ethiopia, Yugoslavia and 99 other countries by the time he came to Bowdoin.

"Crowds greeted me everywhere," he said.

Perhaps only in a Bowdoin winter of the 1960's would he have much appeal but we did make a lot out of him at the fraternity. We laid on a big dinner (an excuse to get the cook to do roast beef, as I remember), and treated him like, well, a king, cheering wildly at his installation. We had a very powerful punch for special occasions like this. He crowned himself king in the student union and he was carried off on the shoulders of the football team to the stirring strains of "Onward Christian Soldiers."

The old duffer was pleased beyond words and tears came to his eyes when he told us how much better we had treated him (clapping and cheering when he put the crown on his head) than those louts down in Cambridge. "They were rude to His Majesty at Harvard" was all we could get out of him but not to worry, we were told, the real people had showed up in "great numbers" when he arrived in Harvard Square.

The recollection of all those people bustling about in anticipation of his arrival brought a smile to his face, surpassing, no doubt, the rudeness of those Harvard chaps who, we all knew even at that early age, were not up to the challenge when it came to basic humanness.

Now, all those people were undoubtedly in Harvard Square to begin with and would have been there whether His Majesty was there or not, but in his mind, they were there because he was there. I don't know what the exact scientific term for it is, but people who take things literally in this way are not exactly all there, for reality does not always depend on one's presence, real or imagined. Still, if everywhere you went there were a lot of people you thought were there to see you, it might make you happy.

A lot of consultants are like Bishop Tomlinson. And I admit that on occasion, especially when pitching an account in a distant state, I may have sounded like that as well. Some political figure gets elected and would have gotten elected if the consultant had never been born, yet the consultant takes credit for the success of the candidate. It's an occupational hazard and all of us are guilty of this type of hubris to some extent (although I should note that some struggle more successfully with this than others!).

I have tried to keep ridiculously bloated claims to a minimum in this book. At the same time, I honestly believe there were some outcomes in Maine politics during the last three decades which would not have occurred had I stayed at Vassar College and practiced my magic in New York or had I continued to teach at Dartmouth and tried to influence political events in New Hampshire. In many ways, consultants only have ideas, will, concepts and game plans to offer. They can provide the conceptual road map to victory even though others have the harder task of actualizing the plan. Consultants also sometimes provide the will to adopt a tactic or strategy that gets a candidate to see the stark choices in front of them and the ramifications of one course of action or another.

In candidate races, of course, the candidates themselves are the ones who act on the good advice (and avoid bad advice) and carry it out. Only they can make even the best ideas come true. Perhaps the best way to think of it to be fair to both consultant and candidate is to think of the consultant as helping the candidate by providing him or her with the concepts, which if actualized, can help to put the candidate in a position to win. Sometimes consultants can provide very important concepts.

Consider Bill Cohen getting to Congress. Bill has been kind enough to say publicly that without me and my idea of getting him to walk across the state of Maine, he would not have made it to Congress in 1972.

He gives me too much credit.

Like all candidates, he had to do the hard work himself. I do think though that getting him to walk 600 miles from Gilead to Fort Kent not only put him in a position to win that race, but it also resulted in a shift in perceptions about what a Republican candidate was: younger, more vigorous, more moderate, closer to working men and women. But as I walked along with him one day, partway through the walk (I had promised him I would walk with him the first day, the last day and one in between) and listened to the blood and fluids from his broken blisters slosh around in his work boots, I knew in my heart it was really his effort, not my idea, which deserved the credit.

In any case, he and the walk then became the standard against which Republican candidates were measured, and the wave of successful candidates from the 1970's and early 1980's—Dave Emery, Olympia Snowe and Jock McKernan—all were more like him than previous Republican candidates and all walked to meet the voters to show they cared about the average person and wanted to hear their views directly. The walk truly changed the way politics in Maine were conducted for a whole generation.

For the record, I have indicated that in any case, the walk itself was not my idea, but that of one of my students at Bowdoin, Bob Loeb, who had seen Dan Walker walk across Illinois to capture the March Democratic primary and later get elected as governor in 1972. Walker in turn had gotten the idea from Lawton Chiles who walked across Florida in 1970 to become a U.S. Senator.

But, sitting on a park bench with Bill Cohen in Brunswick during the early summer of 1972, I guess I turned the idea into a potential feasible political reality by convincing a skeptical candidate that this was a good way to spend his summer.

Twenty years later, I played another small but, I believe, conceptually significant role in getting Angus King to a position where he *could be* elected governor. Angus might have been elected if he had followed his original strategy of waiting to do television advertising in the fall of 1994, but I doubt it.

I believe Angus was in a position to win the last 10 days of the campaign precisely because he followed my advice to advertise in the spring, creating his own "Independent Primary" which he then "won" and thus was able to frame the choices for the fall as between himself and Joe Brennan, bypassing the Republican alternative. Angus too has been kind enough to suggest that this was one of the key decisions in his struggle to become Maine's second independent governor but this in no way should be taken as diminishing his own enormous personal effort.

By following up his "victory" in the "Independent Primary" and by advertising all summer long, when the first public polls came out around Labor Day, he was in second place and thus a viable candidate who, not incidentally, had a plurality of Republican votes. For many Republican voters, by Labor Day, he had become "their candidate." I can't take credit for all his hard work or for the excellent advertising of Dan Payne or for the support he earned from thousands of Maine people all across the state.

I also believe I was one of the very few of his friends and advisors who told him that Susan Collins capturing the Republican nomination in 1994 was a good thing, not the calamity others (who had anticipated a Jack Wyman victory) were predicting. I know he thought her primary victory might well prove fatal to his chances.

Over the last 25 years, I have been most fortunate through both participation and doing tracking polling to be in a position to follow the actual—as opposed to the perceived—political careers of Dave Emery, Peter Kyros, Bill Hathaway, Mark Gartley, Jim Erwin, Ken Hayes, Pat McGowan, Hal Pachios, Barry Hobbins, Rick Barton, Leighton Cooney, Harold Silverman, Jack Wyman, Jock McKernan, Olympia Snowe, George Mitchell, Ed Muskie, Bob Monks, Joe Brennan, John Baldacci, both Jim Longleys, Tom Andrews, Susan Collins and Tom Allen, as well as many others who didn't make it to electoral office.

Thanks to the marvelous mystery predictive machines of Peter Burr and Dave Emery, and ongoing tracking, I have almost always known who was going to win before the polls closed and I have seen most turning points in most candidate races. I have enjoyed this part of politics immensely.

I also believe I have had some discernible effects on many of the referenda in Maine over the last 20 years. In terms of ballot measures, I believe I have had even more experience in gauging what happened, when and why; I also think I was at the very center of a majority of the most important ballot measure campaigns since World War II in Maine.

Ballot measure campaigns are a lot more fun than candidate campaigns and it is much easier to gauge your impact because the client is a cause or a concept, not a person who is acting much more as a free agent. Control is the key to successful ballot measures such as referenda and bond issues, and good consultants are able to achieve far more control over the outcome if they know what they are doing and can get the client to follow a potentially winning strategy.

For example, the Save Maine Yankee campaign in 1980 was the beginning of a whole new scale and approach to referenda politics. Skip Thurlow, the head of Central Maine Power (CMP), was a first-rate company manager, and I do not believe that the company has been in as good hands since, but he did not have the best political instincts and had no concept of what he was up against with the anti-nuclear activists of the early 1980's.

Without shaping the initial decisions of that campaign and especially to insist on the hiring of the firm of Winner Wagner to run it, I think the plant would have been voted down by the electorate. I was deep inside that one and at the center of every strategic decision in the campaign (as well as in the next 1982 Save Maine Yankee II campaign when Jack Havey and John Christie of Ad Media did the very effective television commercials).

I believe Bruce Reeves would have won the 1981 Elected Public Utilities Commission (PUC) referendum if I had not gotten New England Telephone to contest it. I say that categorially because without my insistance, there would not have been a serious statewide campaign mounted against the Elected PUC ballot measure. CMP was not going to and New England Telephone believed the cause was doomed before it started.

When I did an initial poll, the Elected PUC concept had the support of 70% of the people. But I convinced New England Telephone they could win and indeed showed them how to win. Most important I convinced them that without them, the measure would pass but that with them it would fail. There was then a whole team—New England Telephone, Tony Buxton, Roger Mallar and Jack Havey, who did much of the lion's share of the work on a day-to-day basis. They deserve far more credit than I for making the campaign a success. But there would have been no meaningful campaign against the elected PUC concept if I hadn't, by sheer force of will, made one happen.

I think John Cole would have made the Wild Wild East a lot tamer if I hadn't made the 1983 Moose Hunt referendum a referendum on the Wild Wild East. I'm pretty sure George Smith and I were the ones who prevented the NRA from adopting a destructive, divisive strategy which would have most likely lost the race.

To his credit, Dr. Gus Garcelon, founder of both the Sportsman's Alliance of Maine and the Natural Resources Council of Maine, although vice president of the NRA, saw that "The Maine Way" was the right way. George Smith and Jack Havey put together a very effective team to turn this most likely loss into a 60% to 40% win. Much of the credit for the success of the effort should go to Beryl-Ann Johnson and Kathy Guerin of Ad Media, who found the gorgeous hunk of a game warden, "Chuck," and turned him into a media darling, thereby changing tens of thousands of votes, especially among women in the home in the Portland Designated Market Area (DMA). In fact, after the election, I did a focus group with 15 women, and 12 of them claimed they had voted for Chuck! That didn't happen by accident.

I have to believe Bob Reny of Reny's would still have Sunday Sales bottled up in committee in the Legislature if Rett Stearns of Porteous had not come to my office with Harold Pachios. I told them both that they would never win in the Legislature given Reny's power in the Legislature on this issue, but once they took it outside the Legislature, Bob Reny would only have one vote. I believed that the people of Maine wanted to have stores open on Sunday and they would vote to do so if the situation were taken out of the Legislature and put in their hands.

I must say I was very wrong on several counts and it turned out that Bob Reny actually did have more votes outside the Legislature than I thought, as the mom and pop stores throughout the state raised the specter (see "Imaginary Horribles") of their going out of business if the measure passed! "Enjoy your *New York Times*. You won't be able to get it here anymore if this passes." That was the closest ballot measure campaign in which I have ever been involved.

Without George and Edie Smith collecting as many signatures as they did, the measure would not have gotten on the ballot. The campaign itself was ably managed by John Cleveland, Bob Cott of Creative Design did marvelous work with the media, and Rett Stearns raised enough money to make the campaign not only viable, but victorious.

In 1991, there was a $35 million bond issue for public land acquisition on the ballot. This type of bond issue had already been defeated once (and later, in 1994, would be defeated again). Hard-core environmentalists were in charge of the campaign and insistent on using posters with no humans in them ("Our members don't like to see people in the woods!").

I believe I was able to convince The Nature Conservancy people (especially Carol Baudler) that the referendum could not be won going this route. I insisted that there had to be a coalition of hunters and fishermen, those who wanted to drive their RV's and campers into "the wilderness" and even the elderly who wanted to look at the foliage from tarred roads. Without this reorientation and the polling which went with it, I'm not sure the bond would have ever passed, even though when it did pass, it did so with great gusto (see "Straits of Florida").

Again, the Maine branch of The Nature Conservancy, led by Kent Wommack and Mason Morfit (who raised the money); Roger Williams and his team at Roger Williams Advertising, including Jane Williams and Betty Angel, who did the ads; and political figures such as Pat McGowan and (then) TV host Angus King played important roles. So did Sherry Huber, who helped out on many fronts. But the basic strategic concepts critical to the eventual success rested with this political consultant and his team.

Most recently, I believe Carolyn Cosby would most likely have won The Gay Rights scrap in 1995 without some timely intervention from "Dr. Demento." I had the most incredible time getting any input into that campaign that I have ever had. I offered my services *pro bono* (always a very bad idea for a consultant!). First I was turned down by the gay men. Then I was turned down by the lesbian women. Then I was turned down by the people raising the money. Then I was turned down by the campaign coordinating committee. Only very late in the game did the campaign manager come and talk to me, and even then I had to be further vetted by their media man Will Robinson of McWilliams Cosgrove. To his credit, he saw some use for me.

Defeating the Cosby measure was a very close-run thing and heroic efforts were made by many, many people. The committee was ably led by

Pat Peard, who did a magnificent job in holding the various factions together. The Maine Won't Discriminate Committee worked very hard by raising the money necessary to fight the discrimination, by excellent and inexpensive media, by hundreds of activists and a superb field organization headed by Joe Cowie, and the courageous intervention (early, when it really mattered) of Governor Angus King. Angus didn't even want to see polling numbers, he wanted to do what he thought was right. And there were dozens of Maine Won't Discriminate volunteers who did the tracking polling so that every night the TV commercials were on, their impact could be tracked.

I would not in any way want to diminish this broad spectrum of activity, nor would—or could I—take credit for the total outcome. But in the last week of the campaign, *after everything had been done*, we were still behind and behind by 2–1 in the coastal counties of Sagadahoc, Lincoln, Waldo, Knox, Hancock and Washington counties. My insistence on creating and using the "Lobster Boy" commercial (which was superbly put together by Will Robinson) proved of considerable importance. It only ran at the very end of the campaign and was counter to everything most in the campaign wanted to use.

But the nightly tracking done by the campaign's volunteers showed its powerful theme, "It's just not Maine," coming from the angry lobsterman, turned those 2–1 margins in favor of the referendum to 60% to 40% against it in the coastal counties. Few in Maine would make the connection between my involvement and the outcome, but in my political heart of hearts I believe that without those final voter switches, the Cosby measure would have passed.

Since 1972, I have been involved in most major political ballot measure battles and when I was not on the strategic inside of them, I was tracking the progress of them. I honestly believe that no one in Maine has seen more data about more elections, both candidate and ballot measures, *as they were taking place.*

Reporters and pundits are good during and after the fact and at guessing how things are going out, and many of them, such as Mal Leary and John Day, are particularly good at picking up movement on their own, but seeing every election clearly from beginning to end puts me, I believe, in a pretty good position to say what worked and why in a particular situation.

And, did I tell you about all the people who were waiting for me and

Bishop Tomlinson at National Airport the last time we went to Washington?

There were thousands and boy, were they glad to see us!

Enough of Bishop Tomlinson and my growing resemblance to him in my advancing years. I'll let the reader judge the "insider" quality of the observations which follow, but I honestly believe that it would have been very difficult for anyone else to put together this book.

In addition to my own observations, of course, this account is based on hundred of interviews with political professionals and staff in on- and off-the-record discussions during over 20 years of politics. And, as the acknowledgment section indicates, I have had a great deal of help from a number of other longtime participants and observers of the Maine political scene. I have learned so much from so many people.

Without them, this book would never have been able to provide the wide range of insights from so many different points of view. I have included observations and inside information from a very large number of people and in the process, I have learned a great deal about Maine politicians even as I wrote about them. At the end of the book, there is a long and grateful acknowledgment section where all their contributions are noted. Dozens and dozens of people contributed thoughts, ideas, dates, and added many phrases and terms which enriched the central lexicon portion of this work.

Here I would especially like to thank Paul Mills, Maria Fuentes, Barry Hobbins, George Neavoll, Bob Tyrer, Paul Franco, Ted Curtis and Mert Henry; their contributions were truly heroic and very insightful as they read the entire manuscript at various stages of preparation and added a great deal to each successive draft.

In fact, I learned a lot more from them than they learned from me and if this work has any lasting value, it will be in large part because of their contributions. Paul Mills, for example, sent me so much material there was enough for a second book! I hope he will write it. Jim Bradley, my research assistant at Bowdoin, was also a terrific help as he worked two summers on the research and then the manuscript, copyediting, proofreading and helping out with the statistics. Ariane Bailey and Chris Stearns ably assisted me in getting the final manuscript ready for the publisher.

Twelfth, this work is written from a consultant's point of view. It is not written as a government text. Nor is it a League of Women Voters paean to democratic process. Please don't be offended by the occasional cynicism. "Do unto others as they would do unto you, but do it first" is standard operating procedure on many political levels. Politics is like a kaleidoscope: turn it a little and the color and designs change. I have chosen to turn it toward the insider players and their "gun for hire" views and away from the coloration of the League of Women Voters.

This dimension runs me smack up against what I call the "Paradox of the Consultant." Consultants prize their independence. And they love working for money. And they love their self-image as "professionals," that is, working for money. But since they get paid for services rendered, consultants can be fired. Many are. It's much harder to fire a volunteer. And most consultants know that candidates and causes may tolerate them, even like them, but they are not always appreciated. Good consultants have more than a tinge of ego to go with their cynicism. To outsiders (and especially to candidates), paid consultants may sound egotistical and didactic but in the heat of the battle, when there are really touch decisions, they do have to make more right decisions than wrong, or over time they will not be paid consultants anymore.

But consultants are also strangely appreciative of loyalty. They don't always get it. God knows they don't always deserve it, but when it comes back from political figures or causes, they certainly appreciate it. Even if they are well paid for their efforts and pride themselves on being professionals, they still like the sense that they were important to the candidate or the cause. And they like being recognized for that importance. This is especially true if that praise comes publicly and after—not before—victory had been attained. This work tries to capture this sometimes bittersweet relationship between consultant and candidates and causes.

Finally, this is also very much a work in progress.

I hope there will be future editions. I hope that everybody who reads this will accept the fact that this is meant to be a well-meaning first step. I have not consciously left out anybody who was a player in Maine politics during the last 45 years, although I have left out party chairs unless they had some discernible impact on specific races and I have not always included everyone who was a campaign manager or operative for a single race.

I, and the people who read this and commented on it extensively, have undoubtedly left out people. I apologize beforehand to them. I have tried to be fair to all participants and apologize in advance for not giving everyone the credit they deserve. I have not purposely left out anyone. If you think I have left out someone or underestimated their particular contribution, write me and I'll try to make amends in the next edition.

Let me know what other dimensions I have missed so that they can be filled in. I invite readers of this work to submit additional information—names, facts, phrases, aspects of the various subcultures—for what will hopefully be the next edition of *An Insider's Guide* to me at the Department of Government, Bowdoin College, Brunswick, Maine, 04011.

Who ran for what and who won and why and who helped them? That is the focus of my study. I hope readers will suspend some of their preexisting prejudices and assumptions (which we all have when it comes to politics) and whether they agree or disagree with aspects of this work, take it in its entirety as trying to advance our collective knowledge of how Maine politics works and why.

I hope they find the journal enjoyable and thought provoking. I hope they will truly find this "An Insider's Guide."

An adversary

is not

necessarily an enemy.

RICHARD M. NIXON

Stephen 'Steve' Abbott   Lawyer from Orono who captained the Harvard football team and who has been a campaign aide for Republican candidates such as Jock McKernan and Olympia Snowe and is now chief of staff for Senator Susan Collins.

Linda Elowitch Abromson   Mayor of Portland, golf champion, and Democratic candidate for Congress in 1990. She finished fourth in the primary race for the First District with 11% of the vote. Insiders know her for her opposition to the United States sending 5 AWACS planes to Saudi Arabia in 1980 and for her dedicated fight for basic human rights. Her husband, Joel, State Senator from Portland, led the effort to expand the state's anti-discrimination ordinance to include gays and lesbians.

Our Academic Dean   Paul A. Fullam, Colby College professor of history and senatorial candidate against Margaret Chase Smith in 1954 (getting

42% of the vote), the year Muskie won the governorship. Credited by many Democrats for help in starting the Muskie revolution. (See also "Paul 'Haze' Hazeltine" and "John C. JCD Donovan.")

AC/DC   Someone who works for both Republicans and Democrats. "She's AC/DC all the way."

Ace   As used in this lexicon, any person who, since World War II, has won at least five major elections (Congress, governor or the U.S. Senate) without a loss. The most successful aces (in order of most victories without a loss) are Olympia Snowe, Bill Cohen, Ed Muskie, Jock McKernan, Charles Nelson and Stan Tupper. Of aces with one loss, Margaret Chase Smith is the champion, winning House races in 1940 (including 4 contests in six months!), 1942, 1944 and 1946; and Senate races in 1948, 1954, 1960 and 1966.

Acid Rain   According to Governor Angus King, this is something Ohio produces and dumps on Maine, and Maine produces and dumps in the middle of the Atlantic Ocean. First discovered as a campaign issue by Senator George Mitchell in 1982, but made into a superb ad by Don Ringe for Congressman Dave Emery. Voters have yet to grasp this as an actionable issue, however.

Ad Media   Augusta-based commercial and political ad firm. President is Beryl-Ann Johnson, creative director is Jack Havey and production director is Kathy Guerin. Perhaps the most sucessful Maine ad firm in terms of political impact. Doing work for the Republican state committee in the 1960's, Independent Jim Longley Sr. in 1974 and Democrat Chuck Cianchette in 1994, Ad Media also became the premier Maine firm in terms of ballot measures, winning such diverse and truly contested efforts such as the 1982 Maine Yankee II referendum, the 1981 Elected PUC referendum, the 1983 Moose Hunt effort, the BIW Drydock referendum of 1977 and the 1984 anti-ERA campaign.

Andrew Adam   Independent candidate for governor in 1990, received 9% of the vote, probably costing Joe Brennan the election, by drawing Democratic support in Franco-American areas such as Lewiston.

Glenn Adams   Associated Press reporter, fair, objective, spinnable. Consistent.

Mary Adams   Garland, Maine, "plucky housewife" who headed the political action committee named Save Our State in the 1970's which led the successful fight to repeal the uniform property tax in 1997. Subsequently became a major conservative activist and ran for governor in 1994 finishing 6th, getting 8% of the vote in the Republican primary but carrying the counties of Piscataquis, Penobscot and Hancock. In 1996, because of her extensive grass roots experience, she was asked by opponents to lead the campaign against the forest compact and formed the PAC Stop the Backroom Deal. Vote 2C. 2C got 23% of the vote and she declared victory when her efforts and those of Johnathan Carter kept the compact total below 50% (47%).

The Adams Option   Jim Brunelle's term for the 2C option in the 1996 forest debate referendum. Named for Mary Adams of Garland who led the "Stop the Backroom Deal" group to oppose both the Green Party initiative and Governor King's forest compact. Brunell wrote "The Adams option is the know nothing approach." Two months before, "The Adams Option" had been the position of most of the entire forestry industry.

Added-Value Opportunity   A chance to get extra political mileage out of an event. "It's an added-value opportunity. Go to the funeral and talk to the scorps, they'll be there with nothing to do."

ADI   Area of dominant influence, geographic survey area created and defined by Arbitron based on its measurable patterns of television viewing. Roughly corresponds to Nielsen's DMA's (designated market areas). Maine has three ADI's: Portland, Bangor, and Presque Isle.

Advice Is Worth What It Costs   Saying of Richard Nixon. The golden credo of political consultants. "He used his brother-in-law for the media because he didn't charge anything. So he lost by 10 points; advice is worth what it costs." (See also "The Best Advice Is That for Which You Pay.")

Affirmative Action Babe   Derogatory phrase for a woman in politics who wants to be treated like a man, only better. Any female in politics who wants special treatment because she is a woman. "She really galls me; she talks about equality and no special treatment but she's really an affirmative action babe when all is said and done." (See also "Tough As Any Man and Twice As Smart.")

Afflict the Comfortable, Comfort the Afflicted   This is supposed to be the credo of reporters but many often do the reverse by revering most incumbents.

AFL/CIO   Largest trade union organization in Maine (approximately 50,000 members), now headed by Charles "Chick" O'Leary. In Maine today, the state AFL/CIO generally rises and falls with the Democratic tide and is not usually thought of as an independent variable in most races. Played a more substantial role in the 1970's and 1980's by providing campaign workers, money and organizational skills. Still can provide useful validation and numerous workers. AFL/CIO identification polls are famous with some insiders for often getting Democratic candidates such as Duke Dutremble and Joe Brennan to believe they are ahead.

The Agency   Wilmington, Delaware, political consulting firm headed by Mike Harkins and Chris Perry. Hired by Bob Monks to give Bill Cohen help in the 1972 Republican primary and was kept on by Cohen in the general election. The Agency was a very important factor in Cohen's 1972 win, especially in the primary that year. (See also "Michael 'Mike' Harkins" and "The Littlest Gunslinger.")

Aim High with Hildreth   Slogan of former governor (1945–1949) Horace Hildreth Sr. when he ran for governor again in 1958. Hildreth was one of the first Maine politicians to use television commercials extensively. This slogan was usually accompanied by images of skyrockets shooting off into the night. Of course, owning some of the TV stations didn't hurt!

Ain't Beanbag   Short version of "Politics ain't beanbag," meaning it's a rough sport with lots of contact and bruised feelings. Often used as an excuse by those who want to use negative ads. "Hey, this ain't beanbag, throw all that stuff at her at once and see how much of it sticks."

Ain't It Odd   Coastal saying used in politics ironically, often to indicate satisfaction with a planted news story. "Ain't it odd, the *Casco Bay Weekly* picked up on that theme."

Air War   TV and radio messages as opposed to field work and get-out-the-vote efforts. "We're creaming him in the air war, forget the other stuff."

Madeleine Albright   Former member of Senator Ed Muskie's staff, later ambassador to the United Nations and in 1997, Secretary of State.

All Against All   Key precinct system using regression analysis first used in Maine by Peter Burr when working on the Dave Emery campaign of 1974. Peter correctly projected the outcome as 40.1% Emery, 39.6% Kyros, thus accurately anticipating Emery's razor-thin margin of 50.1% to 49.9%. Emery and Burr worked together until 1984, when both established their own updated data banks and developed their separate ways of analysis, including nonlinear and graphical analysis techniques. By combining the results of all modern elections in every Maine town against the results of all modern elections in every other Maine town, the resulting equations are much more accurate than normal random polling. Burr has been very successful using his approach to predict the outcomes of such important referenda as the Moose Hunt, Maine Yankee I, Sunday Sales and the very close 1994 governor's race, as well as assisting the Democrats in legislative district reapportionment. Emery has used his equations more consistently on behalf of Republicans, including reapportionment and many House and Senate seats and predicting the correct outcome of the 1994 Longley–Dutremble congressional race the weekend before that election. "All against all won again, projected King the winner by noon and half the people hadn't even voted yet." (See also "Grid/Outcome System.")

All-Around Eminence Grise   Jim Brunelle's name for General William C. Lewis, administrative assistant to and close friend of Senator Margaret Chase Smith from 1940 until his death in 1982.

All Qualified Candidates Are Not Attractive and All Attractive Candidates Are Not Qualified   Wit and wisdom from 8-term Congressman Bob Hale as reported by Don Larrabee.

All the Big Mistakes Are Made Early   In most ballot measure campaigns, the big mistakes are usually made at the beginning of a campaign, often by one's closest supporters as they frame the debate incorrectly or turn a potentially successful referendum into a losing one by seeking the unattainable. "Forget October panic, with referenda, all the big mistakes are made early." (See also "October Panic.")

All the Coffins Opened   Refers to a situation when there is a political opening and people who have been out of politics for 20 or 30 years say they are thinking about running again. "When Cohen retired, all the coffins opened."

Carol Allen   (now Carol Martel-Reiss). Campaign manager for the anti-Sunday sales referendum of 1990.

Scott Allen   Political reporter for the *Boston Globe*, formerly of the *Maine Times*. A big Rolodex guy with a very sure hand when it comes to politics. (See also "Big Rolodex.") One of the fairest and hardest working reporters. Excellent balance and sense of fair play.

Thomas 'Tom' Allen   Former Democratic mayor of Portland. Received 23% of the vote in that party's primary for governor in 1994, losing to Joe Brennan, then ran for Congress in the First District in 1996 beating Dale McCormick in the Democratic primary and Jim Longley Jr. in the general election, getting 56% of the vote.

All's Fair in Love, War and Politics   Hard-core consultant's view of the way life should be on the campaign trail. Politics, love it or leave it! "I say go with the negative ad, all's fair in love, war and politics."

Almost Doesn't Count   (1) Refers to the misfortune of Waterville's Democratic mayor, F. Harold Dubord, when at the depth of the Depression in 1934, he came within 1% (1,200 votes) of upsetting veteran Republican U.S. Senator Frederick Hale. Dubord's near miss made it possible for Ed Muskie subsequently to claim the title of Maine's first popularly elected Democratic U.S. Senator in 1958 (since before 1916 the Senate had some Democrats but these were elected by the Legislature and not by direct election). Dubord became a Maine Supreme Court Justice after Muskie was elected governor.

Almost Doesn't Count   (2) Refers to the misfortune of Waterville's former Democratic Mayor Richard Dubord (Harold's son) when in the recounted 1962 Democratic gubernatorial primary he lost to Maine State Grange Master Maynard Dolloff. Dolloff in turn lost the election (after another recount) to incumbent John Reed. In 1964, this Dubord edged out Ronald Kellam to win the Democratic party nomination and ultimate legislative election to become Maine's first Democratic attorney general in 50 years. Also, Dick Dubord was one of Ed Muskie's best friends; his untimely death in 1970 may have contributed to Muskie's somewhat off-balance and ultimately futile Presidential campaign in 1972.

Alpha Wolf   The primary political operative in a group of political consultants. Powerful, aggressive and in command, the Alpha Wolf is seldom challenged in that particular circle. "I used to think it was just posturing but he really is the alpha wolf. (See also "Big Buck.")

Amazon Warmonger   Soviet press term for Senator Margaret Chase Smith for her strong support of U.S. defense budgets.

And I Eat Red Meat   Susan Collins on why Maine Republicans should choose her in the 1996 Republican primary for U.S. Senate over R.A.G. Monks and John Hathaway, both of whom said they didn't eat meat. "I'm younger, I'm energetic, I'm female and I'm not rich. And I eat red meat."

Richard 'Dick' Anderson   Former executive director of Maine Audubon and charter Brennan loyalist. Dick served under Brennan as Commissioner of Conservation. Long history of working on important environmental issues with a lot of accomplishments going back to the Public Lots effort of the 1970's. Has also been very active on many referenda such as the widening of the Maine Turnpike and the Forest Compact. Now a consultant with Barton, Gingold, Eaton and Anderson in Portland.

Thomas 'Tom' Andrews   Portland legislator who ran for Congress in 1990, winning the Democratic primary with 36.3% and the general with

60.1%. Reelected in 1992 with 65% of the vote despite being outspent by over $600,000 in his race against Linda Bean. Lost to Olympia Snowe in 1994 in race for U.S. Senate. Then became director of People for the American Way. Now a consultant in Maine and Washington.

Andro   Short for Androscoggin County, one of the most important political areas in Maine because of its swing nature and its ability to project the outcome of any statewide race. "Get her up to Andro and keep her there for a week. It's key."

Anecdotal   Individual or personal observations as opposed to polling and the law of large numbers. "It's anecdotal; I don't care if the candidate heard it in Bangor or not, we just asked 500 people all over the state and they could care less about taggets or whatever the hell they are." (See also "The Law of Large Numbers.")

Angel   The party in a coalition who will pay the bills when the campaign is over no matter how little is raised by the coalition. "Don't worry, we'll all get paid, NYNEX is the angel on this one. They want those schools wired and they're in this all the way."

Apparently the Public Doesn't Want Public Servants Anymore   Dave Rawson, after voters in 1994 chose Angus King over Joe Brennan for governor.

Arc of Uncertainty   Belt of voters from Bethel to Lincoln to Danforth whose attitudes toward the Forest Compact of 1996 determined much of the flow of that election but not its outcome, which was determined by women voters who work at home in the Portland suburbs. They had been for the Compact, giving it 51% of the vote but changing their minds the last weekend in the face of national Sierra Club ads and pulling the Compact down to 47%.

Arch Conservative   What Democrats call Republicans whom they want to push to the edge of the voting spectrum. "John Hathaway is an arch conservative."

Benjamin Arena   Ran for Congress as the Democratic nominee in Maine's old Second Congressional District in 1948, received 32.8% of the vote.

Armpit Shot   The election night photo with the candidate's arm high in the air celebrating victory. "I want to be in the armpit shot. Forget all those field people, keep them off the stage."

Lorin 'Doc' Arnold   Political reporter and columnist for the *Bangor Daily News* in the 1950's and 1960's. Along with Peter Damborg of the Guy Gannett newspapers, one of the deans of political correspondents during that era.

Arranging the Chairs   Consultant-speak for "rearranging the deck chairs on the Titanic." A useless, often dangerous job for a doomed campaign or candidate, but one worth a bit of pocket change if handled properly. "Don't look at me, I'm just arranging the chairs; everybody who could get off has already gotten off." (See also "Keeping the Store Open.")

Artifact   A fragment or portion of a poll, taken out of context and dropped to the newspapers or fund-raisers in order to create an opposite impression from what the entire poll conveys. This is most often used by losing campaigns and by consultants trying to play with the heads of the opposition. "They say he's ahead with women in Penobscot County? It's an artifact, forget about it."

As Maine Goes, So Goes the Nation   One of the most dubious of dubious political statements. Had some validity in earlier times when Maine held its general elections in September, voted Republican and saw the subsequent national elections choose Republicans. In the four closest Presidential races since World War II, however, Maine has not voted with the winner any of them. Still, it is a myth which dies hard and on the campaign trail, it is still heard.

Ash Heap of History   Where all defeated politicians and discredited consultants go but from which this book rescues them and gives them a kinder resting place.

The Ask   The point of a political fund-raising letter or direct mail piece. "Always put the ask at the end in the PS."

Assistant Purveyor of Slime   AFL/CIO president Charles O'Leary's name for John Day after Day saw traces of plausibility in FBI agent Gary Aldrich's charges of womanizing against President Clinton.

Attack Ad   Your opponent's television commercial characterized by negative attacks on the candidates, which causes you favor. This is opposite of *your* attacks on your opponents which are called "contrast ads" (See also "Contrast Ads.")

Attack Politics   Going over to the offensive by criticizing your opponent. This is best done if you are reasonably well known. If you are unknown, nobody will care about your attack. "Attack politics don't make any sense; your name ID is 4%."

David 'Dave' R. Ault   Republican candidate for Congress in 1968. Lost to Horace Hildreth, Jr. in the primary, getting 18% of the vote (but beating Gary Merrill). Later a Cohen aide.

Phyllis Austin   Believed by some consultants to be the best in-depth reporter in the state. Although she has definite points of view, her reporting is usually fair, objective, and extremely well researched even when she is writing about people and causes she dislikes. Probably puts more time into one of her feature pieces than any other reporter in Maine. Has an uncanny ability to get quotes right without using tape recorders or taking many notes. Phyllis came to Maine in the early 1970's as a State House correspondent for the Associated Press (AP). She later became a regular contributor to the *Maine Times*. Her 1972 story on Senate President Ken Macleod and his new office furniture is legendary with political insiders, remembered with awe even 25 years later. Her more recent (1996) "SAM I AM" is a classic of superb in-depth political analysis. Skeptical but always receptive to "the true gin." (See also "True Gin.")

Authority Figure   A generic type or specific individual who has the credibility to carry a particular message or promote a particular candidate.

Used in polling to find the right message senders. "Ken Curtis was a perfect authority figure for the turnpike referendum among yuppies." An authority figure may be believable for one product but not another. The Olympic champion Joanie Benoit, for example, may be very believable as a spokesperson for a sports drink or running shoe but perhaps less so for a bank, if viewers believe they would not be treated as well as she in the bank of her choice.

Auto Pilot   Not leading, just going through the motions. "For his second term, he was on auto pilot."

Avails   Short for availabilities, the TV time which can be bought. Often used by media consultants to stampede unknowing candidates into putting money up front and into their hands. "We've requested the avails but haven't placed any order yet. We'd better hurry up, the avails are going fast from what we hear. You'd better get the check here by Federal Express."

B

B-Roll Background video for TV commercials without sound. "Just use that b-roll stuff; they can imagine what seagulls sound like."

Babe Babe Dutremble, longtime Democratic mayor of Biddeford (1974–1979) and state representative (1977–1980, 1986–1994). Father of "Duke" Dutremble. (See also *"The* Duke.") Returned to the Maine House in 1996. Major power in York County and avidly courted by smart candidates of both parties.

The Baby Sitter An alleged incident involving Republican John Hathaway and a 12-year-old girl. The #1 issue of the Republican senatorial primary campaign of 1996, it sank not only Hathaway's bid for the

Republican nomination, but also that of Bob Monks, who hired a private detective to check up on the six-year-old incident in Alabama. By keeping above the fray, Susan Collins solidified her lead and won the primary going away.

Backdooring   To go around the campaign manager or chief of staff to get to the candidate or officeholder. "Don't worry, I don't care if Jackie doesn't like it, I'm good at backdooring."

Back-to-the-Earthers   Remnants of the Hippie culture of the late 1960's and early 1970's. This political subspecies is distinguished by people who have never met an organic vegetable they didn't like or a nuclear plant that they did. While scattered throughout the Pine Tree State, they can often be found concentrated in the backwaters of Waldo County, at Druid gatherings celebrating the solstice or at the Common Ground Fair passing out pamphlets protesting most aspects of modern life. "Let the back-to-the-earthers amuse and intrigue you but don't count on them voting for you." (See also "Tree-huggers.")

Bad Clients   In the world of consultants, these are men and women with egos too big to follow advice, who pay poorly and/or are never on time and who always act like their successful campaigns were due to their good looks and acumen. "At the risk of generalizing, self-made millionaires usually make bad clients."

Bad Shit   Good Old Boy (GOB) phrase for very bad news; in politics, campaign disclosures which cannot be easily or well spun. "That part about the 12-year-old boy is bad shit."

Bag Lady   Someone charged with the responsibility of picking up campaign money. In Maine politics this term does not have as negative a connotation as it does elsewhere. "She's a great bag lady; she won't leave the room without the checks."

Bag Man   Male bag lady.

Dennis 'Dennis the Menace' Bailey   One of the most effective press secretaries cum strategists of the last several decades in Maine politics.

Goes beyond a normal press secretary's function to play additional roles within the dynamics of a particular campaign. Close working relationship with Steve Campbell. One of the few people who can consistently spin that *Portland Press Herald* reporter perhaps because Bailey plays in a rock band. Worked for Representative Tom Andrews, Tom Allen and Governor Angus King. A player.

Balanced Data   Polling data which has been balanced for such demographics as sex, party affiliation or ethnicity. "You were behind on the raw data because you are doing poorly with women, but when we looked at the balanced data you were actually ahead by a little. Close the gender gap George, and you win."

John Baldacci   State Senator (D-Bangor) winner of the Democratic congressional primary in 1994 with 27% of the vote, won general election in Second district with 46% of vote. Reelected in 1996 with 72% of the vote. A major force in the Democratic party as of 1997.

Rosemary Baldacci   Smart political operative and sister of John Baldacci. His actual and de facto campaign manager in his important races of 1994.

Ballot Match-ups   The portion of a poll which puts candidates, including those who might not even be in the race, head to head to see which one starts out ahead with which groups. Often the press is badly gulled by leaked ballot match-ups because they do not know how many people actually know both candidates which is the most critical break in any match-up.

Ballot Measure Campaign   A referendum campaign as opposed to a candidate campaign; something which is on the ballot but not human. "To be honest, ballot measures are usually 200% more fun than candidate campaigns."

Ballotgate   December 11, 1992, incident in which Ken Allen, top aide to House Speaker John Martin, eventually pleaded guilty to two counts of burglary and ballot tampering in the Statehouse election-fixing scandal in connection with two closely contested elections for the Maine House.

Bangor Baptist Minister Reverend Herman "Buddy" Frankland who ran from the pulpit for governor in 1978, hoping to do what Jim Longley Sr. had done earlier. Endorsed by the *Bangor Daily News*, he still only got 18% of the vote, finishing third. Republicans believe, however, that he did enough damage to Republican candidate Linwood Palmer to help swing the election to Joe Brennan.

Bangor Billy Congressman William S. Cohen before he got elected.

Bangor Daily News (BDN) Maine's second largest daily (69,000 + as of 1997). In the 1960's it used to be the largest. Insiders usually expect it to endorse Republicans or conservative Democrats. Among them, it is known for its inordinately high opinion of its ability to change voters' minds. This is usually based largely on the newspaper's endorsement of Independent Jim Longley for governor in 1974, but overlooks the paper's subsequent endorsement of others who did not triumph. These ranged from the Independent Buddy Frankland in 1978, to Republican Susan Collins for governor (twice) in 1994. For many years, insiders sometimes referred to as the "Bangor Deadly" for its penchant for publishing ads for the weekend retail sales occurring in Bangor designed to lure Canadian residents south to avoid Canadian taxes, and for keeping the general public up to date on the number of road kills of moose across the northern tier of counties and the results of any pigeon-racing finals. It has much more allure for political junkies since 1970 than previously as the reporting of hard political news increased.

Bank Phone bank, used to contact voters. Previously bank meant bank as in where you put your money, but since the campaign reforms of the 1970's, candidates can no longer get money on their good looks and name ID from their local bank. "Get the banks up and running; the primary is only 6 weeks away."

Bar Barbara Bush, wife of President George Herbert Walker Bush.

Richard 'Dick' Barringer Professor of government and head of the Edmund S. Muskie Institute of Public Affairs at the University of Southern

Maine. Also a pundit. Ran for governor in 1994 and finished third in the Democratic primary with 9% of the vote. Then baptized Joe Brennan "a progressive" and supported him. Editor of *Changing Maine* (Portland: University of Southern Maine, 1990), a book on Maine's contemporary scene and recent political history and former head of the Maine Department of Conservation under Governor Brennan. A player in Democratic politics for over a decade.

Clyde Bartlett   Democratic candidate for Congress in the 1st District in 1962. Received 43% of the primary vote, losing to Tom Maynard, who for health reasons withdrew. The ultimate nominee, Ronald Kellam, lost to Stan Tupper.

Frederick D. 'Rick' Barton   Winner of the Democratic primary for Maine's First Congressional District in 1976 with 24% of the vote. The primary was so crowded he did not have to attain his age (27) in order to win. Beaten 57% to 45% in the general election by Congressman Dave Emery.

Barton Works   Clever campaign slogan for Rick Barton in 1976. Helped him to win the primary against David Bustin, Neil Rolde, Bruce Reeves, Gilbert Boucher, James Mitchell, and Donald Lowry, all of whom thought they could beat Congressman Dave Emery. Barton later worked as a political consultant.

Barton Works, Briefly   Clever Republican epithet for Rick Barton's congressional campaign after his smashing defeat by David Emery in 1976.

Base   Short for base of support, a candidate's or cause's strongest support segments. "We won't lose our base this time no matter what, so why worry about it?"

Bat Shit   GOB phrase meaning to go crazy. Usually refers to the actions of a candidate as opposed to the campaign staff who do not have that luxury. "Ed went bat shit when he heard about the staff screw-up."

Bates College Ward   Ward 3 in Lewiston situated next to Bates College. Not a good predictor of statewide or Franco-American results but a nice tie-in with Gorham and some other suburban areas.

BBs   George Bush, Howard Baker delegates from the moderate wing of the Republican party in Maine. "Those BBs have bbs for brains; I'm for Ronnie."

Be Careful What You Wish For   There are many examples of this admonition, but none more illuminating than the wish of William Hathaway in early 1972 that the citizen referendum on the big box be held in November that year. At the time, Ed Muskie was running for president and Hathaway, rightly I believe, assumed that with Muskie at the head of the ticket, Democrats would be swept into office and since Hathaway was challenging Margaret Chase Smith for the U.S. Senate, he wanted to be one of them! In 1971, Bob Monks had challenged Maine's big box ballot (on which a voter could vote a straight party ticket by checking a single box at the top of the ballot) because he, rightly, believed that it fostered straight party voting, especially by Democrats. When that challenge failed in court, Monks supported a citizen initiative to have the public vote on the issue, and the effort collected enough signatures to bring the issue to the Maine Legislature for ratification or public vote. The Maine Legislature chose to put it out for referendum. Hathaway wanted the vote in November so that the big box would still be in place even if the voters chose to eliminate it. The Republicans wanted a vote on the big box in June so that they would have a better chance of getting rid of the big box and it would be a dead issue by November. Governor Ken Curtis was willing to have the vote in November, but the Republican Attorney General, Jim Erwin, who had run for governor twice and would again (1974) was adamant that the vote be held in June and threatened to sue Curtis if he didn't have it then. Curtis then said the vote would be held in June. Hathaway was livid and lost his temper with Curtis. But irony of ironies, Muskie dropped out of the presidential race, the people of Maine voted overwhelmingly (63% to 37%) to get rid of the big box in June so it wasn't on the ballot in November when Republican Richard Nixon crushed George McGovern. Had the big box still been in place, it is doubtful that Hathaway would have beaten Margaret Chase Smith. (See also "Big Box.")

Linda Bean   Republican candidate for Congress in 1988, lost to Ted O'Meara in the Republican primary, getting 48% of the vote. In 1992, she won the Republican primary with 46% of the vote, losing in the general election to Tom Andrews, getting 35% of the vote. One of the heirs to L. L. Bean, she has long been active in conservative politics in Maine.

Edward Beauchamp   Ran for Congress in Maine's 2nd Congressional District (CD) in 1946, received 39% of the vote in the general election.

Because George Bush Picked the Other Guy from Indiana As Vice President   Why Senator Richard Lugar ran for President in 1996. Senator Lugar had high hopes for his chances in Maine, hopes which were dashed in the Yankee Primary.

Bedfellows Make Strange Politics   Those who sleep together sometimes have opposing political views.

Been There, Done That   Consultant-speak for "I've already done that. I'm not going to do it again." "Put up lawn signs? Been there, done that. Count me out."

Behind the Ask   When the real purpose for a political request may be obscured by the intial "ask." "Forget his name, behind the ask is his affiliation."

Severin Beliveau   Former legislator and very prominent Democratic rainmaker and counterpart to Merton Henry (see "The White Rabbit"). Severin Beliveau has spun more political stories and intrigued more behind the scenes than any other Democratic operative in contemporary Maine politics. One of the few blots on his copybook is an unsuccesful run for governor in 1986 when he got 24% of the vote in the Democratic primary. Apparently some of his lobbying clients hurt him in the Democratic primary! Perhaps he should have run as a Republican. A major player and rainmaker with great behind-the-scenes skills. Someone you really want on your team when something needs to be fixed in Augusta in a variety of venues.

Bellweather Precincts   Important locales which tell how an election is going. "Ward Four in Portland is always a bellweather precinct." (See also "Key Precinct.")

Rick Bennett   Republican candidate for Congress, 1994. Got 40.7% of the vote in losing to John Baldacci after winning a 4-way Republican primary that year with 29% of the vote. Later elected to the state senate in 1996.

Stan Bennett   Of Oakhurst Dairy fame. Has raised money for Republicans, Independents and Democrats over the last 25 years.

Larry Benoit   Chief of staff for Congressman John Baldacci and before that, staffer for Senator George Mitchell and Senator Ed Muskie. Longtime (26 years), talented, major player. He was campaign manager for Peter Kyros in 1974, George Mitchell in 1982 and again in 1988. Became Senate Sergeant-at-Arms in 1994.

Berl Bernhard   Campaign manager of Ed Muskie when he ran for president in 1972. Also partner in the law firm of Verner, Liipfert, Bernhard, McPhjerson and Hand, one of the many places George Mitchell currently hangs his hat.

Georgette Berube   Respected Democratic state senator from Lewiston who for many years was a player in statewide politics by virtue of her pivotal endorsements, including Bill Cohen in 1978 and Susan Collins in 1996. Ran for governor in 1982 and received 23% of the vote in the Democratic primary, finishing second to incumbent Joe Brennan. She and Sherry Huber share the distinction of being the first women to seek the Maine governorship. But both lost their respective 1982 primaries, Berube to incumbent Joe Brennan, Huber to Charles Cragin.

The Best Advice Is That for Which You Pay   Consultant's credo. This is a variation on the saying "The Only Good Advice Is That for Which You Pay." Consultants believe that if candidates only listen to themselves and their friends, they will do badly come election day. An objective observer who knew the dynamics of politics might or might not agree. (See also "The Only Good Advice Is That for Which You Pay.")

The Best Welfare Program Is a Job   Joe Brennan's significant and oft-repeated insight which preceded Clinton's espousal of the issue by 26 years.

Bet Against the Box   Polling slang for superstition during the final weekend of a campaign when the polling data shows your client clearly winning but you don't want to tempt the fates by proclaiming it too loudly or too firmly so you say the opponent could win. "Don't mind him, he always bets against the box the day before an election."

Better to Be Feared Than Loved   Statement of Machiavelli, one of the patron saints of political consultants. (The other, of course, is Rumpelstiltskin.) In Maine politics, he got it half right: It is better to be loved *and* feared. "George Mitchell was feared and loved, a nice combination if you ask me."

Better to Be Lucky Than Good   GOB phrase relating to deer hunting. Applies to politics and love as well. "He won? Well, I suppose it's better to be lucky than good."

James 'Jimmy B' Betts   Effective Democratic grass roots organizer. Close to labor groups and sometimes known as "The King of the Street People" for his ability to develop grass roots activity. Important player in the Gay Rights referendum of 1995, the Turnpike-widening battles of 1991 (on one side) and 1997 (on another) and a variety of candidate campaigns. One to watch for the future.

Albion Beverage   Finished fourth in the 1948 Republican Senate primary with 5% of the vote.

Bi   A political consultant who works for both Democrats and Republicans. "She's bi, but she's good at what she does so both sides want her help, even though they don't really trust her."

Hattie Bickmore   Energetic Republican party chair who subsequently went to Washington during the Reagan years and only returned recently to the Maine political scene to work at L.L. Bean's. An early supporter of Cohen, Snowe and McKernan and the first woman chair of the Maine Republican pary. Insiders regard her as someone who brought zest and humor and important insights into Republican politics.

Biddeford Journal Tribune   Most important paper in York County; now does some good political reporting although its editorial endorsements are far too predictable.

Biddeford Urinal   Unkind Republican name for the *Biddeford Journal Tribune* in the 1970's and 1980's for its penchant for endorsing any and all Democrats no matter how qualified their Republican opponents.

Big Board Politics   Elected offices for governor, Congress and the U.S. Senate. "It's a big jump from state rep to big board politics; not very many make it successfully."

Big Box   (1) In Maine, prior to 1972, there was a big box at the top of the ballot enabling a voter to vote a straight party ticket by checking the box of the Democratic or Republican party. Because the Democrats had many more people who voted a straight ticket, the successful citizen initiative to eliminate it in 1972 opened up the political landscape and paved the way for a number of successful Republican candidates such as Bill Cohen, Dave Emery, Olympia Snowe and Jock McKernan, especially among Franco-Americans. Since 1972 Maine has used the Massachusetts or office-block ballot, one that generally encourages ticket splitting. Bob Monks deserves a lot of credit for doing away with the big box, first by challenging Governor Curtis's delay in scheduling a referendum on it in court (Kelly vs. Curtis) and then by supporting the citizen initiative itself. Jim Brunelle is correct that Monks's effort may have hurt some Republicans that first time out (because with Nixon at the top of the ticket that year, Margaret Chase Smith probably would have been re-elected) but it helped others such as Cohen. (See also "Be Careful What You Wish For.")

Big Box   (2) As an undergraduate political science major at the University of Maine at Orono, Olympia Snowe once wrote a term paper criticizing the "Big Box" as anti-democratic. For this she was criticized by her professor, Ken Hayes. Hayes later took his criticism one step further, running against her in 1988 when she was in Congress. Hayes turned out to be wrong on that score as well, losing 2–1.

Big Buck   The biggest, strongest, often sexiest figure in a political as well as woods setting. Folklore overlooks the fact that it is the female of the species that keeps the deer family together and safe for 11/12ths of the year. This fact of nature is often ignored by male political figures who style themselves the most important of the consultants. (See also "Alpha Wolf.")

Big Bucks   Lots of money for consulting. In colonial America, the skin of a deer was known as a "buck" and was used for currency, hence "lots of money." "We're getting big bucks for this campaign."

The Big Easy   Any candidate who goes for sex over policy. "He's such a big easy, don't let Loretta near him, she'll change his position on the ERA in a flash."

Big Ed   Affectionate nickname for Governor, Senator, Secretary of State, and Vice-Presidential candidate Edmund S. Muskie (D-Waterville). "Big Ed was a giant of Maine politics in every way."

Big Five   Refers to the largest Maine counties in terms of population: Cumberland, York, Penobscot, Kennebec and Androscoggin. The remaining counties are usually clustered together in four other pods for polling purposes: Aroostook, Hancock/Washington, Lincoln/Sagadahoc/Waldo/Knox, and Franklin/Somerset/Oxford/Piscataquis.

Big Green Machine   Flatbed truck used by Congressional candidate Abbott O. Greene in 1972 from which he gave speeches. Reportedly chained to a fire hydrant by persons unknown but thought to be Cohen stalwarts.

Big Guy   Davis Rawson's nickname for Congressman Dave Emery after his raft sank in the Kennebec during his campaign for the U.S. Senate in 1982.

Big Mo   Momentum, what a candidate or cause likes to feel, movement in a positive direction. More and more people accepting the candidate or cause as their own. "We've got big mo, the numbers are going our way. Let's go campaigning some more." (See also "Head of Steam.")

Big Pigs Get Slaughtered, Little Pigs Get Fed   Wise consultant credo.

Big Raft   From Mahayana "Big Raft" Buddhism for its tendency to include many different people and points of view. "The Democrats get into trouble when they depart from a big raft philosophy." (See also "Big Tent.")

Big Rolodex   A reporter who has a lot of contacts and uses them on political stories instead of touching base with only a half dozen of his or her favorites. Few Maine reporters really are big Rolodexes, mainly because it is a lot of work to keep up with a big Rolodex. On the national scene, David Broder of the *Washington Post* is known as a big Rolodex.

Big Tent   An inclusive party. "The Republicans always have members who don't want it to be a big tent party. That's when they get into trouble." (See also "Big Raft.")

The Bikers   The more than 13,000 motorcycle riders in Maine. A secret weapon of Jock McKernan and Olympia Snowe. Famous with the general public for their September "Toy Run" for underprivileged children, insiders know them for their key role in helping both McKernan and Snowe win very close elections in 1990, and Snowe in her three-way race against McGowan and Carter in 1992.

Billy C   Insider nickname for Bill Cohen as Congressman (see also "El Supremo.") "Billy C likes to wear double knit dungarees now, but he buys them on Lisbon Street."

Billy Wonderful   Nickname for Bill Cohen after he was on the cover of *Time* during the Watergate hearings. "Billy Wonderful was in town last week, working the crowds. He was on top of his form but a lot of Republicans didn't like his being against the President."

Bio   A biographical spot, an ad which tells who the candidate is and where he or she came from. A bio spot can do more to establish a candidate's credibility than an issue ad. "In 1994, Olympia used a very strong bio ad; Andrews never had one so she got to define him in the Bangor DMA."

Birdie   The source for much political gossip. "Birdie told me about that, don't tell anybody."

Brenda Birney   Famous with political insiders of the left and right for, as a state representative, suggesting that welfare recipients go out and collect bottles from Maine roadsides to make money.

Neil Bishop   Republican conservative undaunted by successive defeats. Ran for governor in 1948, gaining 10.5% in the Republican primary. Ran again for governor in 1952, receiving 27.2% of the vote in the GOP primary. Lost to James Reid in the Republican Second Congressional District primary in 1956, lost to Senator Ed Muskie in 1970 (getting 39%) after winning the Republican primary with 60% of the vote. Previously (in 1954), Bishop had headed up "Republicans for Muskie," a position with a more positive outcome.

BIW   Short for Bath Iron Works, the single largest private employer in Maine and in point of fact the single most powerful corporation at least in terms of hardware and firepower. Kept in business by the quality of the ships they build, a pervasive fear of Soviet expansionism, and the past ability of Senators Smith, Muskie, Mitchell, and Cohen to prevent Mississippi from taking over the FFG and DDG programs (see also "FFGs"). Now depends on the good efforts of Senators Olympia Snowe and Susan Collins.

Blacks   In Maine, black ducks, the totem bird for those who hunt. Not to be confused with mallards. Urban Maine politicians have to know the importance of these birds if they wish to curry favor with rural hunters. "I know it's the Feds that set the limits, but the blacks are in trouble."

The Blaine House   Short for the Blaine House mansion, former home of James G. Blaine, termed "the continental liar from the State of Maine" by the Democrats of his era (a nice piece of negative campaigning that!). Blaine was actually born in Philadelphia and thus began a tradition of Maine politicians who were "from away." Donated by Blaine's heirs to be the governor's mansion, it has become a Mecca for Maine politicians great, near great and not so great. Ironically, Blaine served in Congress and the U.S. Senate but was never governor. In most of Maine political history, there have been really only two basic kinds of politicians: those who want to go to Washington and those who want to go to the Blaine House. More recently, there is a third type, of which we have but one example. Angus King, who wanted to become governor but didn't want to live in the Blaine House. He achieved both wishes in January, 1995.

Blainemobile   Name for campaign Winnebago of candidate Jim Longley Sr. when he ran for governor in 1974. Reporters always tried to avoid riding in the Blainemobile because there was no escape from it. Actually, except for Jim Longley Sr., there is something of a Maine political tradition of using a Winnebago as a campaign vehicle and then losing the race. Duke Dutremble used one, Joe Brennan used one and Bob Monks used one, to name just a few candidates who were not successful, although, of course, there may have been more to their stories than the selection of a campaign vehicle.

Raymond J. Blair   Associate editor of the *Times Record*, who covered the 1954 Maine senatorial election in which Margaret Chase Smith defeated her pro-Joe McCarthy opponent, Robert Jones of Biddeford. Blair wrote that Jones would need to "uncork a miracle." Jones wasn't able to, losing 96,457 to 19,336.

Dennis Blais   Head of the CIO Textile Workers Union in the Lewiston area during the 1950's and 1960's. An active and influential Democratic Party member.

Mr. Bland   Davis Rawson's name for Jeff Butland (R-Cumberland), president of the Maine Senate 1994–1996, who defeated Merle "The Pearl" Nelson in 1992 for the seat which propelled him to a position only a heartbeat away from the governorship. (See also "Jar Head" and "Butthead.")

Blocker   Short for **Assigned Blocker**, staffer or volunteer assigned to keep specific people away from the candidate, to "block" their access by distracting, if possible, and by physically obstructing, if necessary, the undesirable. "When Emery finished the walk, I was the blocker to keep that state senator out of the photo. He didn't like it one bit, but it had to be done; he hadn't walked before with Dave, why should he try to hog the glory?"

Blowout   Any campaign victory 60%–40% or better. Actually, 55%–45% is a strong victory as well but seldom regarded as such. "It will be a blowout; Baldacci will win in a walk." (See "In a Walk.")

BNAS   Brunswick Naval Air Station. Located in Brunswick, this naval base is the home to various P-3 Orion squadrons which during the period under review, tracked Russian submarines in the North Atlantic. A magnet for any and all candidates who want to sound tough on defense, BNAS is almost always commanded by naval officers who see the value in having friends on the Armed Services committees of the House and the Senate and who treat most candidates and all office holders as if they were visiting royalty. " I love going to BNAS with the senator; if he asked for it, they'd give him a P-3."

The Boffin   Professor Will Hughes of Bowdoin College, professor of physics, who with one 60-second commercial in 1980, changed 90,000 Mainers' minds and saved Maine Yankee, not just from that referendum but for the next 20 years. The plant was never behind again after his television debut. "I tell you The Boffin will carry the day; he looks like a foreign-born scientist and they tested off the chart as authority figures."

Bolsheviks   In Maine politics, not an ideological term. To insiders, "Bolsheviks" are zealots who will use any tactics and techniques, including not telling the truth, to win for their cause. "It doesn't matter what the facts are, they're Bolsheviks, anything goes for them."

Bombay Mahal   Brunswick, Maine, restaurant which serves as Governor Angus King's real kitchen cabinet. "The governor met again with the group at the Bombay Mahal. Even the Godfather of Calcutta was there."

Bookends   Senators Olympia Snowe and Susan Collins for their position in Maine and their Republican and moderate political philosophies as balances to the California duo of Senators Diane Feinstein and Barbara Boxer, who are Democrats and very liberal.

Booze for News   Don Larrabee's phrase for the habit of politicians to reward reporters with gifts of alcohol at Christmas. See Don's account in his delightful *It's News To Me* (Washington: Trades Unionist Printing Co., 1989).

Boss   Good, excellent, first rate. "That was a boss speech."

Steve Bost   Former Democratic state senator (D-Orono) who went on to support Ross Perot for President and became New England head of his Reform Party, and briefly ran under that banner for the U.S. Senate in 1996 until he discovered that Ross Perot had no intention of helping him to become senator. Bost then returned to the Democratic fold by supporting Joe Brennan in his race for the U.S. Senate.

Both Be the Same As One   Maine coastal expression for no difference between candidates. "Them running for the Senate? Both be the same as one."

Bottom Feeders   Consultants who work for tiny amounts of money or on insignificant projects. "I like him but he's strictly a bottom feeder. He does city council races for God's sake."

Gilbert R. Boucher   Democratic candidate for Congress in the 1st District in 1976. Received 9% of the vote.

The Boys from California   Winner, Wagner, Mandabach, the ballot measure consulting firm from Los Angeles which has played an important role in Maine electoral politics starting with Save Maine Yankee I and running through the Turnpike Referendum and the Ban Clear Cutting Referendum. Winning 90% of their races, they are the premier ballot measure firm in the U.S. "The boys from California have a formula and they stick to it no matter what. That may be why they lost the first Turnpike Referendum but it's why they won all those others."

Dieter Bradbury   Environmental reporter for the *Portland Press Herald* and *Maine Sunday Telegram*. Strongly pro environment although he can write a fair story if he sets his mind to it. Usually, though, he's best if he's on your side of the issue, otherwise almost impossible to spin. Often seems to have the story written by the time he calls.

Brag Wall   Penchant of politicians, elected officials and consultants for putting faces of famous people on their office walls. "Did you see her brag wall? She has Emery and Brennan both right over her desk."

Brain Lock or **Brain Freeze**   An inability to think due to campaign overload. "When Mitchell announced his retirement, the calls came in so fast and furiously, I got brain lock."

Brain Trust   The 1969 and 1970 group of Washington and national advisors to Senator Ed Muskie as he prepared for his Presidential bid in 1972.

Joseph E. 'Joe' Brennan   Cumberland County Attorney, State Representative and Senator (D-Portland), and Attorney General, Brennan first ran for governor in 1974, losing in the Democratic primary to George Mitchell with 26% of the vote. Subsequently elected governor 1978 with 48% of the vote after defeating Phil Merrill and Richard "Spike" Carey in the Democratic primary with 52% of the vote. Reelected governor in 1982 with 61% of the vote and winning every county in the state (after getting 76% of the primary vote against Georgette Berube, the first Democratic woman to seek the job). Ran for Congress in Maine's First District in 1986, winning with 53% of the vote and again in 1988 with 63% of the vote. This was the highest percentage of the vote ever gathered by a Democratic candidate for the 1st CD in a contested race.

Also ran for governor and lost in 1990 (received 44% of the vote) and again in 1994 (34% of the vote). Won the Democratic nomination for the U.S. Senate in 1996 with 55% of the vote, finishing second in the general election with 44% of the vote. Al Diamon believes he may run next for mayor of Portland! Although Brennan ended up losing four major races, he should really be remembered not for losing those races but for having won so many others and for caring enough for the people of Maine to keep trying.

Brennanistas   Name given to die-hard supporters of Congressman and Governor Joseph Brennan (D-Portland). Republican insiders believe requirements for membership in this group include: (a) agreeing with everything that Governor Brennan did or did not do, (b) badmouthing Angus King, Jock McKernan, Olympia Snowe, and all Democrats living in the west end of Portland, and (c) writing off Lewiston as not important to Democratic statewide victories, especially those involving Joseph Brennan. A more objective assessment would highlight their true loyalty to a man who in private was very engaging, always very loyal to them, quite concerned about people and their plight and who always asked for their help. (See also "McKernanistas.") True insiders recognize two phases of Brennanistas. Phase One Brennanistas (1978 and before) include the earliest supporters such as Davey Redmond, Arthur Stilphin, Jerry Conley, E. O. Kelleher, John and Dave Kerry and David Flanagan. Phase Two Brennanistas (post 1978) include Barry Hobbins, Dick Anderson and a host of others. Within the Brennanista group, some still keep a close tally on who was in Phase One and who was in Phase Two.

Dave Brennerman   State Representative, executive director of the Democratic Party under Barry Hobbins (1981–1984). Now Vice President for Governmental Affairs, UNUM.

Owen Brewster   Elected to the U.S. Senate in 1946 with 64% of the vote. Lost the Republican primary for Senate in 1952, getting 49% of the vote. One of the very few incumbent major office holders to lose a primary in recent Maine history.

Bridge Over Troubled Waters   Campaign theme song of Bill Cohen's 1972 congressional race. Diane Cohen, who was an integral part of the Cohen team effort and a player in the primary and general elections, is generally credited with choosing the theme song.

Broadcast TV   Network TV as opposed to cable TV. CBS, NBC, ABC and FOX are examples of broadcast TV, while CNN and ESPN are examples of cable. Usually cable TV is much cheaper to buy but often much less effective in reaching the mass of voters in a political campaign. Still, cable can be used to keep from going dark due to a lack of funds to stay on broadcast TV.

David Broder   Perhaps the best political reporter in America for the last several decades. When writing about the Maine scene he almost always picks up the right nuances and figures out what is really happening. "Baker was dead after the Portland mock convention and Broder picked it up first." (See also "Big Rolodex.")

A Bronze So Far from Home   Insider's phrase for putting a good face on a bad campaign, taken from the statement by Michael Dukakis, after he got clobbered in the Iowa primary of 1988. "Only two committee people voted for you? Call it a bronze so far from home if the press calls."

Ralph 'Bud' Brooks   Republican candidate for Congress in 1st District during 1966. Got 21% of the vote in the 7-person primary. Early supporter of Nelson Rockefeller.

Brother   A term of semi-endearment used consistently by only two Maine political insiders, George Campbell and Severin Beliveau, the latter almost always attaching the term to the addressee's last name as in "Brother Potholm, I have a client who could use your services."

The Brothers   Often applied to Jock and Robert "Bobby" McKernan, the former governor and congressman and his brother and account executive at the political media company of Smith and Haroff. But for a swing of a few thousand votes in the First District congressional election of 1982, "the Brothers" might have been John and Dave Kerry, Democratic activists from Saco. John lost to Jock by less than 6,000 votes in 1982. Dave continues to be a player in Democratic primary politics in the First Congressional District.

Craig Brown   Major Democratic activist credited with managing Tom Andrews's successful campaigns for Congress in 1990 and 1992.

Marion Fuller Brown   Longtime Republican national committeewoman and a major power in York County. Almost singlehandedly killed billboards in Maine (thus freeing up campaign money for TV!). A player in Republican Party circles.

James 'Jim' Brunelle   Columnist for the *Portland Press Herald* and commentator on MPBN's "Maine Watch." Jim is a respected political observer and very knowledgeable as a political historian. Originally a statehouse reporter for the Maine Broadcasting System which in the 1960's included WCSH. Compiler of two editions of *The Maine Almanac* (1978 and 1979). Knows a great deal about Maine history, and his columns and commentary always enlighten as well as amuse. In private conversations, he has a good sense of humor and seems to enjoy politics. *But in public, and from a strictly consultant point of view,* he can be something of a killjoy. For three decades Jim's doleful countenance has glowered over the Maine political scene like the ghost of Cotton Mather. Jim doesn't like modern campaigns, negative advertising, TV advertising, expensive campaigns, long campaigns and/or any of the other aspects of modern politics which make them fun and lucrative for political consultants. On air and in his columns, he doesn't seem to share in the sheer joy of partisan and ballot measure struggles.

BS   Bullshit. What candidates talk and voters expect, may demand, no matter what they tell reporters. "Most voters have no tolerance for honesty when it comes to Medicare or Social Security. Don't be a hero, give them the usual BS. Look what happened to Tony Payne."

Bud   (1) GOB name for "buddy." "Bud, we *will* do something about the coyotes if I'm governor."

Bud   (2) Bud Leavitt, late, beloved sportswriter for the *Bangor Daily News* and fishing buddy of Ted Williams. Very important authority figure for the GOB's. As such, Bud was a major factor in the passage of Maine's $35 million bond for parks and wildlife in 1987.

Buffalo   From the saying "It's not how far the buffalo flew, it's that the buffalo flew at all." Consultant-speak for a tired or old-fashioned candidate who does not win. "What do you want from me, I got the buffalo 49%."

Chipman C. 'Chip' Bull   Democratic candidate for the 2nd CD in 1984. Ran against Olympia Snowe in most whimsical fashion, passing out wooden coins with "Official Bull Chip" on one side and "Chip Bull, Democrat, Congress" on the other. Chip Bull was an original and provided more delight to political insiders than his 23% total in the general election would suggest. Unfortunately, his campaign faltered when he admitted that he did crossword puzzles all day as a USDA bureaucrat. "Politics needs more Chips as far as I'm concerned."

Bull Roar   Bullshit, as spoken by abnormally polite candidates in private, or most candidates in public.

Bullet Poll   Channel 6/*Bangor Daily News* Bullet Poll which polls Maine citizens by machine and whose results are sometimes unpredictable. In 1994, for example, the election day Bullet Poll showed Joe Brennan winning 35% to 32%, although King actually won by that amount. Insiders usually get advance word of what's going to be released so there is ample time both to spin and to release one's own data in order to take the edge off any bad news.

Bullshit Meter   Ability to smell out falsehood from a candidate. "For a scorp, she's got a pretty good bullshit meter." (See also "Scorps.")

Bundling   A method of campaign giving which circumvents the $5,000 PAC limits by channeling funds to candidates outside the PAC itself by using individuals. Invented as a technique by some environmental groups, it is perhaps used most effectively in Maine by Emily's List, which gives money only to pro-choice Democratic women.

The Bunker   Campaign headquarters or the location where the campaign manager holes up to get away from the press and his or her own field people. "I think he's in the bunker and doesn't want to talk with anybody right now."

Bunker Mentality   A state of siege feeling which comes over losing candidates and causes. The principals refuse to believe incoming bad news and turn inward to reinforce their own notions that everything is going to be all right. "When they got in their bunker mentality mode, they wouldn't even talk to their pollster."

Burned   Exposed by a reporter. "I thought we were off the record and he burned me." In reality, there is seldom anything truly off the record.

Burner Man   Nickname for Charles Webster (R-Farmington), state senator and architect of the 1991 government shut-down who ran for governor in 1994, getting 6.9% of the vote in the Republican primary, finishing 7th out of 8. Charlie's day job was as a furnace repairman.

Lee Burnett   Political reporter for Biddeford's *Journal Tribune*, he is regarded as extremly fair and very thorough, often digging deep on political stories. Has good sources across the political spectrum. He is also famous with insiders for his "what does this mean for Maine politics" questions which usually strike the interviewee as coming out of left field. "Elvis has been sighted in Memphis. What does this mean for the Maine Senate race?" Spinnable and fun to talk to. Usually writes some good, balanced stories. Works as hard as any Maine journalist.

Burnout   TV commercials which have lost impact. "That's a burnout; the numbers have stopped moving. Pull the sucker."

Lucille Burr   From Falmouth, she is a one-woman key precinct. Lucille has never been wrong about the outcome of a major political race in Maine in the last 25 years. Picked McKernan over Kerry, Longley over Dutremble, and foretold the passage of Sunday Sales. Smells a winner two years out!

Peter Burr   Authentic mathematical and political genius who worked behind the scenes in Maine politics for two decades, supporting Democrats, Independents and Republicans, and helping the Democrats in two of their redistricting efforts for the Maine House and Senate. For two decades, Peter has astounded friend and foe alike with his ability to predict the outcomes of political races. He called Cohen's 60%-40% victory over Bill Hathaway based on numbers from Monhegan Island alone and in 1996, on June 20, called the U.S. Senate race from Concord, N.H., giving Collins a 47% to 45% victory over Brennan with 8% going to the other candidates. Called King's 1994 three-point victory over Joe Brennan at one o'clock in the afternoon on election day. A player.

Ken Burrill   Exceptional Republican fund-raiser of note and charter member of the Maine sand and gravel crowd. (See also "Sand and Gravel

Crowd.") Major fund-raiser and strategist for the Collins for Senate and Maine Citizens for Jobs and Safety efforts. A player. One of the very best fund raisers in the state.

David 'Dave' Bustin   Longtime Democratic Party activist and party chair. Very close to Joe Brennan. Ran for Congress in 1976, getting 12% of the vote in the 1st District primary.

Butt Man   Democratic name for Republican presidential candidate Bob Dole for his support for and from tobacco interests. Even though Maine Democrats were not overly enthusiastic for Clinton in 1996, they really disliked Dole. "Butt Man just gave me another reason to vote for Clinton."

Butthead   Democratic insider name for Senate President Jeffrey Butland (R-Cumberland). "Beavis and Butthead give me acid indigestion." (See also "Jar Head.")

Anthony 'Tony' Buxton   Major political player. Democratic insider and party chair as well as a member of the Preti, Flaherty, Beliveau and Pachios law firm. Involved in many of the most important political events of the last several decades ranging from being campaign manager for George Mitchell in 1974 to overseeing the massive transformation of electrical utility reform in 1996. Has one of the better grasps on the realities of Maine politics.

Buzzy   Affectionate nickname for Duane "Buzz" Fitzgerald, former corporate lawyer, former head of the Bill Haggett for Governor exploratory committee, former head of Bath Iron Works (see also BIW). A big-time supporter of Tom Andrews and later Angus King. Loves to speak out on public issues. Now into corporate consulting as a member of The Portland Consulting Group.

By Remote Control   Consultant-speak for trying to influence a campaign (and getting paid for it) from afar, without having to attend campaign meetings. "She's a great asset, but she tries to do everything by remote control, and so she's never there when the decisions are really made."

James E. 'Jeb' Byrne   Augusta UPI bureau chief, news secretary to Governor Clausen, assistant to SBA Director Bernard Boutin, editor of the Federal Register.

C

Cable   Cable TV, often used to considerable effect in local races, does not have much of a demonstrable impact on congressional or statewide races due to the fragmentation of the audience. At the same time, major candidate races usually feature it, especially if the campaign does not have enough money to stay on network TV. It remains hard to measure its impact in any given situation. It can be an effective supplement to broadcast, but candidates often mistake it for a substitute.

Jean Cabral   Head of "What Ever Happened to Local Control?"—a voter interest group concerned with issues of local control, generally active on a number of referenda in the 1980's.

Pamela 'Pam' Cahill   Republican State Senator from Bath who ran for governor in 1994, getting 5.8% of the vote in the Republican primary. She remains a popular force in moderate Republican circles.

Cake   Easy, simple, as in "a piece of cake." "The term limits referendum was cake, nothing but cake."

Helen Caldicott   Australian anti-nuclear activist who came to Maine to predict that the election of Ronald Reagan as President and Bill Cohen as Senator would lead to nuclear war. This opinion, delivered to Maine children in Yarmouth, caused quite a stir and did not help the senatorial campaign of Libby Mitchell for whom Dr. Caldicott was appearing.

Pat Callahan   Low-key anchor and political debate moderator on Channel 6 in Portland. Always seems prepared and gives candidates a fair hearing in debates.

Cameo   As in "cameo" appearance, a brief visit by a candidate at a function he or she would never attend if they were not running for office. "He's off to see the docs; it's more than a cameo, they've got the green." (See also "The Green.")

Campaign Finance Reform   Something George Mitchell advocated the year (1988) he set the Maine state record for PAC contributions. Also something of a cottage industry for Common Cause. (See also "PAC.") Something Tom Allen advocated the year after the AFL/CIO knocked off his opponent with $1 million in negative ads.

Campaign Secrets   Really good gossip, usually of interest only to political insiders but very interesting to them. "He's on the horn, pushing campaign secrets out the door like there's no tomorrow. I got them all."

Campaign Sex   Like any other kind of sex, except often fueled by the aphrodisiac of time being speeded up by events and by the danger of discovery and thus being on the 6 P.M. news. "I don't think regular sex can ever be as good as campaign sex."

George 'Jorge' Campbell   Portland city councilor and mayor (1997) who was the principal rainmaker for Tom Andrews in 1990 and 1992. Raised over $1 million during the turnpike referendum of 1991. Jorge briefly ran for Congress in 1996 as a Democrat but quit, reportedly saying "I can't take any more meetings with hippies in their yurts at 11 P.M. with their dogs farting in my face." For insiders, the highlight of his brief campaign occurred when his three ex-wives endorsed him. George is, in real life, a major political player and now a member of Pierce Atwood.

Steve Campbell   Political reporter for the *Portland Press Herald* and *Maine Sunday Telegram* and author of the *Telegram's* "Washington Watch" column. Steve is one of the two most widely watched print scorps (the other being John Day of the *Bangor Daily News*). Steve is regarded by political insiders as spinnable in that he will take new information and weigh it within the context of an existing story. Hasn't always had warm relations with all members of the Maine delegation in Washington, and his column sometimes seems remote and often based on "What others are saying about Maine figures." His in-depth pieces on Maine political figures, especially biographies, however, can be exceptional, among the best done in the state. His portraits of Tom Andrews during his losing 1994 Senate effort and Jim Longley Jr. in 1996 stand out. A player.

Canadian Imports   Something which comes from Canada, like fish or lumber. Usually opposed by Maine politicians although all are most happy to have Canadian consumers shop in the Bangor mall and vacation in Old Orchard Beach.

The Can-Do Candidate with the Can-Did Record   Margaret Chase Smith's campaign slogan in the 1940's.

Canine Appetite for Fame   A politician who wants to see his or her name in the paper on almost any subject even if subjected to ridicule. "He may have used the Christian Civic League to satisfy his canine appetite for fame, but they got a lot more publicity than they would have gotten otherwise."

Richard 'Spike' Carey   Democratic representative and State Senator from Waterville. Ran for governor in 1978 and received 12% of the vote in the Democratic primary. A strong opponent of the state's lottery as a candidate for governor in 1978. Later became Lottery Commissioner under Governor Joseph Brennan. He also served four terms as mayor of Waterville.

A Caring Place   Governor Jock McKernan's 1986 description of Maine.

Donnell 'Donnie' Caroll   Democratic candidate for governor in 1994, received 2% of the vote in that primary.

Alan Caron   Longtime Democratic activist and player. Helped the Natural Resource Council of Maine (NRCM) defeat the Maine Turnpike widening with an initiative in 1991 by making it a referendum on Governor Jock McKernan when McKernan was at his political and popular low point (28% approval rating). Was a consultant for the Portland Gay Rights campaign of 1992 and the Lewiston Gay Rights campaign in 1993. Served as Joe Brennan's political and communications director during his race for governor in 1994. Now president of The Portland Consulting Group. (See also "Natural Resources Council of Maine.")

Carpet Bombing   To go up on all TV stations with over 1,000 Gross Rating Points (GRPs) per week. "Andrews tried carpet bombing OJ but it was too late." "The June 1996 carpet bombing of the Greens wrecked their referendum and drove up their negatives."

Paul Carrier   Political reporter for the *Portland Press Herald* and *Maine Sunday Telegram*, and co-author of the weekly political gossip column (with Nancy Perry), "People and Politics." A ten-year veteran, he is regarded as fair and likely to take what is happening at face value without giving events his own spin. Paul was the former press secretary for New Hampshire Senator Gordon Humphrey. Gets high marks from candidates and former candidates for his coverage of their campaigns.

Donald 'Don' Carrigan   Host of Maine Public Broadcasting Network's "Capitol Connection." Don is very likable and objective and known to political consultants as "The King of Softballs" for his caring, welcoming, non-threatening style of asking questions and for treating all his political guests as if they were worthy of respect. Expected to become the host of "Maine Watch" during the fall of 1997.

Carry a Tribe   When a person on a letterhead committee or fund-raising letter brings with him or her a group. "Hell, throw him on, he carries a tribe. We're light on Greeks from Bangor."

Everett Brown 'Brownie' Carson   A Democratic and then environmental activist since his student days at Bowdoin College. He ran in the Democratic primary for Congress in 1972 (getting 33% of the vote) as an anti-war activist after having served in Vietnam and having been wounded in Laos. He lost to Peter Kyros in that primary but is largely credited with weakening Kyros for Jadine O'Brien's challenge in 1974 and Kyros's subsequent loss to David Emery. In 1984, Brownie became executive director of the Natural Resources Council of Maine. A major player on Maine political scene for 20 years, he has opposed many development projects (such as the Big A), helped to win the "Stop the Widening" Maine Turnpike campaign of 1991 and supported the 1996 Forest Compact. Brownie is a serious person with a serious agenda. To some insiders, however, he often seems to have a most Manichaean view of the world and takes himself, as opposed to his causes, far too seriously. Brownie is also known for an impressive ability to spin a variety of editors and political figures, some of whom seem truly frightened by his tone and judgmental stances.

Jonathan Carter   Green Party candidate for Congress (getting 8.8% of the vote and probably costing Patrick McGowan the Second District seat in 1992), and candidate for governor in 1994, getting 6% of the vote. Trained as a botanist and originator of the Ban Clearcutting Referendum, he seems to really enjoy the blood sport of politics. Self-made and a player.

Casco Bay Weekly   Maine's most "progressive" newspaper. Given away free, which may tell you something about the free market system and/or its current value on Maine's political landscape. Still, with columns by Al Diamon and others, no hard political news is really required to make it a good read.

James 'Jim' Case   Prominent Democratic party fund-raiser, served as chair of Phil Merrill's abortive senatorial campaign in 1995–1996 and when Merrill quit the race, supported Joe Brennan. But before that, Case played a series of important roles during the 1970's and 1980's. Insiders know him as one of the few people who could get Ed Muskie to do something he didn't want to. Along with Charlie Micoleau, Larry Benoit and Phil Merrill, he masterminded Ed Muskie's 1975 "race" against Bill Cohen. A longtime player. (See also "The Election Nobody Saw.")

Castle or the Outhouse   All or nothing, go for a big political prize or nothing. "I'm running for the U.S. Senate or I'm finished. It's the castle or the outhouse."

A Cat Fight   What Senator Margaret Chase Smith said she wanted to avoid when she ran against Democrat Lucia Cormier in 1960 and therefore refused all but one invitation to debate her lesser known opponent. Still, *Time* put both on the cover of its September 5, 1960 issue. To this day no state has since seen another election in which both major parties nominated women for the same U.S. Senate seat.

Mary Cathcart   Congressional candidate in Maine's Second District Democratic primary in 1994, receiving 13% of the vote. Elected to the State Senate in 1996.

Cattle Call   Consultant-speak for a situation where clients have various consultants brought in one after the other to pitch them. "I don't do cattle calls anymore. They can hire me or not but I won't do that parade."

Cattle Shows   Insider name for nonbinding "straw vote" conventions in which Presidential candidates appear at a "forum." "The 1979 cattle show at the Portland Expo pushed Howard Baker down and moved George Bush up in the Republican sweepstakes."

CDs   Congressional Districts. The political building blocks of the state of Maine. Currently (since the 1962 election) Maine has two Congressional districts. The 1st District consists of the counties of York, Cumberland, nearly all of Kennebec, Sagadahoc, Lincoln and Knox. The 2nd District consists of the counties of Waldo, Hancock, Washington, Aroostook, Penobscot, Oxford, Androscoggin, Franklin, Somerset and Piscataquis together with Wayne, China, Monmouth and Albion in Kennebec County.
    After the 1930 census, Maine had three CDs. The 1st CD consisted of

York, Cumberland, Sagadahoc and Oxford counties. The 2nd consisted of Lincoln, Knox, Waldo, Androscoggin, Kennebec, Franklin and Somerset; while the 3rd had the counties of Aroostook, Piscataquis, Penobscot, Hancock and Washington.

After the 1960 census, Maine had been reduced to two CD's, the 1st consisting of York, Cumberland, Sagadahoc, Lincoln, Knox and Waldo counties; while the 2nd held Hancock, Washington, Penobscot, Aroostook, Piscataquis, Somerset, Franklin, Oxford and Androscoggin.

After the 1980 census, because of net population inflows into the 1st CD, part of Waldo county was included in the 2nd CD, a process completed with the reapportionment following the 1990 census.

The Center Holds   To understand Maine politics, you have to appreciate the fact that the Republican far right and the Democratic far left, while they drive a lot of comment, debate and get tons of coverage in the free press, actually don't win general elections in Maine. It is almost always voters in the middle of the political spectrum who determine outcomes of statewide races. "Forget it, once the primary is over, the center holds. You're positioned just right to be the next Senator."

Central Planner   Mary Adams's name for Kay Rand during the debate over Governor King's forest compact in the Ban Clear Cutting referendum of 1996. This is apparently a bad thing in Garland, Maine, Mary's hometown.

Cetacea Productions   Good Maine TV production house with a hard-to-pronounce, and -remember, name. Located in Falmouth, Maine.

Bruce Chalmers   From Bridgton, one of the premier Republican fundraisers. Suspect with some Republicans for having supported George Mitchell, a Bowdoin contemporary, for the U.S. Senate. Nevertheless, an unsung hero of the Republican party.

The Chameleon   Jack Wyman, who was a liberal Democrat, a conservative Republican and lots of other things in between, and who, upon becoming a prison chaplain with former White House aide Chuck Colson, said, "Thank God, I'll never have to go and kiss the White Rabbit's ass again." Jack was one political figure with a genuine sense of humor and one who could laugh at himself and his own canine appetite for fame. He also showed a lot of political courage in trying to bridge the gap between Right to Life and Pro Choice, an effort almost nobody in politics other than he has attempted in Maine politics during the past four decades. (See also "Canine Appetite for Fame.")

Champion of All Champions   Democratic Senator John Stennis of Mississippi's name for Margaret Chase Smith after she got 67% of the vote in her 1972 primary battle with Bob Monks. Five months later, she was defeated by Democrat Bill Hathaway.

Liz Chapman   Usually fair and insightful reporter for the *Sun Journal*. Often writes her best material when she is on deadline. Steady performer. Spinnable but only with good material. Does good investigative pieces with an eye toward how things will affect the average person. Many insiders view the *Sun Journal* political reporters, as a group, as very fair in covering different points of view in political contexts.

Philip Chapman Jr.   Finished second in the Republican primary for governor in 1956 with 29% of the vote. Lost in the next Republican gubernatorial primary with 38% of the vote in 1958.

Richard R. Charette   Winner of the 1986 Democratic primary for Congress in the Second District with 58% of the vote. Lost in the general election against Olympia Snowe, getting 22% of the vote.

Cherry   A virgin candidate. "He's a cherry, but I think he's a quick learner. He did okay on Lisbon street his first time out." (See also "Lisbon Street" and "Nugget.")

CHFE   Citizens for a Healthy Forest and Economy, the organizational arm of opposition to Maine's clear cutting ban initiative of 1996. Won that three-way referendum with 47% of the vote but failed to get the 50.1% necessary to avoid a run-off election in 1997.

A.M. Chiaravalloti   Finished third in the Democratic primary for the second Congressional district seat in 1950 with 6% of the vote. Lost two years later in the same primary, with 41% of the vote.

Chicken Off That Bone   To get all the mileage out of a campaign tactic. "We got all the chicken off that bone; let's get off the private eye story."

Dana W. Childs   Democratic candidate for governor in 1966. Got 19% in the Democratic primary. Originally a Republican, in 1965, he became the Democratic House Speaker in part because of the Goldwater debacle.

Chin Music   From baseball, throwing a pitch near the batter's head to push him or her back from the plate. In politics, any warning shot. "The senator threw a little chin music at him and that was the last we heard from that scorp during the entire cycle."

Chinese Fire Drill   Descriptive term of Harrison Richardson, aka "Horse" for any campaign situation which is truly messed up. Why Chinese fire drills should be any more confused and messed up than any other group's fire drills is not clear, but this description, not withstanding its political incorrectness, is firmly established on the Maine campaign trail. "You should have seen Jasper and all his volunteers in the wrong city. It was a Chinese fire drill from beginning to end." (See also "Horse.")

Christian Civic League   With one of its founders, William DeWitt Hyde, the Christian Civic League was originally dedicated to a vigorous, Teddy Roosevelt style of muscular Christianity. In the 1980's, it became the handmaiden of Jasper Wyman. This organization probably gets more publicity than any other religious organization in Maine for its political activities. It manages to get its opposition to gay and abortion rights a lot of ongoing publicity and can, through the use of its phoning techniques, cause local legislators a lot of heartburn. Executive director in 1997, Michael Heath.

George Christie   Campaign director of the coalition which passed campaign finance restrictions in 1996.

John Christie   Delightful, incisive, longtime player on the Maine scene. While at Ad Media, he worked on such referenda as the ERA, the elected PUC, Moose Hunt and Maine Yankee. As head of John Christie Associates, along with Bill Bell, Dana Connors and Tony Buxton, he won the bond issue for the "rehabilitation of Certain Rail Lines in Maine," known forever after as "The Toy Trains" referendum. Christie now heads Maine Business Publications with a circulation of 50,000. One of the best storytellers in the state.

Chronic Campaigner   Someone who perpetually runs for public office, even if they no longer have much chance of winning.

Carolyn Chute   Best-selling author of *The Beans of Egypt, Maine* and founder of the Maine Militia. Against "corporate welfare." Few politicians have read the book and fewer still will attend target practice with the militia. Of this I am quite sure.

The Cianbro Boys   The Cianchette brothers, Ival "Bud" (Republican), Ken "Lunk" (Independent) and Alton "Chuck" (Democrat), major financial and political players in both parties and bulwarks against trade union expansion economically and politically. In political circles, Chuck is best known for his Buddha-like serenity and straightforward honesty. Chuck is also justly famous for flying to Eagle Lake to tell Speaker John Martin he was going to oust him, and for spending $133,000 to be elected to the Maine Senate in 1992, a record expenditure for that body. "Worth every penny of it," said many Maine people but not, apparently George Christie, who pushed for campaign finance reform with that case firmly in mind. The Cianchette family's influence in Maine politics dates back to the 1930's.

Alton 'Chuck' Cianchette   Former Democratic State Senator from Palmyra and longtime player on the Maine political scene, endorsing candidates and causes and having a major statewide impact. A major player for pro-business activities. After he more than doubled the previous state legislative spending record in 1992 by spending over $133,000 on his primary and general election races, he became a true hero to Maine's consultants.

Citizens' Hours   Political art form invented in early 1973 by Dr. Demento. Congressman goes to small town and personally holds open office hours for citizens. Many real people show up and many sightings of UFOs are reported, but the press is awesome and "citizens' hours" are eventually duplicated by all other major officer holders, although other elected officials quickly figure out that sending flak catchers out in his stead makes a lot more sense. Dave Emery's "town meetings" in grange halls were perhaps the highest achievement of this art form. Tom Allen and John Baldacci still do them regularly. (See also "Flak Catchers" and "Dr. D.")

Civilian Time   Nine to five, Monday through Friday, weekends and evenings off. Unlike campaign time which runs 15 hours a day and night, seven days a week, civilian time has rest periods. Campaign time is not driven by the sun and moon but by the news cycle. "He never got the message—we're not on civilian time. We had to let him go, even though his mother donated the max to the campaign. We told him that if he didn't come to the headquarters on Saturday night, not to bother showing up Sunday."

Civilians   Another name for voters, to distinguish them from political operatives. Richard Nixon was very perspicacious when he wrote about how being "in the arena" gave you something in common with others in that arena but which sets you apart for all others who are not in the political arena. "She's just a civilian, don't worry about it." Since Ross Perot, it would appear that this fundamental difference between civilian and political operative has blurred, but it has not.

F. Davis 'Pop' Clark   Winner of the Democratic primary for governor in 1946, he lost the general election with 39% of the vote. In 1948 he was the Democratic nominee for the Congressional seat from Maine's third district, losing the general election with 29% of the vote. Subsequently a Maine District Court judge.

William 'Bill' Clarke   (1) Independent candidate for U.S. Senate in 1996, received 3% of the vote.

William 'Bill' Clarke   (2) Longtime columnist ("Some Log Rolling") for the Gannett papers. Had a conservative slant but really cared about the Maine woods and was a strong authority figure for the GOBs. Bill saw in coyotes a threat others saw only in Eboli. In this, he was joined by Gene

Letourneau, outdoor writer for the Gannett papers, author of *America's New 'Wolf'* and another authority figure for men and women who hunt and fish.

Class   (1) Socio-economic status, an important statistical segment in polling. "It's a class thing; Andrews and McKernan do better in the suburbs than Emery and Brennan."

Class   (2) Political style. "Mitchell had a lot of class."

Clinton 'Doc' Clauson   Elected governor in Maine in 1958 with 52% of the vote after winning the Democratic primary with 51% of the vote. Thought to be the only state IRS director ever elected to major office in Maine history. He was also the first chiropractor to be elected to statewide office in Maine.

Mr. Clean   Columnist Richard Wilson's 1970 term for Senator Ed Muskie for his interest in environmental matters and legislation to clean up the country's air and water.

Clean Numbers   True numbers. Often referring to polling numbers but sometimes referring to campaign specifics. "Okay, Governor, your opponent has an ad on saying you pardoned three felons who committed more crimes. What's the clean number? Twelve? You have to be kidding. We're in big trouble."

John Cleveland   Democratic state senator, former mayor of Auburn and campaign manager of many successful ballot measures including Sunday Sales and a variety of tax cap referenda as well as the telecommunications bond issue of 1995. He has won every referenda he has managed, an outstanding record given the fickleness of the Maine voters on various issues. A player.

Client Voice   Voice consultant uses with client depending on his or her perception of the client's status needs, often based on the Frank Sinatra satori from another age, "Treat a dame like a lady and a lady like a dame." However used, the client voice is designed to establish the superiority of the consultant in understanding the situation. "The word on the street, Congressman, is that you are a colossal asshole. Don't compound things by yelling at your staff."

Clock   To beat badly, hurt another candidate's chances. "She clocked him in the debate."

Close the Sale   Get the endorsement. "Close the sale, Congressman, we need their support. Tell them what they want to hear; they're not policy wonks."

Closed Loop   The tendency of a candidate to surround him or herself with likeminded people, forming a closed loop of information and point of view. The closed loop is most pronounced as candidates begin to lose ground to their opponents late in the campaign. "You can't get through to them; it's a closed loop over at headquarters." (See also "Bunker Mentality.")

Clown   Anyone associated with a political campaign who doesn't seem to know what he is doing. "Where did you get these clowns? They don't even know how to leaflet."

The Clubs   The social clubs of Lewiston, Maine, many of which are on Lisbon Street. It is always a test of one's candidate to send him or her into the clubs for the night, getting them to buy rounds of drinks for the patrons and listening to "the real Maine." "I sent him to the clubs and he screwed up badly. Talked about himself all night long and was stingy with the drinks. They hated him. We'll lose Andro now."

CMP   Central Maine Power, once a Republican political powerhouse made a political eunuch by Peter Bradford just as it was becoming a Democratic milk cow. Later headed by David Flanagan. Now seeking to sell off all of its generating facilities!

Mr. Coffee   Brian Clark, famous for his national ads for the Mr. Coffee coffee maker. Brought into Maine to do Maine Yankee II commercials.

Frank Coffin   Democratic Party chair and integral part of the Muskie revolution. Ran for Congress in 1956 in Maine's 2nd District, winning the primary with 70% of the vote and the general election with 53% of the vote. Reelected in 1958 with 61% of the vote. Ran for governor in 1960, losing to John Reed in the general election, getting 47% of the vote. Later a respected federal appeals judge.

Ralph Coffman   Former Democratic representative from Old Town, changed to an independent and then ran for governor as a write-in candidate in 1994. As of 1997, he was attempting to form an "Independent Party" via petitions. He will need 26,000 signatures, or 5% of the number of votes cast in the last gubernatorial election.

John Coghill   Democratic nominee for Congress in Maine's 3rd CD in 1946. Lost the general election, getting 27% of the vote.

Leonard J. Cohen   Gannett newspaper columnist, editor, and political pundit in the 1950's.

William S. 'Bill' Cohen   Bowdoin grad and mayor of Bangor, elected to Congress in 1972 (with 54% of the vote) after winning the Republican primary for the Second District with 61% of the vote. Reelected in 1974 (with 71% of the vote), 1976 (with 77% of the vote), elected to the U.S. Senate in 1978 with 56% of the vote in a four-way race. Reelected in 1984 with 73% of the vote and again in 1990 with 61% of the vote. A true warrior and modern political ace. Of the four "Titans" of post–World War II politics, Cohen is the only one never to have lost an election, nor to have been behind in any contest. Prevailed in a truly wondrous and unexpected victory in an insider contest when he beat George Mitchell to the cabinet of Democratic president Bill Clinton, becoming Secretary of Defense in 1997.

Kenneth Colbath   A Democrat, he ran for Congress in Maine's 3rd CD in 1954 (40%) and 1956 (39%) losing to Cliff McIntire.

College Tour   Bowdoin has its Mitchell, Andrews, Allen and Cohen; Bates has its Hodgkin and Muskie; Colby has its Maisel, Merrill, and Corrado. UMO has (all in the class of 1970) Snowe, George Smith and Steven King (but not his namesake Angus), John Reed, Ken Hayes and Gene Mawhinney. USM has Barringer and Coogan. Dartmouth has Angus King and Jock McKernan (Celtic tribalism at work!).

Susan Collins   Ran for governor in 1994, winning the Republican primary but losing the general election with 23% of the vote. Ran for U.S. Senate in 1996, winning the Republican primary with 55% of the vote and taking the general election with 49% of the vote.

Colson's Dictum   Charles "Chuck" Colson of Nixon White House and Watergate fame once said, "Get them by the balls and their hearts and minds will follow." Consultants who want to sound tougher than they are sometimes quote Chuck but seldom footnote the source. Chuck now works with Jasper Wyman.

Coming to a Polling Place This Fall   Effective campaign slogan for Angus King in 1994. Created by Dan Payne, the slogan played during the spring and summer and let voters know that they would have a broader choice of candidates in the fall than were appearing in the party primaries.

Command Research   Political consulting and polling company headed by C.P. Potholm. Active in Maine politics since 1980 in both candidate and ballot measure campaigns, having fun in most. (See also "Little Money, Little Fun").

Common Cause   A full employment interest group for liberal causes and the consultants who defeat them. "Common Cause put my kids through school; I don't know about you."

Communist Sympathizer   Term used by Jack Lait and Lee Mortimer in a 1952 book called *U.S.A. Confidential* to describe Margaret Chase Smith for her attack on Senator Joe McCarthy. They were forced to retract their charges, pay $15,000 in damages and pay for advertisements in Maine papers which stated that the charges "were mistaken and should not have been made."

Ralph Conant   Democratic candidate for Congress in 1990 in Maine's 1st District. 1.7% of the vote in the primary. Did get 37% of the vote in the Democratic primary in 1984, losing to Barry Hobbins.

Concerned Maine Families   Group concerned about homosexual rights and marriages. Sponsored the unsuccessful referendum to restrict gay rights in 1994. (See also "Lobster Boy.")

Congo Dave   Name given to Dave Emery by Peter Burr when he worked for the Congressman. Often used by the younger members of his staff such as State Senator Mary Small (R-Bath). Thought to be a corruption of "Congressman." Dave Emery deserves far more credit than he currently gets on the Maine political scene. Upsetting four-term Congressman Peter Kyros in 1974, he subsequently decimated entire cohorts of Democratic challengers including Rick Barton, Harold Pachios, and John Quinn (who in turn cleaned out dozens of other Democratic challengers in their primaries). Ran against George Mitchell for the U.S. Senate and lost, in part because of the quality of Mitchell's campaign effort but also because 1982 was the nadir for President Ronald Reagan. Subsequently a distinguished member of the Arms Control and Disarmament Agency, he oversaw the destruction of many of America's chemical and biological weapons. Dave has always remained true to his Maine heritage and his love for the state. (See "David F. 'Dave' Emery" for his political biography without the editorial comment.)

Gerard P. 'Jerry' Conley   President of the Maine Senate (1983–85) and major Portland player. Original Brennanista and important supporter of Tom Andrews when he ran for Congress against Jim Tierney and Libby Mitchell. Insiders also know him for his deep distrust of moose hunting and things GOB as well as for his sense of humor.

Dana Connors   Distinguished-looking former head of the Department of Transportation and now head of the Maine State Chamber and Business Alliance. Well liked. Led the fight to widen the Maine Turnpike in 1997.

Maynard G. Conners   Republican candidate for Congress (2nd CD) in 1970, got 35% of the vote against Bill Hathaway in the general election.

Conservation Law Foundation   Small (500 members in 1996) environmental group. Not a significant factor in Maine politics as of that date.

Conspiratorial Focus Group   A focus group in which the participants are asked to construct a campaign, first for a ballot measure, and then against the same measure. A very effective tool for discovering the efficacy of various authority figures and influence vectors.

Constitutional Political Alliance   Umbrella group supporting and created by Hayes Gehagan, who ran as an Independent for U.S. Senate in 1978, getting 8% of the vote against Bill Cohen and Bill Hathaway.

Consultant on Consultants   A grand job, one of overseeing the work of other consultants on a campaign, and a grand title. First coined by Dr. Demento during the 1994 gubernatorial campaign. When asked what he did for Angus King, he said he was a "consultant on consultants." (See also "Dr. D.")

Consultant-Speak   Vocabulary for political insiders and wannabes. What this lexicon is filled with.

Contract on America   Democratic name for the Republican "Contract for America" in 1994. "Jim Longley says it's a contract for America; I say it's a contract on America."

Contras   Anti-Sandinista rebels in Nicaragua, the support for whom was a key conservative Republican litmus test for Maine Republicans in the late 1970's and 1980's. Insiders still describe with great mirth the scene in which two prominent conservatives, when asked to actually locate Nicaragua on a map, pointed in the general direction of Surinam.

Contrast Ads   Negative ads done in a nice way by your candidate. "Angus King's contrast ads with those empty reservoirs worked like a charm."

Control or Control the Agenda   The ability to manage one's own political destiny. Difficult to achieve in a candidate race (as opposed to ballot measures where one can control much more of what happens). "Brennan knew he could control the agenda in the primary and that gave him a tremendous advantage."

Leighton Cooney   Schoolteacher who ran for Congress against Bill Cohen in 1976. Got 19% of the vote and subsequently became director of the Bureau of Public Improvements (BPI).

COPs   Children of privilege, campaign shorthand for upscale college students who don't want to do hard work on the campaign but who want to talk policy with the candidate. "This campaign can't use any more COPs; get me some high school kids who want to go door to door."

Angel Cordaro   A consultant who likes to have a candidate in the race, regardless of the candidate's party or ideology. "Hell, I was sitting by the pool like Angel Cordaro with no horse in the derby and he called me up so I said sure. I don't have any idea where he is on the issues; it's too late for that."

Gayle Corey   Longtime aide to Edmund Muskie and after he retired, George Mitchell. Beloved staffer on Capitol Hill with a great sense of what was important in politics. Sister of "Buzz" Fitzgerald. Gayle Corey passed away in 1996, a few months after Muskie. To Don Larrabee, she epitomized the very best in Capitol Hill staffers. See his *It's News to Me.*

Lucia M. Cormier   Democratic candidate for U.S. Senate in 1960. Unopposed in the primary, she received 38% of the vote against Margaret Chase Smith in the general election. Later became "Collector of Customs" in Portland, following in the footsteps of Joshua Chamberlain! She was also the Democratic nominee for Congress in the 1st District in 1950, losing to Robert Hale, the incumbent, but getting 46% of the vote.

Cornerback   Insider term for a valuable player who in campaign strategy sessions "has no memory." In the National Football League, the cornerback is effective to the extent that he can blot out past failures and concentrate on the task at hand. You would be truly amazed at how much of candidate or ballot measure strategy sessions are taken up with fighting old battles (usually with an eye to settling old scores). Cornerbacks look ahead, not backwards. "She was a terrific cornerback. I don't think he would have become governor without her skill."

Coronation   A campaign situation in which the incumbent basically has no opposition. "Basically, Angus wanted a coronation for his second term."

Anthony 'Tony' Corrado   Colby College professor of government and nationally known expert on campaign reform. Author of *Creative Campaigning*, *Paying for Presidents* and *Financing the 1992 Election*. Worked with Jimmy Carter, Walter Mondale, Bob Kerry and Bill Clinton. Major pundit.

Correct Me If I'm Wrong   Consultant-speak for "I'm not wrong. Just be quiet and listen." "Correct me if I'm wrong, but I don't think most of the people of Maine want their candidates to dress like they got their clothes in the local Goodwill store."

Carolyn Cosby   Led the 1995 referendum effort to prohibit Maine communities from enacting laws protecting civil rights of gays and lesbians and a 1997 effort to ban same-sex marriages. The first effort was defeated by voters, the second was enacted by the Legislature without being submitted to voters. Insiders are always interested in problems facing the state such as same-sex marriages of which, at the time of the effort, there were none in the state.

Cost Per Point (CPP)   The average cost of each rating point delivered for a specific television schedule in a specific ADI or DMA. "The great irony of TV commentators decrying the high cost of modern elections is the fact that the CPP's are—by far, far, far—the largest single expense of major races." (See also "ADI" and "DMAs.")

Counter-intuitive   Goes against conventional wisdom, what distinguishes the mundane from the perspicacious. What keeps political consultants in business.

Counter-productive   The suggestion your rival makes about how to improve the state. "Gambling in Maine would be counter-productive to the long-term economic health of the state."

The County   Aroostook County and heartbreaker of many politicians from Bangor south. Requires lots of attention since its citizens, like Gaul, are divided into three distinct parts: the Republican south, the Democratic St. John's Valley, and the swing middle of Caribou/Presque Isle.

Courage   Political courage is taking a tough position on an issue you know will cost you lots of votes. "Tom Andrews showed courage on Loring."

Cowboy   A consultant who does what he or she wants even if it is not in the candidate's best interest. To many staffers, most consultants are, at heart, cowboys. "What a cowboy, he just wants to save his ass. He leaked that story and put his own spin on it."

Joseph 'Joe' Cowie   Democratic activist and campaign coordinator. Widely regarded as the grass roots organizer and campaign manager who propelled Tom Andrews to his Congressional victory. After Andrews's defeat in his U.S. Senate bid, Joe became head of Andrews's fire brigade for Citizens for the American Way's, "Expose the Right!" when it briefly confronted the Christian right-wing in such "key" places as Iowa and New Hampshire. Joe was no doubt looking forward to lunching with Stephen Spielberg at Spago, but Tom Andrews did not let this happen. Cowie is known as the best overall supervisor of grass roots activity operating in Maine today.

Peter Cox   Longtime publisher of the *Maine Times,* famous with Republican insiders for his passion for the environment and for his tortured editorial endorsement of any and all liberals. His editorial support for Senator Bill Hathaway in 1978, for example, even though Hathaway favored building the Dickey Lincoln dam and opposed public financing while his opponent Bill Cohen opposed Dickey Lincoln and supported public financing, is regarded as an Orwellian classic. While the endorsements of the *Maine Times* count for little in the law of large numbers, they have always been sources of considerable aggravation and mirth for political insiders of both parties. Olympia Snowe became so angry at the paper's coverage of her that for a number of years she refused to speak to its editorial board or its reporters. Still, the *Maine Times* really kept the environmental agenda front and center for much of the 1970's and 1980's and for that, he deserves a lot of the credit. Peter began as a campaign volunteer for Frank Coffin's gubernatorial campaign in 1960. Consultants love this guy!

Crack Campaign Staff   Sarcastic term for the candidate's staff when they screw up. "Our crack staff and press secretary Duke, they just sent out a press release on education with seven spelling mistakes in it." Another version of this term means a staff which is high. "Our crack staff? I think it's alcohol, not cocaine but I can't be sure long distance."

Charles L. 'Charlie' Cragin   Republican candidate for governor in 1978, finishing second in the Republican primary with 38% of the vote. Next time around, in 1982, he won the Republican primary with 38% of the vote but lost the general election with 38% of the vote. Later chairman of the U.S. Veterans Affairs board of appeals. Noted in Maine legal circles as the first graduate of U. Maine Law School to be hired by one of Portland's old-line firms.

Elizabeth 'May' Craig   From the early 1930's until 1966 when she was replaced by Don Larrabee, she was the Washington correspondent for the Gannett newspapers. Her "Maine in Washington" column and news dispatches could make or break many a member of Maine's Congressional delegation. A strong crusader against miscegenation laws and for the rights of women reporters in the Washington press corps.

Robert L. Cram   Republican candidate for Congress in 1970, getting 19% of the 1st District primary vote.

Henrietta Page Crane   Grand dame of the Republican party, active from the 1950's until the 1980's, serving in various organizational capacities including National Committeewoman. Big initial supporter of Margaret Chase Smith and Dave Emery.

Crap Shoot   A political situation where the polling says both candidates could win. "I told Billy it would be a crap shoot against Muskie. Why take a chance? Wait two years and have a straight shot against Hathaway." (See also "Straight Shot.")

Crave to Pave Crowd   Davis Rawson's term for the construction lobby that always wants to pass transportation bond issues. (See also "Sand and Gravel Crowd.")

Creative Demagoguery   Untrue but believable statements or strategy in a ballot measure campaign. What bad consultants engage in. "I can't believe they have no regard for the truth, what creative demagoguery."

Creative Design and Marketing   Ad firm which creatively won various elections for Dave Emery and also won the Sunday Sales referendum. Bob Cott and Ken Krause are principals.

Crisis du Jour   Crisis of the day. For consultants, every campaign has some kind of crisis, whether self-inflicted or not. "Don't worry about it, Governor. The crisis du jour is the scheduler vs. the field woman."

Robert Crocker   Augusta Bureau Chief, Associated Press, in the 1950's and 1960's.

Cronies   What the press and Republicans often call the friends of Joe Brennan. Joe makes a very fair point when he asks, "Why do I have cronies and everybody else has friends?" Actually, the enduring loyalty of those who have supported Joe Brennan through thick and thin is one of the more refreshing aspects to Maine politics since World War II.

Burton Cross   Republican governor who lost to Ed Muskie in 1954, only the fifth time since the Civil War that a Democrat had won the Blaine House (others were Alonzo Garcelon in 1878, Frederick Plaisted in 1910, Oakley Curtis, 1914, and Louis Brann 1932 and 1934) and the first time in 20 years. In 1952, Cross won a three-way Republican primary for governor with 40% of the vote and won a four-way general election with 52% of the vote.

Cross of Gold   William Jennings Bryan's memorable class warfare speech in 1896 pitting Democratic workers against corporations and asking voters not to crucify working men and women on a "cross of gold." Bryan's running mate was Arthur Sewall of Bates, grandfather to Maine

Governor Sumner Sewall. Currently in Maine politics, it refers to any candidate, male or female, with a gold chain around the neck. "Did you see that guy running for mayor? He's a cross of gold fellow."

Cross-Dressers   Democrats who turn Republican and Republicans who turn Democrat. Does not apply to whatever it is Independents do. "She's a cross-dresser now."

Cross Maine Bear   King Harvey's name for Burton Cross during his 1954 race with Ed Muskie. Harvey thought Cross's personality and comments were costing him politicially and compared him to a cranky Maine bear. Cross eventually did lose the race to Ed Muskie.

Cross-Tabs   Short for cross-tabulations; in polling, the segmentation of the voting population by age, sex, income, education and other categories. "Collins looked good in the head to head but there were some initially major weaknesses in the cross-tabs, such as with working women."

Crows   The press, from Eugene McCarthy's bold 1968 statement, "The press are like crows. They all sit on one wire until one flies off to another, then they all fly over there." May also explain the press and its fascination with road kills. (See also "Scorps.")

Cruel Yuppies   Polling name for those upscale voters in the arc around Portland, in places such as Cumberland and Yarmouth, where the voters go for candidates who are more likely to cut federal programs no matter what party the candidate belongs to. "The cruel yuppies put Longley over the top and he didn't even know they were there."

Crush   To win by a margin bigger than 55% to 45%. "I don't just want to win, I want to crush those guys."

Cuomo   To agonize over a political decision until the opportunity is lost, as in "She Cuomoed the Senate race again." (See also "Hamlet.") Governor Cuomo, having passed up numerous chances to run for President, became a talk show host following his defeat in 1994. "God, it looks like Colin Powell is going to Cuomo."

Leland B. Currier   Ran for governor in the Democratic primary in 1946 (43%), 1948 (42%) and 1950 (38%). In 1950, ran in the general election as a States' Rights Democrat and received .4% of the vote. This was before Maine adopted its "sore loser" law in the late 1960's that has since prohibited a losing primary candidate to then file as a non-party candidate in the general election. Currier then ran again as a Democrat for Congress in Maine's 2nd CD, winning the primary in 1952 with 59% of the vote and losing the general election with 33%.

Curse of the Francos   Although the Franco Americans are the most important swing vote in Maine politics, they have seldom elected one of their own to major office such as Congressman or Congresswoman, Governor or Senator in Maine. In fact, unless you count Margaret Chase Smith and Jim Longley Sr. as Franco Americans, they have not elected a Franco American to major office since World War II. It is often said by Franco insiders that this is due to internal rivalries within the Franco-American community, where the subculture says, "You can do well but not too well." A variety of Franco candidates such as Elmer Violette and Duke Dutremble have not done as well in the Franco communities as one might expect given their ethnicity, and have subsequently lost their races for U.S. Congress and in the case of Violette, the U.S. Senate. In fact, in his 1994 race against Jim Longley, Duke Dutremble actually ran behind the vote total of Tom Andrews in Biddeford (70% to 72%) and elsewhere. In Maine, the Franco propensity for division is often contrasted with the Irish or Jewish voters who tend to place ethnicity or religion above jealousy, to the advantage of Irish or Jewish candidates. Prior to World War II, Franco-American office holders included Democrat Alonzo Garcelon, governor in 1878, Democrat Edward Carl Moran, 2nd District Congressman from 1933 to 1937, Republican Charles Boutelle in Congress 1883–1901 and Democrat Louis Brann, governor from 1933 to 1937.

George Curtis   Finished third in the Republican primary for the 1st CD in 1958, receiving 28% of the vote.

Kenneth M. 'Ken' Curtis   Elected governor in 1966, winning the Democratic primary with 56% of the vote and defeating John Reed in the general election with 53% of the vote. Reelected in 1970 after beating Plato

Truman in the primary with 63% of the vote, he narrowly (50.1% to 49.9%) defeated Jim Erwin. Previously ran for Congress, winning the 1st District Democratic primary in 1964 with 66% of the vote but lost the general election with 49.9% of the vote. As Maine's governor from 1967 to 1975, Curtis is perhaps best remembered for the state income tax, reorganization of state government and for appointing James Longley Jr. to a statewide cost management commission. (See also "Don't Blame Yourself, Kenny.")

Later he became ambassador to Canada after his early support for the Georgia governor, who became President Jimmy Carter. Subsequently Curtis became head of the Maine Maritime Academy from which he had graduated in 1953. Curtis was Davis Rawson's choice to be Senator Ed Muskie's replacement, and Rawson thought he would or should be appointed by Governor Joe Brennan. Since Curtis had worked against Joe Brennan in various races and openly opposed some of his policies, this was certainly not the political wisdom of the moment (although some Democratic insiders were pushing for Curtis as well). Nor did it come to pass. Some Democratic insiders believe Curtis might well have challenged Brennan's appointee to the U.S. Senate, George Mitchell, in 1982 except for Curtis's heart attack in late 1981. Curtis remains highly regarded by both Republicans and Democrats and is one of the nicest people in Maine politics.

Theodore 'Ted' Curtis   Republican State Senator from Orono and important Party player in the 1960's and 1970's. Served as 1960's campaign coordinator for the Republican State Committee and John Reed. Nominated for the Maine Legislature while stationed in Vietnam. A strong force for numerous constitutional reforms, including the 18-year-old vote, the Equal Rights Amendment and the abolition of the Executive Council. Insiders know him as the first person to suggest to Olympia Snowe that she should run for Congress when he told her Bill Cohen was running for the U.S. Senate.

D

Politics is like football. You have to be

smart enough to understand the

game and dumb enough to think

it's important.

GENE McCARTHY

D Triple C   DCCC, the Democratic Congressional Campaign Committee which supports Democratic candidates for Congress.

Thomas 'Tom' Daffron   Longtime aide to Congressman and then Senator Bill Cohen, now administrative assistant to Senator Fred Thompson. For two decades, Tom has been a Maine political player of note and one of the best tacticians in Maine politics. In addition to Senator Cohen, Daffron has been at the heart of various Republican candidates' campaign efforts, including those of Charlie Cragin, Ted O'Meara and Susan Collins. He played a particularly important role in helping Collins overcome her primary and general election opposition in the 1996 Senate campaign. Thought by some insiders to be one of the most gifted (though underpaid) consultant in the post–World War II period in Maine politics.

Damage Control   Process of trying to mitigate the electoral fall out from some campaign mistake. "Did you see those boys around Muskie trying damage control after he cried in New Hampshire?"

Peter 'Pete' Damborg   Political writer, *Portland Press Herald* and *Maine Sunday Telegram*. Press secretary for Jim Erwin in 1974 and later aide to Governor Longley and executive director of the Maine State Employees Association.

Peter Danton   Thirty-five-year friend and confidant of Joe Brennan, chief of staff for Governor Brennan 1985–1986. Important player in that era.

Joanne D'Archangelo   Former executive director of the Democratic Party, now executive director of the Maine Women's Lobby. Democratic field activist.

Thomas 'Tommy D' Davidson   Democratic state representative from Brunswick. Very effective street campaigner. Some Democratic insiders believe that he will be the next Congressperson from the 1st District when Tom Allen moves up to run for governor or the U.S. Senate. Important player in southern Maine political circles.

Richard 'Dick' Davies   Longtime Democratic activist and president of Public Policy Associates. Former state legislator (1974–1982), worked on a number of Democratic campaigns including Phil Merrill for Governor, Joe Brennan for Governor and Senate, Elizabeth Mitchell for Senate, Jim Tierney for Governor and Dale McCormick for Congress. Also worked to eliminate the big box ballot, to shut down Maine Yankee, to pass the ERA, to widen the Maine Turnpike, and to pass a variety of jobs and affordable housing bonds. A player.

James V. Day   Finished second in the Republican primary for the 1st CD in 1956 with 38% of the vote.

John Day   Longtime political columnist and reporter for the *Bangor Daily News*. Washington bureau chief but returns to Maine to cover major elections. Conservative and thus a nice antidote to the more natural liberal bias of much of the media's political reporters. Tends to form passionate attachments (the McKernan extended family and Bob Tyrer) and inveterate antipathies (Joe Brennan) but is really, at heart, an equal-opportunity savager. One of the brightest and most creative of the Maine reporters, Day has two lists, one for sources, which is very small, and one for enemies. That one has many names. On the top of that list, Steve Campbell recently replaced Al Diamon. (See also "Big Rolodex" and "Rasputin.") Rarely able to disguise his sources from political insiders. This often causes heartburn to friend and foe alike. A player and for 25 years arguably the most important print reporter in the political sphere. Spinnable in little doses, especially for a free game of golf.

Day Late, Dollar Short   Short for "A day late and a dollar short." Any campaign suggestion that is too late to do any good. "Sure we would have liked to mail all gun owners in that cycle, but frankly we were a day late and a dollar short."

Day of Betrayal   Jonathan Carter's hyperbolic designation of June 14, 1996, the day Governor King's Compact for Maine's Forests was achieved by the governor, the major landowners, The Nature Conservancy, The Audubon Society, and the Natural Resources Council of Maine. This day appears to have coincided with the bottom falling out of the Green Party's public levels of support for its clear-cutting referendum.

D.C. Guys   Consultants from Washington, D.C., who, whether they are Republicans or Democrats, think that they know more than the Maine state operatives of either party. Since the Republican and Democratic national committees have incredibly incestuous relationships and sweetheart contracts with these consultants, the committees usually withhold campaign contributions and donations unless they are "hired" by the Maine campaigns. "Those D.C. guys are at it again. They don't know jack shit." (See also "Jack Shit.")

Dead Cat Bounce   A strange, almost mystical state which descends on a candidate who knows he or she has definitely lost and that there is nothing he or she can do to reverse the situation. When accepted, this knowledge brings the candidate inner peace, and because the candidate looks more relaxed and at ease, it is often accompanied by a rise in the polls. "Ironically, Dave Emery and Tom Andrews got the same dead cat bounce in their senatorial campaigns."

Dead Man Walking   A candidate who is finished politically but who still has to face election day. "Did you see the clip of Monks the night before the election? He was dead man walking and he said on the air that he was going to finish third. I can't believe it."

Dead Smoke   Campaign information which is old or out of date. "There's nothing in that column except dead smoke."

The Dean   Short for "The Dean of the Statehouse Press Corps," Mal Leary. "The Dean is pretty fair and he knows a lot of history so he can put things in perspective; I trust him."

Declaration of Conscience   (1) Senator Margaret Chase Smith's June, 1950 attack on the tactics of Senator Joseph McCarthy of Wisconsin and on the lack of executive and legislative leadership against those tactics. The speech was a powerful, courageous statement not only on the slandering of "communists" but "fascists" as well, not only of right-wing attacks on the left but left-wing attacks on the right.

Declaration of Conscience   (2) Senator Margaret Chase Smith's June, 1970 speech delivered after her visit to Colby College in May. This time she attacked the excesses of the left and raised the spectre of disorder.

Declaration of Conscience   (3) Book by Senator Margaret Chase Smith and General William Lewis setting forth the high points of her career, bookended by the two Declaration of Conscience speeches.

Deep Background   What reporters say they will put you on right before they write a column in which any moron or civilian can figure out that their source is you. "Deep background, John? I know what that means; even Kent Ward will figure out your source."

Deep Pockets   A client with lots of financial resources. "In the term limits referendum, Betty Noyce had deep pockets and there was no heavy lifting involved."

Deep Shit   GOB term for big trouble. What George Bush should have said instead of "Deep Do Do" if he had really wanted to be President of the United States for a second term. Probably caused him to run third in Maine in 1992. Nobody can claim to be "country" and use "Deep Do Do" instead of "Deep Shit," even if they like pork rinds and Patsy Cline.

Define   To paint yourself in the most positive way and your opponent in a less advantageous way. An essential part of contested political contests no matter how much editorial writers say they don't like the process.

The Deformed Transformed   Forget Lord Byron, this is what every political consultant should strive for. In addition to making a little money and having a little fun, a consultant should always try to actually improve a candidate's performance and/or appearance. "Talk about the deformed transformed! A year ago he couldn't put two sentences together without a TelePrompTer, now he's running for the U.S. Senate. I take some credit for that."

Robert 'Bob' 'Dice Man' Deis   Chief Eastern strategist for Winner/ Wagner and Mandabach Campaigns of Los Angeles, America's premier ballot measure campaign firm. Won Save Maine Yankee I (1980) and Save Maine Yankee III (1987), lost turnpike-widening referendum in 1991 but won the complicated three-way campaign against the clear-cutting initiative (1996) with 47% of the vote. These guys roll the dice successfully 9 out of 10 times, having won over 100 campaigns in 22 states. "Dice Man" is also one of the fairest and most effective political operatives on the Maine political scene and one of the few national political consulting operatives actually located in Maine. "Check it with the Dice Man; he knows the score."

John Delahanty   Son of Thomas and a longtime effective Democratic political operative and fund-raiser. Worked for Muskie, Mitchell, Brennan, Baldacci as well as Compact I and Compact II. Works for Pierce Atwood.

Thomas E. Delahanty   Democratic nominee for the second district Congressional seat in 1954, he lost the general election with 46% of the vote. Close confidant of Muskie whose final act as governor was to name him to the Superior Court in 1958.

Deliverables   Voting groups which can be gotten by one strategy or action. "Forget their hard core, we're going after the deliverables only."

Delusions of Adequacy   Campaign staffer's self-images not borne out by campaign results. "He was lousy as a field man and now he wants to be the press secretary. He's got delusions of adequacy."

Demagogue   To appeal to the most primitive instincts and beliefs of a particular group. "You have to demagogue them a little; they're the city committee in Brewer, for heaven's sake."

Demagoguery   Wild assertions, attacks, claims, and promises made by one's opponent. "Maine people will not fall for such demagoguery."

Mr. Democrat   Some Democrats' name for Rep. Louis Jalbert's (D-Lewiston). The "Dean" of the Maine House, and a major force on the appropriations committee, he served from 1945 to 1953, and from 1955 to 1984. He wished to have one of the bridges from Lewiston to Auburn named after him. Due to the civic intervention of Auburn Mayor Jack Linnell and Lewiston Mayor Bob Clifford, the bridge was called the Vietnam Veterans Memorial Bridge. Rep. Jalbert's name is on a building at the Central Maine Technical College in Auburn, which was founded through legislation he sponsored in 1965.

The Democratic State Committee   An auk masquerading as a donkey.

Demographics   Standard polling grouping by such variables as sex, age, income, and education which enable a pollster to segment the population into meaningful groups. Also very useful in TV placement. "Clear cutting was initially opposed in 1996 by every major demographic group."

Demonize   To paint a candidate in such a negative light that he or she never recovers. Often used as a motivational technique to arouse true believers. "Tom Andrews demonized Linda Bean with that toxic waste ad and she was history." (See also "True Believer.")

Henry J. Desmarais   Democratic candidate for Congress in 1st CD, received 34% of the vote in the primary in 1964.

Al Diamon   *Casco Bay Weekly* columnist, media personality and follower of the Maine political scene. Al almost always has an interesting column no matter what your political point of view. Basically a libertarian with strong anti-gun control, anti-government spending views, and adamant free speech positions, he is liberal on such social issues such as gay rights and pro-choice on abortion. Unless he is writing about you and yours, he can be wickedly funny and often trenchant. Even then, he sometimes is. It is rumored among political insiders that he once wrote a positive column about an elected official but that has not been verified as of press time. He is particularly adept at pulling up previous verbatim quotes of candidates and office holders when they later change their opinions on those subjects. His predictable cynicism turns off some insiders, but most read his column with relish.

G. William 'Bill' Diamond   State Senator (D-Windham), Maine Secretary of State and candidate for higher office. Ran for governor in 1986, losing in the Democratic primary with 21% of the vote, and for Congress in Maine's First District Democratic primary in 1994, obtaining 23.8% of the vote.

Diamond Lil   Lillian Caron O'Brien, the first woman to become mayor of a major city in Maine when she won that office in Lewiston in 1975. Part Cherokee Indian with a Franco last name, courtesy of her first husband, and an Irish one thanks to her second, she therefore hit two of the three most important ethnic groups in the state. Diamond Lil was a major tactical player on the Maine political scene for two decades. She also worked as a staffer for Bill Cohen. "Diamond Lil was one of a kind, we really miss her, she could rustle up a demonstration in an hour." One of the most engaging people in post-war Maine politics.

Dickey Short for the Dickey Lincoln Dam whose plans dominated the environmental landscape of the 1960's and 1970's. Supported by Democrats such as Muskie, Hathaway, and Mitchell, it was opposed by the state's environmentalists and most Republicans. The Dickey Lincoln School project would have flooded 100,000 acres of Maine's north woods at a cost of over $1 billion. Nobody seems to have decried its passing. "I love Dickey as an issue; it sticks it to the *Maine Times* in the worst way. They hate the dam but they hate Republicans. I bet they go with the Democrats anyway." Also responsible for the memorable *BDN* headline in 1979: "Carter to Brennan: Dickey Now in Your Hands."

Didactic Focus Group Focus group in which an effort is made to see how easily a group can be "taught" new political information. Often used to test the limits of messages. "The didactic focus group won the election for us. It showed what we could not do and still expect to win."

Paul Dillaway Longtime GOP state committee stalwart, executive director of the party and a major fund-raiser.

Edward 'Ed' Dinan Current president and CEO of Bell Atlantic Maine. Major insider of note. Almost everybody goes to Dinan for support for themselves and/or their causes. A player.

DINKs Polling and advertising term for a "dual income, no kids" category of people, this group forms the basis for the "Cruel Yuppies" in polling psychographics. (See also "Cruel Yuppies.")

Dip and Ship White hunter term for dipping an animal skin or head for shipment and then sending it off. In Maine campaigns it often means "get it done quickly" as "Forget making the dubs perfect, dip and ship, we need to be on the air tonight."

Dirigo Latin for "I Lead." The state motto of Maine and the central core self-image for Maine political figures Ed Muskie, Margaret Chase Smith, Bill Cohen and George Mitchell. What Maine people say they want in their elected officials and usually do.

Dirt for Hire   John Day's characterization of the Democratic senatorial campaign for hiring a private investigator to research the background of Susan Collins.

Dirt Nap   Dead, finished. "His political career took a dirt nap when he was indicted on drug charges."

Dish   (1) To give a story to a scorp, playing one reporter off against the other. "Dish this one to Campbell; we dished the last one to Day."

Dish   (2) Logging term for a chainsaw moving to the left or right as if it had a life of its own. In politics, means a campaign moving off in its own direction, away from the game plan. "I tell you, Dick, she's dishing. You've got big problems."

Disloyal   What, in the minds of staffers, all political consultants are, as in "You disloyal pigs, you're only in this for the money." This contrasts with staffers who are only in it for job security.

Distribution   In polling, the distribution of opinion means how widespread is an opinion. "Jobs are the number one issue in each of Maine's 16 counties."

DMAs   Designated Market Areas. Units of measurement, used by Nielsen television ratings, that are designed to show the market areas or reach of television stations. In Maine, there are three DMAs. The first, Portland, accounts for approximately 60% of the viewing public. The second is Bangor, which accounts for 30%; and the third is Presque Isle, which has the remaining 10% of Maine TV viewership. DMAs are roughly comparable to Arbitron's Areas of Dominant Influence (ADIs).

DNC   Democratic National Committee. Famous for sending people from Washington to Maine to tell Maine Democratic candidates how to appeal to Maine people. "They want us to push gun control! Can you believe that? Where do they get these DNC types?"

Do a Beckel   To fail at politics and become a pundit. Named for Bob Beckel, who as Walter Mondale's campaign manager in 1984 lost 48 states and then became a national commentator on politics. "I saw him at BIW, I swear to god, he's doing a Beckel. He's telling them how to do PR."

Do a Connally   Spend a lot of money running for President and do very poorly. Refers to John Connally, who ran for President in 1980 and spent $26 million to get a single delegate. "Gramm is going to do a Connally." (See also "Do a Gramm.")

Do a Duke   To not respond to your opponent's negative ads even if it means losing an election. Named for Duke Dutremble who did not respond to Jim Longley Jr.'s attacks during the final 10 days of the 1994 1st CD race. A rare event in politics, although those who are 20 points ahead often take the moral high ground and don't go negative, but few candidates refuse to go negative if it means losing the election. "Don't do a Duke; hit him right away."

Do a Gramm   Spend a lot of money running for President and do very poorly. Named for Phil Gramm's embarrassing run for the Presidency in 1995 and early 1996. "You don't want to do a Gramm, do you?" (See also "Do a Connally.")

Do a Haig   For a candidate or consultant to run around in a frenzy asserting that, a la Al Haig, he or she is "in charge." "Did you hear about it? The Congressman kept saying, 'I've had enough of you damn consultants, I'm in charge, I'm in charge.' It was something to see."

Do a Larry King   To be very easy, almost disgustingly so, on a political figure. "It was awful, he did a Larry King on our opponent."

Do a Rollins   Referring to a classic miscue by Ed Rollins, who in the aftermath of Christie Todd Whitman's victory in the 1993 New Jersey governor's race, got carried away with his own importance and bragged that the Whitman campaign had paid money to Afro-American ministers "to suppress" the black vote. In consultant-speak it means stepping on your story of triumph with some terrible revelation. "Keep your mouth shut at the victory press conference; let the candidate have her day. Don't even bring up the walking-around money story. Don't do a Rollins."

Do Nothing   Often the best advice a consultant can give a candidate. This piece of advice is also one of the most likely pieces of advice to be ignored by said candidate. "Loeb made fun of your wife, Senator? Do nothing."

Do Unto Others What They Would Do Unto You—But Do It First   Consultant advice to Christian and non-Christian candidates alike.

The Docs   Doctors who, in political terms, tend to be very cheap when it comes to individual donations to campaigns or causes, except those involving national health care plans.

Dodge   Short for "Dodge City." Consultant-speak for the place where the action is and where any campaign showdowns will take place. "I'm coming to Dodge to kill him, not wound him. Who's coming with me? The road to the Blaine House doesn't run around Joe or under Joe; it runs right through Joe. Let him bring his guys and we'll bring our guys and we'll take Dodge. Let's go."

Dog in the Fight   Denotes a political situation where one has a candidate one is supporting. Often used to feign objectivity as "I've got no dog in the fight but I think she'd make a pretty good senator."

Dog Race   Consultant-speak for a sure loser. "It's a dog race for sure, but I like the guy."

Dogmeat   A candidate headed for defeat. "She's dogmeat, no question about it. Head for the hills."

The Dogs Bark but the Caravan Moves On   Consultant-speak for "Let the reporters and editors make their noise, we're going to win anyway. "I guarantee you nobody will read that editorial, let alone remember it. The dogs bark but the caravan moves on."

Dogs on a Roof   A messy situation. Refers to some double-decker houses where the dog on the upper floor is allowed to go out onto the roof of the lower floor to defecate. "What a screw-up; it was dogs on a roof, a lot of dogs."

Doing the Gates   Standing at the mill gates in Westbrook, Rumford, Millinocket, Jay, and other paper mill towns. This time-honored Maine tradition is disliked by candidates and mill workers alike and continues to have a life of its own for reasons that remain obscure. Imagine how interested you would be in talking to some political yobo after finishing an 8-hour shift of work.

Maynard C. Dolloff   Democratic candidate for governor in 1962. Won the primary with 50.3% of the vote and then lost the general election to John Reed with 49.9% of the vote after a statewide re-count.

Done Deal   An election won. "It's a done deal; we're carrying Penobscot and Cumberland. It's all over and the scorps haven't figured it out yet."

Donkey Party   The Democrats. "The donkey party is after your bank book. Head for the hills."

John C. 'JCD' Donovan   Bowdoin professor of government, a campaign manager for Ed Muskie (along with Frank Coffin), and Democratic state chair and candidate for Congress in 1960. Beat Roger Dube with 76% of the vote in the 2nd District primary but lost to Stan Tupper in the general election with 47% of the vote. A major participant in the Muskie revolution.

Don't Blame Yourself, Kenny   Polly Curtis's comment to her husband, Governor Ken Curtis, on election night 1974 when Jim Longley won after having been given a political platform by Ken Curtis in the form of the Maine Cost Management Survey. Quoted by Willis Johnson, *The Year of the Longley* (Stonington: Penobscot Bay Press, 1978).

Don't Bullshit a Bullshitter   Don't use client talk on a consultant. "You need a 15% markup on the placement? Don't bullshit a bullshitter, Bob."

Don't Get Mad, Get Even   Family motto of the Kennedy family. Often cited by Maine consultants to deflect candidates from making mistakes in the heat of anger. "Look, Senator, I know it would make you feel better to send that letter but don't get mad, get even. In two weeks, you'll be re-elected and you don't have to let him in the door."

Don't Rely on Them for Anything   Sage advice when asked about using a state legislator on a ballot measure campaign. "Some of them will work for their own re-election but for this referendum, don't rely on them for anything."

Don't Skimp on the Sauce   A phrase used by Congressman John Baldacci to describe his method of making spaghetti. Also a phrase used by some of his Democratic primary opponents to describe the manner in which the cigarette manufacturers contributed to Baldacci's Congressional campaign in 1994. To his credit, Baldacci later stopped taking tobacco money.

Don't Trade a Record for a Promise   Margaret Chase Smith's slogan when she ran for the U.S. Senate in 1948 and received more votes than her three male opponents combined.

The Double Man   William S. Cohen's novel written with Gary Hart. According to Democrats, Cohen would have had to be a double man to have enough time to write all those novels and still be a full-time U.S. senator. "When did the Double Man write that? On the red eye from California?"

Allan Dowd   Reporter for Reuters and Maine Public Radio. Doesn't do analysis but his news coverage is straightforward and very solid.

Down Ballot Races   Races on the ballot such as state senator or mayor which appear below the statewide and congressional contests. "Her media firm has mostly had experience with down ballot races."

Down East Shots   Pretty, scenic shots in campaign advertising, named for *Down East* magazine, famous for only having upbeat stories and pretty pictures between its covers. "I don't want any dark, brooding stuff; give me the Down East shots from beginning to end. Have the candidate run the beach with his dog and this time have him take off his shoes."

Down the Food Chain   Refers to the order of importance of players in a political campaign. "He has no idea how far down the food chain he is; he's just wasting his time."

Jon 'Clogs' Doyle   Longtime Republican activist and Augusta lawyer (Doyle and Nelson) with many briefs for political action. In 1995, his firm received $181,000 from such diverse clients as R. J. Reynolds, CMP and Blue Cross. Major legislative player. Now a rainmaker for both Republicans and Democrats. Show me the money!

Dr. D   Short for Dr. Demento, Dr. C. P. Potholm, professor of government at Bowdoin College. Political pollster and strategist who loves to give political advice. Used as in "Billy, Dr. D wants you to donate one of your kidneys to some little girl. Says it would be a great photo op and you could skip the walk in the Valley this summer." Political insiders sometimes remark: "Dr. D can be amusing in small doses."

Gordon M. Drew   Behind-the-scenes kingpin in the GOP resurgence of 1960; key supporter of John Reed.

Drift   Sometimes even the most insightful and creative pollsters cannot explain a change in the political landscape. That is when they turn to the time-honored phenomenon of "drift," or unexplained movement. "How did they move up over the summer? Drift is the best I can do."

Drink the Poison   To do something very damaging in response to an opponent's or reporter's challenge. "You can drink the poison if you want, Congressman, but I'd waffle until we see what the numbers say on this."

Drive the Ballot   To change people's minds about a candidate or cause. Using "influence vectors" and "authority figures," political consultants lead the voters from one position to another. "Being able to go to church in the morning and go shopping in the afternoon drove the ballot in the referendum on Sunday Sales." (See also "Authority Figure" and "Influence Vectors.")

Drive the Headlines   Make news; have a story which will make the news in a positive way. "Jack Wyman actually was a pretty good candidate one on one, but he had a hard time driving the headlines week to week because the scorps pigeonholed him."

Driveway   In ballot measure campaigns, the transition from one position to the one you want the voters to adopt. "Where's the driveway in our message?"

Drop   When the direct mail arrives. "Time the drop to follow the TV, not go before it."

Dry Humping   Fund-raising term, to go to a PAC or interest group and say all the right things and have them appear to like you but then give you no money. "All that time we spent with the docs? It turned out to be just dry humping. We never got a cent."

Dub   (1) Coastal slang for a poor fisherman, hence a poor performer in any realm. "What a dub, he got the candidate there late and to the wrong address."

Dub   (2) To make copies of TV spots and ship to the stations. "Dub them tonight or you're out of a job."

Dub Around   Coastal saying meaning to fool around, not accomplish anything. "Let's stop dubbing around and get some lawn signs up."

Roger P. Dube   Democratic candidate for Senate in 1952, (getting 35% of the vote) and Congress in Maine's 2nd District in 1956, getting 30% of the vote against Frank Coffin in the Democratic primary. Then in 1960, he lost to John Donovan in the primary, getting 23.8% of the vote.

F. Harold Dubord   Democratic National Committeeman who, in 1946, talked Ed Muskie into running for the Maine Legislature, thus launching one of the most successful political careers in the history of Maine. (See "Almost Doesn't Count" [1].)

Richard J. Dubord   Democratic candidate for governor in 1962. Lost to Maynard Dolloff in the primary but got 49.7% of the vote. (See also "Almost Doesn't Count" [2]).

Political Duenna   Term for Senator Margaret Chase Smith in 1960 by an unnamed Bowdoin College professor who predicted Smith's overwhelming defeat in 1960. In her race against Lucia Cormier, Senator Smith claimed that because a duenna was "an elderly woman who watches over a young woman," the term was as inaccurate as the rest of the prediction.

Duke   Duke Dulac, owner of Duke's Rotary Barber in Augusta, whose barbershop poll gets statewide attention each election fall as the scorps seek a story and candidates' reassurance. Has been correct a number of times.

***The* Duke**   Dennis Dutremble (D-Biddeford), President of the Maine Senate, and candidate for Congress in Maine's 1st Congressional District in 1994. Named for his fondness in high school for the song "The Duke of Earl." Beat three other Democrats in a hotly contested primary but then lost narrowly to Jim Longley in "The Year of the Republican." Turned around and delivered York County to Tom Allen against Dale McCormick in the 1996 Democratic primary for Congress, thereby ensuring Allen's victory in the fall. Major power in York County. One of the few candidates in Maine political history who refused to go negative when he was facing defeat, knew it and could have won had he gone negative. Deserved all the editorial support he got.

The Dunfees   Major Democratic powerhouse fund-raising family, especially in the 1960's, '70's and '80's. Jerry and especially Robert 'Bob' Dunfee were close to Governor Curtis.

Dung Eyes   Maine coastal resident name for those who live inland. "Those dung eyes are for Porteous. I'm having none of it."

James P. Dunleavy   Democratic candidate for Congress in Maine's Second District in 1982, finishing with 33% of the vote after getting 51% in the Democratic primary.

Frank O. Dunton   Finished second in the Republican primary for the 1st Congressional District in 1948 with 10.5% of the vote.

Duopoly   John Rensenbrink's term for the political system dominated by the Republicans and Democrats and the reason for the need to establish a broad-based alternative in the form of the Green Party.

Dust   To dismiss. "The media often dusts good candidates before they get a chance to tell their story. The media likes horse races more than policies."

Dennis 'Duke' Dutremble   Democratic candidate for Congress in the 1st CD in 1994, won four-way primary with 33% of the vote and lost the general election to Jim Longley Jr. getting 48% of the vote. (See also "*The Duke.*")

Robert 'Bob' Dyke   Longtime political reporter for Channel 8 news before the arrival of Jeff Toorish. The best of TV reporters and an exception to the consultant stereotypes of most TV reporters as being in the "Talking Heads" or "Sourceless and Senseless" categories. Dyke often had a good grasp on the background aspects of politics and wasn't afraid of asking politicians tough questions. Honed his skills with ABC News. Excellent natural curiosity.

E

Eagle Award   Any award manufactured for political advantage. Named after the Merrymeeting Waterfowl Museum's giant carved eagle which went to Bill Cohen in 1973 for "his outstanding contribution to the cause of Freedom in the United States and around the world." Award was never given again and the eagle ended up falling apart in Cohen's office. But for years, it kept the attention of Peter Bradford. "Forget it, it's another eagle award."

Earl   Affectionate nickname for former Congressman Dave Emery, name derived from the 350-pound bear of the same name in John Irving's book *The Hotel New Hampshire.*

Early Fringe   TV talk for the 4–5 P.M. or 4–6 P.M. time period which precedes the local news. Many talk shows are found here, and political commercials can often fit into early fringe time slots for less money than around the local news.

Early Money   In politics, the money which comes in early often gives that candidate a big advantage, so "early money" is regarded as twice as valuable as "late money." "Both Spencer and McCormick had early money advantages in 1996, but both failed to capitalize on it." (See also "Late Money.")

Earned Media   Free media, that for which you do not pay but "earn" with press releases and the like. "She's ahead with the earned media but we're beating her on the air."

Easy Choice   Consultant-speak for a candidate you like who has a lot of campaign money and wants you to spend it. "She was an easy choice for me, 7K a month and no heavy lifting, and I liked her position on at least some of the issues." (See also "K.")

Easy Money   Money for which a candidate doesn't have to do a lot, such as the money which comes from the state party or the national party. Actually, "easy money" can sometimes be difficult if the state or national party attaches conditions to it or forces a campaign to use certain vendors. "Duke's easy money wasn't easy after all; those Washington dudes really fouled up the last ten days of the campaign."

Ecofeminists   Women who believe that only women know what's best for Mother Earth.

Ecoterrorists   Unkind name for the Green Party.

Editorials   Perhaps the most overrated political art form because of the changing nature of political campaigns. Although newspaper editorials used to be of great value to candidates in the 1950's and 1960's, with the increased importance of television, they are seldom decisive in the 1990's unless they are taken from the pages of the newspapers and put in 30-second commercials. There are three reasons for this. First, most modern campaigns are decided long before the editorials come out. Second, so few actual voters read the political endorsements (although all insiders read them with eagerness). Third, given the attention span of voters in the age of MTV, the editorials are often complex and too long. On balance, for print editorials to be a major factor in a political race, therefore, they have to appear early enough so that media consultants can highlight the appropriate points they make and put them on TV. In that context, they can still be important. To maximize their impact, editorial writers should endorse at least three weeks before election day.

El Supremo   Tom Daffron's term for Bill Cohen as Senator. "El Supremo is in good spirits today."

El Whacko   Democratic nickname for Governor James Longley Sr. (1975–1979) *after* he became governor. See Willis Johnson's humorous book about Longley, *Year of the Longley* (Stonington, Maine: Penobscot Bay Press, 1978).

Election Cycle   Refers to the fact that most Congressional and statewide elections take place on even years, making the odd-numbered years lean ones for political consultants, although civilians often find them a refreshing pause in the political activity associated with campaigns.

Election Day   The Alpha and Omega of days on the consultant calendar. Prior to 1960 in Maine, that day was the second Monday in September. Beginning in 1960, it was the first Tuesday after the first Monday in November.

The Election Nobody Saw   The 1975 contest between Congressman Bill Cohen, Senator Ed Muskie and their staffs to see if Muskie could get a lead over Cohen as Muskie sought reelection in 1976. Although Muskie was only able to cut Cohen's head to head polling lead from 16 points to 11 with a series of wise political moves, including the formation of the Senate Budget Committee to appear more conservative, the race did not feel right to Cohen and he decided to wait until 1978 to run for the Senate, defeating one-term Senator Bill Hathaway 60% to 40%. Jim Case, Larry Benoit, Phil Merrill and Charlie Micholeau ran the Muskie effort; Tom Daffron and Chris Potholm the Cohen.

Elephant Party   The Republicans. "The elephant party is in control of the labor committee; forget boosting the minimum wage this session."

Eleventh Commandment   Speak ill of no Republican, a credo attributed to Ronald Reagan.

Patricia 'Pat' Eltman   Major Democratic activist and for many years the right-hand woman and chief of staff for Speaker John Martin (D-Eagle Lake) and later, Speaker Libby Mitchell (D-Vassalboro). Pat is one of the most prominent Democratic players and an important field operative for Democratic Presidential (and other) candidates. Always highly sought for her get-out-the-vote efforts. A serious moose hunter. Insiders know her by her spirit name "She who must be obeyed."

Eben L. Elwell   Democratic candidate for Congress in 1966. Received 30% of the vote in the 1st District primary. Elwell was also the Waldo County Democratic Party chair in 1954, and during that campaign he was a key liaison with Republicans for Muskie in the mid-coast area. He later became State Treasurer.

David F. 'Dave' Emery   Republican state representative from Rockland. Ran for Congress in 1974, defeating Peter Kyros with 50.2% of the vote. Emery was the only Republican that year to unseat a Democratic incumbent in a House race. Subsequently re-elected in 1976 with 57% of the vote, in 1978 with 62% of the vote, 1980 with 69% of the vote. Ran for the Senate in 1982, losing to George Mitchell with 39% of the vote. Ran for Congress again in 1990 when he won the Republican primary with 61% of the vote and lost the general election to Tom Andrews with 39% of the vote. (See also "Congo Dave.")

EMILY   Short for "EMILY's List." EMILY is an acronym for Early Money Is Like Yeast, a Political Action Committee (see also "PAC") which gives money to pro-choice, Democratic women. Sometimes referred to as "Yeast Infection" by Democratic male candidates. Republican candidates think about EMILY's list about as often as they think about what is happening on Ganymede or Io.

End Game   The climax of a political campaign. In Maine politics, this usually takes place by mid-October. Only rarely are elections in Maine decided the last week or the last weekend of the campaign. "Hell, for Save Maine Yankee I, the end game was right around Labor Day."

Engaged, Engaged, Engaged   Consultant-speak for "Your damn phone was busy all night long." "Hey, I tried to call you about the press conference but all I got was engaged, engaged, engaged."

Amos Eno   National head of the National Fish and Wildlife Foundation and a major player in Maine environmental and political circles due to his ability to bring funds to Maine for environmental projects.

Entrance Polls   Polling of voters or caucus members as they go to vote. In Maine, these can be very effective, often indicating statewide winners by 2 P.M. or earlier, fully 6 hours before the polls close.

Enviros   Somewhat, but not totally, negative term for environmentalists. As a series of interest groups, enviros actually get a lot of credit for being players on the Maine political scene. Sometimes they are. "The enviros killed the turnpike widening." Sometimes they are not. "Maine Yankee was kept open again, in spite of the enviros." Since about 20% of the Maine electorate self-describes themselves as environmentalists, clearly there is a wide spectrum of belief covered by the term. This is true even though the press almost always incorrectly equates "environmentalists" with the Green Party or the Natural Resources Council of Maine and their spokespeople, in part because they are easy to get comments from and give good quotes.

James S. 'Jim' Erwin   Maine attorney general, ran for governor three times. In 1970, the second time he ran, he won the Republican primary with 89% of the vote, losing to Ken Curtis by a razor-thin 50.1% to 49.9% margin. One good TV commercial could have made the difference! In 1974 he won a three-way primary with 39% of the vote but lost the three-way general election with 23% of the vote in the "Year of the Longley." A classy guy who always was a straight shooter, who told it like it was and never blamed others for his defeats.

Evening in Maine   Generic term for the wave of TV ads created by Dan Payne featuring Angus King's office at dusk and telling the story of how hard he worked to make his business a success. This commercial run changed the dynamics of the race and got rural Republicans to abandon their primary winner Susan Collins so that by Labor Day, King was second to Joe Brennan in the polls and thus a truly "viable candidate." (See also "Morning in America" and "Viable Candidate.")

Every Vote Counts   In 1966, Peter Trafton Snowe, husband of Olympia Snowe, ran for the Maine House from Auburn. The election resulted in a tie with his opponent, Romeo Laberge. When the election was turned back to the voters a second time by the Maine Supreme Court, Peter won. He thus became the youngest person ever elected to the Maine House. Had Laberge gotten one more vote, would Olympia Snowe have become Maine's U.S. Senator in 1994?

Evil Ways   Short for "**As Sure As There Is God in Heaven Your Evil Ways Will Not Prevail.**" Used by Colby College history professor Paul A. Fullam contesting Senator Margaret Chase Smith in 1954 senatorial race. He was wrong, at least in the short term, losing badly to her the year (1954) Ed Muskie became the first Democratic governor in post-war times.

Exit Strategy   Plan for getting out of a political mess before it occurs. "Do you have an exit strategy in case Brennan gets into the race? He still has 40% of the vote in any Democratic primary in his pocket."

Exits or Exit Polls   Polling of voters or caucus members as they emerge from voting. Exit polls, done at the proper key precincts, can be very effective, often indicating statewide winners by 2 P.M. or earlier, fully 6 hours before the polls close.

Expectations Are the Enemy of Prediction   Very important adage of Ward Just. Pollsters ignore it at their peril.

Exploratory Focus Group   A focus group which allows the participants to explore topics with a minimum of direction.

Extremist   Someone far to your political right or left. "Tom Andrews is too much of an extremist for me." "Are you kidding? Tom is a mainstream Democrat, as mainstream as they come."

Ezra   Ezra Smith of Winthrop, father of George and Edie, two of the most stalwart Republican operatives and consultants during the last 20 years of Maine politics, and Gordon, a premier lobbyist. A lifelong Republican, Ezra holds the Maine Guinness Book of Political Records for most effective letters to the editor of Maine's newspapers during his lifetime. Winthrop is also one of the best predictors in the state of 1st District election outcomes.

F

Fish where

the fish are.

MAINE COAST ADAGE

Face Time   Time on TV news. "She got tons of face time last week but this week we can't find her anywhere."

A Faint and Distant Hope   Consultant phrase for a candidate or potential candidate with absolutely no chance to be elected but who might, just might, spend some money exploring the feasibility of such a run. "Him? A faint and distant hope but we're taking a look at things for him."

Sean Faircloth   Democratic candidate for Senate in 1996. Received 25% of the vote in the Democratic primary, finishing second to Joe Brennan.

Fake, It's Such a   John Martin's comment on the term limits law.

Fallout   The negative results of a stupid campaign move. "He fired his media advisor, his pollster and his scheduler. The fallout will continue all next week at least. I think he'll lose 10 points."

Fat Albert   Self-proclaimed name of Harrison "Horse" Richardson (R-Cumberland), Republican candidate for governor in 1974. (See also "Horse.")

Fat Cat Bureaucrats   Republican term for state and federal workers who they consider to be Democrats and who always want to build bigger empires at taxpayer expense.

Fat Cats   Democratic phrase for Republicans. "It isn't the party of Lincoln anymore; it's the party of fat cats."

Fatmouth   Harsh criticism of a staffer by candidate or office holder. "When you leak to the press like that, you just have to expect fatmouth; it comes with the turf."

Sandra 'Sandy' Choate Faucher   Longtime anti-abortion activist associated with the Maine and national chapters of the National Right to Life Committee and a major force—perhaps *the* major force—behind the defeat of the ERA in Maine in 1984. Lately very active on the national scene with various Right to Life groups.

Favorable to Unfavorable   The ratio of positive feelings toward a candidate compared to the negative feelings about that candidate. This is often more important a number than the horse race numbers between candidate A and candidate B because it shows the upside potential of the candidate as more people get to know him or her. "Forget the head to head, our guy has a 4–1 favorable to unfavorable; he's going to win the primary. Watch."

FBs   Faceless bastards, Ed Muskie's term for the staffers who made up his campaign and constituent schedules.

Fear Drives Out Favor   The often effective strategy of ballot measure campaigns if you have the "no" side. The use of exaggerated consequences to concern the voters enough to vote no on a proposition they would have otherwise favored. "The NRA's cardinal rule of politics is fear drives out favor." (See also "Influence Vectors.")

Feather In (also known as **Rotate In**)   Bring a second TV spot on gradually instead of stopping one and then bringing on the second abruptly. "I want to feather in the testimonial ads, start with 1/4 the mix and move up to 1/2 by the end of the week."

Feets   Named for Robert "Feets" Reagan, a hard-charging rebounder who always does what's best for the team, hence anyone who sacrifices himself for the good of a campaign or candidate. A very important role. "Feets went right in there and took the hit for the scheduling mistake. NOW forgave him after he groveled for about 20 minutes. We could use 10 more Feets on this campaign. They save the candidate a lot of aggravation."

Frank Fellows   Longtime Republican Congressman from Maine's third Congressional District. First elected in 1940, he died in office in 1951 and was succeeded by Clifford G. McIntire. When he returned from heading a delegation to Europe after World War II, he reported to Don Larrabee, "They need to harden their currency and soften their toilet paper."

Roy L. Fernald   Lost the Republican primary for governor in 1946 with 20.7% of the vote. Finished fourth in the same primary two years later, receiving 11.7% of the vote.

When Tom Allen sought the Maine governorship in the 1994 Democratic primary, he was hailed in some quarters as the best educated to have ever sought that position. After all, what other Rhodes Scholar had dignified a Maine gubernatorial race? Though not a Rhodes Scholar, Roy Fernald held nine earned college as well as graduate school degrees from the University of Maine, Harvard, and Boston Universities. Robert Ripley was so sure that this record would be nearly unique in its time that Fernald was featured twice in the "Believe It or Not" series, the first time after the then 29-year-old Fernald had earned his eighth degree in 1932 and the second in 1942 by this time Fernald, as a 40-year-old private enlisted member of the United States Army Air Corps, had earned his ninth such degree.

Fernald also established a 20th-century record which was in 1994 equaled but not surpassed by Joe Brennan for being the only person to have run 5 times for Governor, losing hard-fought GOP primaries in 1938, 1940, 1944, 1946, and 1948.

Fernald's most lasting defeat, however, probably came when as a member of the Maine State Senate in 1935, he led opposition to placing "Vacationland" on the state's license plates. "Vacationland" now has the world's record of longevity for a license plate slogan.

FFGs   Abbreviation for Fast Frigate Guided Missile, the U.S. Navy's ship to replace the destroyer. A gun platform that even liberals were forced to support if they wanted to do well with BIW workers.

Field   Short for field organization. Everybody talks about grass roots organization and the field work to set it up. In fact, the very best field operation can only change the margin of outcome by 1–2%. Thus political insiders talk about "Field as Smoke and Mirrors," doing enough to give the press and the candidate the impression you actually are building an organization, and "Field as Therapy" in which the campaign leaders and the candidate are lulled into a less agitated state. With few exceptions, such as the 1995 Gay Rights referendum and Dale McCormick's 1996 primary effort against Tom Allen, it is very hard to track signficant impact for field activity in terms of actual voting shifts. These exceptions are called "Real Field" as opposed to "Pseudo Field."

Fight at the OK Corral   Any big primary or general election battle with powerful "gangs" of important candidates and their supporters. "It's too bad Cohen never ran against Muskie; it would have been another OK Corral."

Fighting First for Maine   Tom Allen's slogan when he ran for Congress in 1996.

Fighting Joe   Joseph Brennan as introduced by Senator Ted Kennedy in 1980. Ted once spent a night at the Blaine House but state historians cannot pin down the actual date or location. "He's a fighting governor; he's 'Fighting Joe' Brennan."

Michael 'Mike' Fiori   Longtime Democratic activist, fund-raiser and charter (since 1974) Brennanista. His personally designed ads for Downeast Pharmacy suggest that consultants will prove essential should he decide to run for governor.

Fire Hydrant Draft   A speech or policy draft circulated with the expectation that staffers and consultants will urinate all over it. "That piece on euthanasia was just a fire hydrant draft but I think there are some good lines in it."

First Cabin   Consultant-speak for level of campaign spending. "It was first cabin all the way; we met at the Sheraton."

First Family   Four possible choices here. There are the McKernans, led by matriarch Barbara McKernan; her two sons, Bobby and Jock; and her daughter-in-law, Olympia. There are the Smiths, led by patriarch Ezra Smith; his two sons, Gordon and George; and daughter, Edie. And there are the Longleys, led by patriarch James Longley Sr., governor; James Longley Jr., Congressman; and Susan Longley, state senator. Since 1996, one would also have to include the Collins family with Senator Susan; her father, state senator Don Collins; uncle, Supreme Court Justice Sam; mother and Mayor of Caribou Pat; and grandfather Sam who was chairman of the Appropriations Commitee when Muskie was governor. Objective historians would probably have to go with the McKernans, but insiders would still have fun with the exercise.

First Tier   In any election cycle there are candidates who are regarded by the media as being serious contenders. These are often called the first tier of candidates, much to the chagrin of those not so named. "The scorps don't think he's in the first tier; it'll be a self-fulfilling prophecy."

Charles Fitzgerald   Independent candidate for Congress in 1994 in the Second District. Got 4.7% of the vote. Green Party activist.

John C. Fitzgerald   Democratic nominee for Congress from the first district in 1946, he lost the general election with 40.4% of the vote.

Fix   For political junkies, that which sustains them, usually some bit of inside information, no matter how inconsequential. It can be a new overnight tracking poll of three people, a rumor of a new, negative spot, or some information unknown to uncaring civilians. "She just got the support of Ralph Brown; he's the town chair in Jonesport." Fixes provide two highs, one when the junkie gets the fact or rumor, and another when he or she passes it on to another junkie.

Flak   Press secretary. The best flak is a true believer in the candidate and his or her mission, but such devotion is hard to come by in real-life politics. "Wills Lyford was a true believer and a stand-up guy for Jock, not just a flak."

Flak Catchers   Any staffer sent into an unpleasant situation to receive citizen ire instead of having the candidate or office holder take the hit. Republicans usually send flak catchers to do the AFL/CIO annual conventions, for example. "I'm not going there. Send in one of our surrogates; we need a flak catcher there." (See also "Feets.")

Flameout   A campaign disaster, usually a candidate fiasco, as in "He picked his nose right in the middle of the debate. Picked it and kept his finger in there for about 10 minutes, what a flameout!"

David Flanagan   Early and longtime supporter and political strategist for Joe Brennan. Brennan's legal counsel when he was governor. Later lobbyist for and then president of Central Maine Power.

Flatlanders   Used primarily in Oxford, Franklin, and Somerset Counties to refer to those people who do not understand their reasons for living in western Maine and who fail to appreciate the allure of ice fishing, snowmobiling, and dog sledding. Also sometimes applied to people who move to Maine "from away."

Flight   Wave of TV. A flight of political TV might run three or four weeks to seven or eight weeks, although most TV flights would lose impact if run as long as six weeks. (See also "Burnout.")

Flip-Flop King of Congress   Sherry Huber's nickname for Jock McKernan when she ran for governor against him in 1986.

Flotsam and Jetsam   Human debris brought together by a candidate or cause. "Without flotsam and jetsam you couldn't keep a campaign office open and staffed."

Fluffer   Tom Hanrahan's name for Fred Nutter, editorial commentator for WCSH-TV. Hanrahan once wrote in the *Casco Bay Weekly*: "Fred "Fluffer" Nutter, the editorial mouthpiece of WCSH-TV, is a legendary softball in the great down pillow of Maine television journalism, but Nutter outdid himself on Labor Day."

Fluidity   In polling, the fluidity of opinion refers to the ease or difficulty with which a particular opinion can be changed. "Abortion views have very low fluidity in Maine."

Flusher   Campaign operative who works to "flush" out votes on election day. Joe Cowie is reported to be the best flusher on the Maine scene. "I want you on the streets; you're supposed to be a flusher today. I don't want to see you in the headquarters until the polls close." (See also "Hauler.")

Fly-Around   Campaign technique of flying around the district or the state to get maximum TV and press coverage in a 24-hour news cycle. Often used at the beginning of a campaign for announcement purposes and then at the end to close the campaigns. "Chris always drove me nuts with his fly-arounds. He makes you start in Presque Isle, then do Bangor, then Augusta, then Lewiston, then Portland, and you end up in Biddeford or Sanford. But he always figures out some excuse so he doesn't have to do it with you."

Focus Group   A political technique borrowed from advertising in which a small group of people (usually 12–15) are jointly interviewed over a 2-hour period about candidates, causes and advertisements. If polling is 90% science and 10% art, focus groups are 10% science and 90% art. Done properly, they can be of enormous assistance in planning a campaign. Done improperly, they can be extremely misleading. Given all the nonsense which comes out of polling, it is difficult to believe, but in politics, more nonsense actually comes out of focus groups.

Howard M. Foley   Republican candidate for Congress in 1966. Lost to Bill Hathaway but got 43% of the vote. Bill Cohen was his campaign manager.

Football Duck   An awkward candidate. From the saying "Like watching a duck make love to a football." "He may be a Congressman but he still looks like a football duck when you put him with real people."

Fork Him/Her   Short for "Stick a fork in him, he's done" or "Stick a fork in her, she's done." A candidate is dead, finished. "Longley's done, fork him."

John P. Fortunato   Finished second in the Democratic primary for the Second Congressional District in 1950, receiving 16.8% of the vote.

Judy Foss   Chief aide of, and mentor to, Senate President Jeffrey Butland (1994–1996). A former Republican state representative from Yarmouth, Judy Foss ran for governor in 1994, finishing 4th in the Republican primary. Judy was widely regarded as having considerable power over the Senate President, especially when he did things other people didn't like. Charter McKernanista (see "Jock McKernan" and "McKernistas").

Four Horsemen of Calumny—Fear, Ignorance, Bigotry and Smear   Margaret Chase Smith in her maiden Senate speech against Senator Joe McCarthy. "I don't want to see the Republican Party ride to political victory on the Four Horsemen of Calumny—Fear, Ignorance, Bigotry and Smear."

Fourth Estate   What scorps were called in a kinder, gentler era. Now a term which seems a bit old-fashioned and upscale, not to say too laudatory. "I don't think the term *fourth estate* really conveys the reality of today's journalists; I prefer the term *scorps*." (See also "Scorps.")

Francos   Short for Franco-American voters, the most important swing vote in Maine politics, with 17% of the population and the group most likely to determine the winning side in a candidate or ballot measure election.

The Frank   The free postage which enables members of Congress to mail their constituents on any subject. Basically it is a form of advertising which targets constituents by using their own money. "Incumbents love the frank; it's one of their best perks."

Herman C. 'Buddy' Frankland   Baptist minister from Bangor who, encouraged by Jim Longley Sr., ran for governor as an Independent in 1978. Endorsed by the *Bangor Daily News*, he got 18% of the vote, finishing third and probably costing Republican Linwood Palmer the election.

William 'Bill' Frederick   Former UPI Augusta reporter, famous for his run-ins with Governor James Longley Sr. Used to get good stories with his pleasing personality and good sources. Frederick was later launched into unemployment twice by Bill Cohen, first because of his role as press secretary to Bill Hathaway in 1978, and in a repeat performance 6 years later when he served as press secretary for Libby Mitchell in 1984.

Free Fall   In political terms, a sharp drop in the polls. "After the Hathaway incident, Monks went into free fall."

Freedom Fighters   Name given to a colorful grass roots movement of selectmen and town officials across the state who opposed the growing state and federal regulatory encroachment and adopted the name when they met in the Grange Hall in the Town of Freedom in Waldo County in January, 1975. They were particularly exorcised about the state property tax and the mandated closing of open-burning dumps. Mary Adams learned a lot about grass roots activism from their activities.

Freeze Frame   The slow-motion shots in commercials which are usually the most important image you want to leave with the viewer. "I loved that freeze frame where the whitewash flows down as the voice over says: 'The Green Party referendum, it's not what it pretends to be.' "

Fried Clam Sex   Reference to an "expert" brought in by Hayes Gahagan in his U.S. Senate bid in 1978 who claimed that his opponents were using subliminal sexual inducements in their ads to get votes. The expert astounded reporters by giving them the example of the Howard Johnson's menu where the press conference was held, a menu with fried clams on the cover. The fried clams were supposed to represent a sex orgy. Reporters filed somewhat incredulous accounts of the press conference but did not order fried clams for lunch.

Friends of Okey-Dokey   Another Davis Rawson name for "McKernanistas," referring to Governor McKernan's very loyal press secretary Willis Lyford and other supporters who found McKernan to be worthy of support and were willing to defend him against any and all criticism.

Friggin'   Maine country slang for "copulation." "Jesus, it's the friggin' bleeding heart liberals wanting to take our guns away again."

From Another Planet   Phrase used by awed consultants when someone else gets a higher fee than they ever imagined possible. "Did you see what Don Ring is getting from the Emery campaign? I tell you he's from another planet."

Front-runner   Candidate who is perceived to be ahead of the political pack. An excellent position to be in for fund-raising purposes. A bad place to be in if your relative position is going to slip in the future. The press likes nothing more than to turn on a candidate previously regarded (by the same reporters) as unbeatable.

FUD   Short for fear, uncertainty and doubt. What you try to sow when you want to defeat a referendum. "FUD, FUD, that's all that matters; hit Carter with FUD and that clear-cutting ban will fall to the ground." (See also "Fear Drives Out Favor" and "Imaginary Horribles.")

Fudge   To not answer a question or to appear to be on both sides of an issue. Thought to be an absolute necessity in politics since every strong stand usually produces a loss of votes. "She fudged that one nicely." (See also "Waffle.")

Maria Fuentes   Executive director of the Maine Better Transportation Association and campaign manager for the Turnpike Widening effort of

1997. Very effective and one of the nicest people in Maine politics. A winner.

Paul A. Fullam   Colby College professor and Democratic nominee for U.S. Senate in 1954, he received 41.4% of the vote.

Full-Court Press   Hitting your opponent with TV, radio and newspaper ads all at once. "Peter Kelley put on a full-court press to get more name recognition in a hurry."

Jamie Furth   Referendum operative and coordinator on Maine Yankee III and Compact II. President of Furth and Company.

G

There's an 800-pound gorilla in the

Blaine House and nobody wants to

take him on.

PETER MILLS

Gaaaaahgggaaaaa! George Neavoll's expression of exasperation concerning insider assumptions that the editorial page editors influence the reporting of political news stories.

Hayes E. Gahagan Republican State Senator from Aroostook County, he ran for the U.S. Senate as an Independent in 1978, receiving 7.5% of the vote. Was defeated in a later attempt in 1996 to return to the Legislature.

Ernest A. 'Ernie' Gallant Ran for Congress in the Democratic primary for the Second District in 1986, received 42% of the vote.

Albert P. 'Al' Gamache Administrative assistant and political advisor to Bill Hathaway, supported Angus King, who used to work for him, in 1994.

King carried Lewiston where Gamache is now a state representative. Longtime important Democratic political operative.

Game Plan   What every campaign should have, but surprisingly few have. Statewide game plans go for $20–30,000. Perhaps this is why so few have them. "Let's sell Jasper a statewide game plan. There'll be no money after that."

The Gang Who Couldn't Shoot Straight   Some reporters' private term for Bob Monks and his senatorial campaign team in 1996, who when gunning for John Hathaway shot themselves in the foot, finishing third (and last) and spending over $2 million in the process, collecting just 13,000 votes. In fairness to the campaign team, it was reported that Bob Monks was not the easiest candidate to manage.

Garbage   Short for "Garbage Voters," voters who during the last week of the campaign tell you they are undecided on the Congressional race, undecided on the Senatorial race, and undecided on the gubernatorial race. They are not going to vote and are hence "garbage" to a pollster since their opinion is of no consequence whatsoever. "Forget that 8%, it's pure garbage."

Gus 'Doc' Garcelon   Founder of the Sportsman's Alliance of Maine and the Natural Resources Council of Maine, past NRA president and the prime mover behind the defeat of the Ban Moose Hunting referendum of 1983. Now gone to the great woodcock cover in the sky, Doc Garcelon is regarded by many hunters as the patron saint of lead shot.

Peter A. Garland   Republican candidate for Congress in Maine's 1st CD in 1966. Won the Republican primary with 25% of the vote and lost the general election with 45% of the vote. Shows what a big difference the arena can make!

In 1960 he was elected to Congress in the 1st District with 53% of the vote, but due to reapportionment he and Stanley Tupper were forced together in the new 1st CD for 1962, and Tupper defeated Garland in the primary with 61% of the vote.

Markhan L. 'Mark' Gartley   Democratic candidate for Congress in 1974, winning the Democratic primary with 66% of the vote and losing to Bill Cohen in the fall with 29% of the vote. Ran again in 1978, winning the Democratic primary with 64% of the vote and losing in the general election to Olympia Snowe but getting 42% of the vote.

Gas   Candidate or office holder press release. "More gas from Kyros's office; I think he's taking credit for Christmas this time." (See also "Hot Gas.")

Eli Gaudet   Lost the Democratic primary for the 1st CD in 1954, receiving 46.5% of the vote.

The General   William Lewis, consort and principal aide to Senator Margaret Chase Smith, who managed her campaigns from 1948 on. Hailing from Oklahoma, he was an attorney and Congressional committee staffer before joining Smith's staff. His nickname is derived from his rank of Brigadier General in the Air Force Reserve and for his command of the political process which radiated from Senator Smith.

Generic Ad   An ad, usually produced by the Democratic National Committee or the Republican National Committee for use in various races (usually Congressional) around the country. Generic ads of this type are about as good as you might think they would be. (See also "DNC" and "RNC.")

Generic Authority Figure   Generalized figure used to validate a position or candidate, i.e., the lobsterman is always used as an authority figure to validate a cause or candidate for coastal Maine. Can be any number of other generic types relevant to a particular situation. "Get some computer guy in the commercial for the yuppies."

The Genuine Article   Mary Adams's term for John Hathaway when he ran for the U.S. Senate in the 1996 Republican primary. "He's the genuine article, that's why I like him."

German War Machine   Tom Daffron's ironic name for any political campaign which is run in helter-skelter fashion. "The press release didn't get out again? The German war machine is at it again."

Get a Grip   Consultant-speak for a seemingly outrageous goal or planned action. "Run for the U.S. Senate? Get a grip."

Get Out   I don't believe you. "He did what at the convention? Get out."

Get the Box   Get the quotation in the box which stands out in any print story. "We got the box, forget the rest."

Get the Show on the Road   Get moving, get out of the headquarters and onto the streets. To get out onto the hustings instead of plotting and planning. "Come on, guys, let's get the show on the road; we've spent two hours talking about jack shit." (See also "Jack Shit.")

Getting Ink or just **Ink**   A term for getting one's name in the paper. For candidates, getting their name identification (name I.D.) up is very important since many voters make their choices based on name identification. (See also "Name ID.") Therefore, politicians often do many things just to get their name in the papers more than their opponent. This strategy is the opposite of what is desirable for ballot measure campaigns where you often do not want ink because the opposing side will get an equal amount of ink. "She got a lot of ink last week for her health-care proposals." This especially makes sense if someone were running for the state senate or state representative where fewer people have usually heard of the candidates than if they were running for Congress or governor.

Gilead   Town on U.S. Route 2, west of Bethel and starting point of Bill Cohen's 1972 600-mile walk across Maine, which changed the political dynamics of Maine for a generation. Cohen persisted on the walk even though the first day's trek with Charles and Marlene Petersen seemed only to expose him to visitors from Canada who were streaming down from Quebec. Cohen went from commanding this small commando unit in 1972 to commanding U.S. armed forces of 1.6 million in 1997.

Girl in the Red Dress   Name for Susan Collins, the Republican nominee for governor in 1994 and now a U.S. Senator. Named in honor of Professor Charles Colgan, associate professor of public policy at the University of Southern Maine's Muskie Institute who, when asked about her candidacy for the U.S. Senate in 1996, indicated that he knew nothing about her except that she wore a red dress. (See also "Lady in Red.")

Give Me a Break   Phrase expressing disbelief as well as disgust as in, "Give me a break, he can't be serious about running."

James E. Glover   Finished third in the Republican primary for the 3rd CD in 1948, receiving 14.1% of the vote.

Go Dark   To go off television. "I hate to go dark when the other guy is up on TV." (See also "Go Up.")

Go Up   To go on television. "We're up, the money will start to roll in now. She'll enjoy campaigning more when she meets people who have seen her on TV." (See also "Go Dark.")

GOBs   Good Old Boys, second only to the Ma Mères in terms of their political power in Maine. Known for their love of firearms and white-tailed deer. Also known for their love of snowmobiles, ATV's, no motorcycle helmet legislation, and Congressman John Baldacci. Also known for their distaste for members of the Green Party, coyotes, taxes, flat landers and anyone not born north of Lewiston or Augusta. True political genius is required to build political coalitions of the GOBs and the Ma Mères, but it can be done. (See also "Ma Mères.") George Smith and Paul Jacques are perhaps the best authorities on GOBs (See also "Smitty" and "Paul Jacques.")

Joseph Goebbels Award   Insider designation for the biggest lie told during any campaign season. "In 1996 the AFL/CIO won the Joseph Goebbels Award for that attack ad on Longley saying he voted for a Congressional pay raise. The dub wasn't even in Congress at the time!" (See also "Dub.")

Going for the GRPs   Going on TV, going for gross rating points. Reaching out for large numbers of voters. (See also "GRPs" and "Wholesale Politics.")

The Gold Coast   Peter Burr's term for the arc of suburbs around Portland which have become critical swing areas determining Congressional, gubernatorial and senate races since Congressman Andrews beat Congressman Emery in 1990, Governor McKernan beat Governor Brennan in 1990 and Senator Snowe beat Congressman Andrews in 1994. In political mythology, the arc runs from Howard Dana's house in Cape Elizabeth to Tony Buxton's in Stroudwater and from Merton Henry's in Standish to Sherry Huber's in Falmouth Foreside. Also known as the "Yuppie Crescent."

The Gold Room   Insider's name for the pleasant second floor sitting room of the Blaine House where a variety of important political decisions have been made. Name comes from the warm, golden light which diffuses the room. "In the gold room, it is possible to imagine one really can make a difference in this state."

Golden Handshake   An unasked-for reward for services rendered, a nice gesture, usually unexpected. "I got a golden handshake from the Congressman. Surprised the hell out of me."

Goldilocks Campaign   In consultant-speak, this is a campaign which is not too "hot" (too close and you could lose) or too "cold" (too easy and no drama) but just right, about a 10-point lead with money coming in and the candidate doing his or her part. "I've had two Goldilocks campaigns in my time, Cohen for Senate in 1978 and Snowe for Senate in 1994. Beautiful, both."

Gone   As in "he or she is gone." Candidate-speak for "get rid of him or her." "That was the last straw, he's gone."

Gone With the Wind   A very expensive TV commercial. "That commercial on acid rain turned out to be another Gone With the Wind." (See also "Jurassic Park.")

Good Clients   In the world of consultants, good clients are those who follow directions, pay on time and are grateful for assistance provided. "Good clients are hard to come by, not just in Maine but everywhere."

Good Shit   Very usable negative information about a candidate. "Chris, did you get that old *Maine Times* article on Monks that I sent you? Boy, is that good shit or what? Monks is a follower of Mao and all. Let's use it at the convention, but I don't want it traced to us."

Denise 'Denny' Goodman   Maine stringer for the *Boston Globe* and *Time* magazine. A classy reporter who usually gets things right when covering the Maine political scene. Knows how to separate good spin from bad and writes accordingly.

Albion D. Goodwin   Democratic candidate for Maine's 2nd CD in 1970. Got 11% of the vote in the Democratic primary.

Goons and Loons Coalition   Davis Rawson's term for the alliance of SAM and Maine Audubon which resulted in a 72% margin for their constitutional amendment to prohibit the Legislature from using fees from hunting and fishing licenses for general revenue purposes. Not a bad coalition to have on your side for virtually all outdoor referenda.

Goose   Angus King III, first press secretary for his father's gubernatorial campaign, and then scheduler. After the 1994 election he served in the Clinton White House.

Gorgeous George   Republican ironic reference to George Mitchell, for two terms the junior Senator from Maine, and the majority leader of the Senate from 1989–1994, the first from Maine to hold that position since Lewiston's Wallace White held it 1947–1949. To many Republican insiders he was legendary for his good press *and* his self-promotion. "The Supreme Court *or* Baseball Commissioner? Come on, give me a break. Gorgeous George is at it again."

John Gorman   President of Opinion Dynamics Corporation (ODC) of Cambridge, Mass., a national polling firm with a great deal of nuclear and referendum experience in Maine.

Harold 'Hal' Gosselin   Longtime, important political operative in Androscoggin county. One of the original Longley Legionnaires and a political power in Lewiston for both Margaret Chase Smith and Bill Cohen. A political reporter for the *Lewiston Daily Sun* in the 1950's.

GOTV   Get-out-the-vote, a popular subculture of politics which places emphasis on identifying one's supporters, calling them up on election day and making sure they vote. Republicans and Democrats spend enormous amounts of money on these efforts every election cycle without much evidence that they have any effect on statewide or Congressional elections. Some insiders swear by it, others feel it is an enormous waste of effort. "GOTV? I've seen it work a few times, like in the Gay Rights referendum, but for candidates in general elections, forget it, GOTV almost always gets lost in the law of large numbers." (See also "Law of Large Numbers.")

Governor   What most people were calling George Mitchell in 1974 until the campaign of Independent James W. Longley weighed in. (See also "The Judge" [2].)

The Governor for Governor   Slogan conceived by John Reed aide Steve Shaw when Reed ran for re-election in 1960.

Gerald J. Grady   University of Maine professor and Democratic candidate for Congress in Maine's 3rd District in 1958. Received 44% of the vote against Clifford McIntire.

A Grand $1,000, the unit of measurement for most consultants. "A grand a month and I take an occasional look at your campaign; for five or six grand, I get serious." (See also "K.")

Grand Old Party or **GOP**   The national Republican Party.

Earl S. Grant   Won the Democratic primary for governor in 1950, but lost the general election, receiving 39.1% of the vote. In 1952 Grant lost the Democratic nomination for U.S. Senate, but ran as an Independent, receiving 6.4% in the general election.

Nancy Grape   Political reporter and subsequently editorial writer for the *Portland Press Herald* and *Maine Sunday Telegram*. Seldom saw a liberal or feminist candidate or story she didn't like. Very spinnable if you are of that persuasion. Fair and decent. Took a strong stand for Maine Turnpike widening in 1997.

Calvin Grass   Republican candidate for governor in 1970, received 11% of the vote in the primary. Handed out tiny fir trees as a campaign gimmick, a tactic later copied by Linwood Palmer who, when not a Republican candidate for governor, owned a tree farm.

Grass Roots   Basic support and organization at the local level. Everybody talks about his grass roots support. Very few candidates have much.

Gravitas   Weight, authority, presence. "God, I wish Colin Powell were in the race, he has more gravitas than all the rest of them put together." (See also "Heavy Hitter.")

Greater Good   Ballot measure term for technique of framing a referendum debate around the exaggerated positives that the measure could bring. "Give them the greater good instead of just the language and we pick up 15%." (See also "Imaginary Horribles.")

The Green   Campaign money. "I don't care if the candidate hates those people, we need the green and we need it bad; we're supposed to go on TV at the end of the week."

Green Party   (1) The true party of all political consultants.

Green Party   (2) Maine party founded by Bowdoin Professor John Rensenbrink in 1984. Received more than 5% of the vote in 1994 when Jonathan Carter ran for governor and thus qualified for the Maine ballot as an official political party. Green positions on environmental, campaign finance reform and economic issues have pulled mainstream environmental groups to the left. Insiders believe that it is really more than a party, however, but has many characteristics of a movement which in the future will continue to play an important role in the life of the state. Consultants love this party for all the controversy it stirs up!

Greendaddy   John Rensenbrink, father of the Maine and U.S. Green Parties.

Abbott O. Greene   Republican candidate for Congress in 2nd CD in 1972. Received 39% of the vote in the primary, losing to Bill Cohen. Also ran for the U.S. Senate, getting 40% of the vote in the 1970 Republican primary against his cousin Neil Bishop.

Hollis 'Skip' Greenlaw   Republican candidate for Congress in Maine's Second District in 1994. Got 19% of the vote, finishing 4th.

Grid/Outcome System   In polling, any numerical system which takes the outcome of races in certain towns and projects them against the outcomes in other towns in order to come up with those towns which most accurately predict the outcome of whole counties or the entire state. (See also "All Against All" and "Key Precinct.")

GRPs   Gross rating points or GRPs, refers to frequency and reach of television. GRPs are the single most expensive aspect of any statewide campaign. " The cost of those GRPs is killing us but we have to have them, we don't want to go dark." (See also "Go Dark.")

Grumpy Old Men   Democrat wag's description of a possible R.A.G. Monks vs. Joe Brennan contest for the U.S. Senate in 1996. This may have also reflected Democratic insider hopes at the time.

Grumpy vs. Weepy   Dave Barry's characterization of the 1996 Presidential election. In his mind, Bob "Bob" Dole and Bill "Bill" Clinton were so uninspiring that Barry wrote: "The major parties could conduct live human sacrifices on their podiums during prime time and I doubt that anybody would notice . . ."

Gunslinger   Any political consultant for hire. In Renaissance Italy such key people were called "condottieri." This group is very important to political campaigns in Maine although elected officials seldom—if ever—acknowledge that fact. (See also "The Littlest Gunslinger" and "The Man the People Found.")

The Guerrilla Tax Fighter   *Kennebec Journal*'s name for Mary Adams. (See "Mary Adams.")

Guys   Generic term for operatives whether male or female. "Hey you guys, let's get this show on the road." (See also "Get the Show on the Road.")

Gypsies   Political operatives who move from state to state, working on different campaigns and having the ability to blend into the local background. "She's a gypsy but she fits right in; we took her to a meeting in Millinocket and nobody knew she was from DC."

H

Hack   A politician or operative who hangs around the process, doing little but trying to stay alive to get the next paycheck. "Look at those hacks hanging around the governor-elect wanting a job in his administration."

Hail Mary   Any last-minute, last-ditch attempt to win an election. Contrary to the misuse of this phrase by General Norm "Storming Norman" Schwartzkopf during the Gulf War (the Allies' war plan was carefully thought out and had a very high probability of success), it means something with little chance of success. "Few Hail Marys succeed."

HAK   Henry A. Kissinger, not a Maine player for long but a big fan of Bill Cohen with something of a flair for self-promotion. "Did you see Monks blow that cigar smoke in HAK's face? Must be getting him back for the Cambodian incursion."

John Hale   Political reporter for the *Bangor Daily News*. Regarded as fair, straightforward, a recorder of political phenomena, not a maker of news. Spinnable.

Robert 'Bob' Hale   Eight-term Republican Congressman from the First Congressional District, he was first elected in 1942 and won successive general election victories in 1944, '46, '48, '50, '52, '54, and '56, facing primary challenges in each of these years, except 1946 and 1952. In 1958 he won the Republican primary, but lost the general election, receiving 47.9% of the vote.

Hall of Shame   Campaign activist's list of people and groups who have led down their side. More often than not, the hall of shame positions are held by supporters, not opponents. "He only raised how much? Put him in the hall of shame for our side."

Frederick A. Halla   Republican candidate for Congress in 1966. Received 6% of the vote in the 1st District primary.

Shawn Hallisey   Democratic candidate for Congress in the Second District in 1994. Received 414 votes.

Halo Effect   The continuing afterglow of a good campaign event which may influence the polling numbers for a short period of time. "He got a halo effect out of that speech but we saw it fade after a week."

Hamlet   To agonize over a political decision and then do nothing as in "Cuomo hamleted himself right out of the Presidency. What a turkey." (See also "Cuomo" and "Turkey.")

Hammerhead   GOB phrase for a stupid person. One who makes political blunders. "What a hammerhead; he talked about gun control to the SAM convention." (See also "SAM.")

Owen L. Hancock   Finished second in the Democratic primary for the First Congressional District in 1956, receiving 24.7% of the vote.

Handi Wipes   Useless staffers. "He's just a handi wipe; send him out for lunch and tell him not to come back."

Handlers   Consultants responsible for a candidate's actions or perform- ance. "She had great handlers but she never listened to them."

Hannibal Hamlin Institute for Economic Policy Studies   Conservative Maine think tank concerned with free market issues. Executive director was Matt Glavin. Disappeared along with the excesses of the 1980's. Named for Lincoln's first Vice President, who came from Hampden and Paris Hill, Maine.

Thomas 'Tom' Hanrahan   Newspaper columnist and television host. His columns for the *Central Maine Sentinel* from the mid 1980's to the mid 1990's were a mainstay of political commentary during that period. Later a commentator on Channel 8 WMTW and Maine Public Broadcasting. Known for his hard-hitting, no-holds barred journalistic style, he also briefly wrote for the *Casco Bay Weekly*. Colorful and amusing. Nicknamed "Unguided Missile" by some insiders for the ease with which one could ignite him and the difficulty in controlling where he would explode. An engaging guy with no fear. Now studying to become a Maine Guide.

Donald 'Don' Hansen   Longtime political reporter and editor for the *Portland Press Herald*. Very knowledgable about the politics of the 1950's, 1960's and beyond. Well liked and respected. Co-author (with Theo Lipp- man Jr.) of *Muskie*. Succeeded Peter Damborg as state house correspon- dent.

Happy As a Pig in Shit   A GOB term. Apparently on Maine farms, pigs are content when they can roll around in mud, manure and other messy items. On the campaign trail, this tends to be used in a more positive vein to describe a candidate who has had a good day or event. "She is happy as a pig in shit; they clapped for her speech." Seems to suggest that candi- dates roll around in human waste but it normally does not have such a pejorative connotation unless you stop to think about it for a while.

Happy Days Are Here Again   Democratic theme song at many levels of political activity including Democratic state conventions in Maine. The song goes back to the 1932 Democratic convention which nominated Franklin Delano Roosevelt. In 1992, Clinton replaced it with "Don't Stop Thinking about Tomorrow."

Happy Fingers   A candidate's compulsion to dial people up at night to discuss the campaign. "I had to take my phone off the hook last night; I was sure he'd have happy fingers again now that the editorial was out praising him."

Hard Rock   Nickname for State Senator John W. Benoit Jr. (R-Sandy River Plantation) from his days as an embattled, but publicly popular, District Court Judge in Franklin and Somerset Counties.

Hard Support   When looking at polling numbers for a candidate, the ratio between hard and soft support is very important. At least half of those who are for a candidate should say they are "very likely" to vote for that candidate as opposed to those who say they are "somewhat likely" to vote for that candidate. "Once Hathaway saw he had Margaret's hard support down to 30%, he knew he had a real chance."

Michael 'Mike' Harkins   President of The Agency, a Delaware Republican consulting firm, founded by Bob Monks and Bill Webster and dispatched to Maine in 1972 to help Bill Cohen run for Congress. His impact was substantial and made a difference in both the primary and the general election. Harkins was thus in at the creation of both Billy Wonderful and his campaign manager, Dr. Demento, as Maine political players. Few others could make such a claim. Or would want to. Now executive director of the Delaware River and Bay Authority.

M. D. Harmon   Editor and editorial page writer for the *Portland Press Herald* and *Maine Sunday Telegram*. Conservative and Republican leaning, he seems to believe Republicans were put on the earth for one purpose and one purpose alone—to cut taxes. Seems never to have met a liberal he liked. Very predictable.

Daniel 'Dan' Harris   Started out as an enterprising political reporter for WCSH, now at New England Cable News Network. While at WCSH, got a fair amount of inside information from good sources.

Leith Hartman   Write-in candidate for governor in 1974, received 889 votes.

King Harvey   Political writer, editor and publisher of note in the 1950's, 1960's and 1970's. His column "Tom E Rot" in the *Ft. Fairfield Review* was read all over the state by those who followed politics. Visiting him was a must for all candidates seeking impact in Aroostok County and beyond. During the annual Potato Blossom Festival, King really was King, with candidates and office holders of all parties coming to his court to pay hommage and get his blessings.

David Hastings   Head of the Greater Portland Labor Council in the 1950's; key suppoprter among AFL union members during that period, active Democrat over the years.

Hatchet Man   Self-portrait of *BDN* columnist John Day. "I am the hatchet man of long standing." Someone who harms a candidate by taking whacks out of their hide. "Every campaign has to have a hatchet man."

A Mere Hatchet Man   Governor Ed Muskie's name for Republican Senator Owen Brewster when Brewster endorsed Republican Fred Payne and charged that Muskie had taken a great deal of union money in his 1958 senatorial campaign.

John W. Hathaway   Republican candidate for U.S. Senate in 1996, received 31% of the vote in the Republican primary.

William D. 'Bill' Hathaway   Democratic Congressman from Maine's second district (1965–1973). Defeated in 1962 when he first ran against Clifford McIntire, he won in 1964 with 62% of the vote. Re-elected in 1966 with 56% of the vote, re-elected in 1968 with 56% of the vote, re-elected in 1970 with 89% of the vote in the Democratic primary and 64% in the general election. Ran for the U.S. Senate in 1972, beating Jack Smith in the Democratic primary with 90% of the vote and Margaret Chase Smith in the general with 53% of the vote. Lost in 1978 when challenged by William S. Cohen. Received 34% of the vote. Class guy.

Hauler   A campaign operative who uses walking-around money to "haul" voters to the polls on election day. "She's the best hauler we've got; send her into Ward 5 for the day." (See also "Flusher" and "Walking Around Money.")

Have His/Her Ears On   Candidate in full campaign mode, really getting into the flow of a crowd, getting rejuvenated by the interaction. Also known as "Flying" or "Sailing." "Tom Andrews really had his ears on that night. The crowd would have followed him to the ends of the earth."

Jack 'The Sun King' Havey   Nationally known portrait artist who did the media for Jim Longley Sr. in his successful campaign to become Maine's first Independent governor in 1974. Known for his very impressive talents, his lavish office and sunny disposition, the Sun King has also been known to burn clients to a crisp if they displeased him. Very succesful in referenda situations, winning the anti-ERA, elected PUC, Moose Hunt and Save Maine Yankee II struggles. A major player.

Susan Hawkes   Partner in the Augusta consulting firm of Hawkes and Mayhew.

Jean Gannett Hawley   Publisher of Guy Gannett Communications newspapers for 40 years. Strongwilled and independent. Insiders believed her to be a major force in Maine politics, with the power to overrule her editors when it came to endorsements although some at the papers during her tenure deny this was the situation. In any case, she was not regarded as being as interventionist as her father, "the Guy," however. He was thought to stuff financial bonuses into the paychecks of reporters whose sympathies he favored and who steered the company through the troubled waters of a bitter newspaper strike in 1952.

Paul Hawthorne   Campaign manager for Jim Erwin when he ran for governor in 1974. Great believer in grass roots organization and had a huge chart on the campaign headquarters wall with town chairs in each town. Unfortunately for Paul and Jim, few actually delivered on election day as many small-town Republicans went for Jim Longley Sr. But, and this really is inside baseball, without Paul Hawthorne and his grass roots organization, it is doubtful that Dave Emery would have been elected to Congress that year because many of those same Republicans who voted for Jim Longley ended up returning to the Republican column and voting for Dave Emery. Exist polling showed that 13% of those who voted for Dave Emery did not know who he was!

Jean Hay   Democratic candidate for Congress in Maine's Second Congressional District in 1994, receiving 4% of the vote. This finish emboldened her, and she then ran for the U.S. Senate in the Democratic primary of 1996, receiving 5% of the vote.

Make Hay While the Sun Shines   Another bucolic Maine image whose political meaning is straightforward, meaning to seize an opportunity while it lasts. "We polled around the clock for the last five weeks of the campaign; talk about making hay while the sun shines."

Kenneth 'Ken' Hayes   Professor of government at the University of Maine for some 30 years and former Democratic State Senator. Ran for Congress in Maine's Second District in 1988, losing to Olympia Snowe with 33% of the vote. In addition to being a solid pundit over the years, he also served as Steve Bost's campaign manager when Steve ran for the U.S. Senate as a Reform Party candidate. He also taught Olympia some political science when she was in his class at Orono.

Haymakers   Negative ads which destroy an opponent by driving up their negatives. For example, Tom Andrew's ad showing someone in a radioactive suit stopped Linda Bean's upward momentum and drove up her negatives to a point from which she never recovered. Likewise, Bill Cohen's ad linking Bill Hathaway to the possible gift to the Indians of the northern two-thirds of the state made his negatives go up sharply in the Bangor TV market. "Haymakers are few and far between in Maine but when you see one, you know it."

Hazel Green's   Former restaurant on Water Street in Augusta and scene of many powerful and not-so-powerful lunches. For many years a popular watering hole for members of the Legislature and for aspiring candidates who thought members of the Legislature can help their campaigns.

Paul V. 'Haze' Hazelton   Beloved Professor of Education at Bowdoin College and unsung campaign advisor to Ed Muskie in Muskie's successful 1956 run for governor. Along with Frank Coffin, Ed Muskie, and others, he was personally responsible for the revival of the Democratic Party in the 1950's and 1960's. Immortalized for his perspicacious insight: "No one can ever appreciate election politics if they haven't driven the candidate from Rumford to Jonesport to Wytopitlock in a single day to meet with a total of eight town committee people. That's truly retail politics."

He Was Honest with Me   Libby Mitchell's comment on Dick Morris, who advised her in her 1984 race for the U.S. Senate against Bill Cohen. She got 26% of the vote despite—or because of—Morris's advice.

The Head and Horns   Top political operative in a campaign, sometimes the campaign manager, sometimes the candidate, sometimes neither. "She's the head and the horns of that operation but nobody knows it."

Head for the Hills   To bail out on an unpopular candidate. "She headed for the hills right after Labor Day; she knew what she was doing."

Head of Steam   Momentum. (See also "Big Mo.") "In that primary, Baldacci got himself a head of steam and pulled away from the pack. Surprised a lot of people."

Michael 'Mike' Heath   Executive director of the Christian Civic League. Active opponent of gay rights. Astonished insiders when he managed to get over 58,000 voters to sign a petition to that effect in 1997 in the "People's Veto." Modest enough to call the outcome "A miracle of God." The utterance as well as the feat indicated to insiders that he had become a worthy successor to Jack Wyman.

Heavy Hitter   A political player who has "weight and substance" and a commanding presence. "Like them or not, Muskie and Margaret Chase Smith were heavy hitters in their day." (See also "Gravitas.")

David Heller   Media maven from Politics Inc. in Washington who did John Baldacci's TV and radio commercials in 1994 and 1996.

Hello   Consultant-speak for a very bad or very stupid idea. "You want to cut Medicare by 25%? Hello."

James S. 'Jim' Henderson   State representative from Bangor, ran for Congress in 1978, getting 36% of the vote in the Democratic primary against Mark Gartley.

Merton 'Mert' Henry   Prominent Republican rainmaker and law partner in Jensen, Baird, Gardner and Henry. Old enough to have been the head of "Youth for Margaret" in 1948 while still at Bowdoin College, young enough to have headed up Susan Collins's 1996 senate campaign and important enough so that no major decision for good or ill has occurred in the Republican Party of Maine for the last 50 years without Merton Henry being consulted. An important player in the rise and success of Bill Cohen, Jock McKernan, Olympia Snowe and Susan Collins. Affectionately known as "The White Rabbit." Husband of Maine's first female judge, Harriet Henry, who was appointed to the District Court bench by Governor Curtis in 1973.

Hermaphrodites for McKernan   Davis Rawson's 1990 suggested group to show how silly gender politics had become in Maine. "Rawson might have a good idea here, check it out, 'Hermaphrodites for McKernan.'"

Hero or You're My Hero   Consultant-speak for anyone who has gotten you paid. "You got the check? You're my hero."

He's Had One Good Term, He's Earned Another   Congressman Jock McKernan's campaign slogan in 1984. Maine people agreed.

A. J. Higgins   Nice, fair political reporter for the *Bangor Daily News*. Not really a scorp with an agenda, he would rather be right than promote a point of view. Some insiders give him very high marks for giving good coverage of third-party candidates.

High Maintenance   A candidate who needs a lot of attention. "Hell, I got a phone call every night when he was walking through Cumberland County; he was a high-maintenance guy in those days."

Highliner   Coastal Maine name for a respected fisherman or woman, hence in politics, an impressive operative. "I hate to say it, but she earned highliner status with that victory."

Horace A. 'Hoddie' Hildreth Jr.   Republican candidate for Congress in 1st CD in 1968. Won the primary with 66% of the vote, lost the general election with 43%. Hoddie was a Portland lawyer, State Senator, and broadcasting executive, as well as the son of a former governor. After his defeat in 1968, Hoddie remained in the spotlight through his frequent appearances on behalf of environmental groups before the DEP. One of the true founders of Maine's modern environmental movement, he helped to block the Machiasport Oil Terminal in the early 1970's. Political insiders know him for his incredibly perspicacious insight into primary politics: "Stress familiar thoughts."

Horace A. Hildreth Sr.   State Senator (1941–1945) and governor from 1945 until 1949, he lost to Margaret Chase Smith in the Republican primary for U.S. Senate in 1948. Later served as president of Bucknell College and was Ambassador to Pakistan. Returned to Maine to run for governor in 1958, beating Phil Chapman in the primary but losing to Clint Clauson in the last Maine September election. One of the first candidates to use TV ads. Of course, owning a couple of TV stations (Channel 5 in Bangor and Channel 8 in Presque Isle) helped lead him to this art form.

Richard 'Dick' Hill   University of Maine professor of environmental studies whose strong credentials with wood energy helped save Maine Yankee when his ads converted many.

Hill, Holiday   Democratic media firm from Boston credited with the 1972 commericals which portrayed Bill Hathway so effectively in his race with Margaret Chase Smith. Insiders remember these black-and-white commericals as among the best in modern Maine political history.

I'm History   I'm not working on that campaign anymore, thank God.

History   (1) What TV reporters seldom know.

History   (2) To be finished, out of things as in "She's history, those commercials finished her off." To be history can also be a positive thing as in

"Boy was he relieved when his lawyer said, 'You're history, the committee went out of business last night at midnight.' "

A Hit   (1) A news story. "We got a great hit on the library bond issue."

A Hit   (2) A blow. "We sure took a hit on that lousy press release."

Hit It, Bo   Political insider phrase believed to have originated from the TV series *The Dukes of Hazzard,* a GOB favorite. Means "let's get out of here." "Oh God, here comes those old ladies again; they want to talk about Social Security. Hit it, Bo."

Hit the Bricks   Street campaigning. "When it came to hitting the bricks, Harry the Horse was the best I ever saw. Absolutely relentless." Actually, if you try to hit the bricks hard in a place like Portland's Old Port, you are most likely to twist an ankle. (See also "Horse [1].")

Hit Them High and Hit Them Low   Go positive and negative at the same time. Put a positive message or biography on TV at the same time you are using a contrast ad to put your opponent at a perceptual disadvantage. "OJ went high and low and hit Tom hard in the Portland DMA. She won the election while Tom was still floundering around on the ground in rural Maine."

Hitler Youth   Unkind Democratic name for the Young Republicans. "Those Hitler Youth are to the right of Attila the Hun." Never mind the mixed historical references, you get the point.

Barry J. Hobbins   Democratic state representative from Saco. Ran for Congress in 1984, getting 36% of the vote against Jock McKernan after winning the Democratic primary with 63% of the vote. (See also "The Hobbit.") Later served in the state senate from 1988 to 1990.

The Hobbit   Barry Hobbins of Saco, Democratic insider, state chairman and TV personality and a longtime Brennanista. While not an "original" Brennanista, Barry was a Brennanista before and after it was cool sticking by Joe through three straight losses for major political office (governor,

governor and senator). Also ran for Congress against Jock McKernan and lost in 1984. (See also "Barry J. Hobbins.") A player and probably the most knowledgeable Democratic insider of the modern period. Terrific sense of humor.

Douglas 'Doug' Hodgkin   Professor of political science at Bates College for over 20 years. Longtime and effective pundit on the Maine political scene and the only known Republican on the Bates faculty.

Hold Her, Newt   Coastal subculture term for a bad idea such as tossing a lobster trap string over the side of your boat with your leg tangled in the warp line. Used by insiders to urge caution on candidates. "Hold her, Newt; do you really want to appear at the UFO convention?"

Barbara Holt   Veteran Democratic operative, most recently campaign manager for Dick Spencer for Senate in 1996. Also worked on various Joe Brennan campaigns.

Hook and Bullet Crowd   Liberal nickname for the men and women of Maine who hunt and fish.

Horse   (1) aka **Harry the Horse**. Republican House Majority leader and candidate for governor in 1974, Harry Richardson (R-Cumberland). Good buddy of "Snort." Horse is regarded by many insiders as having been the best street campaigner of the modern era. He was extremly effective one on one and a relentless morning-to-night campaigner whether the target was female or not. One of the truly great senses of humor in Maine politics. Very engaging guy.

Horse   (2) Generic term for hardworking candidate. "She's a real horse, Senator, a real horse. She hit the gate at 6 A.M. and just kept going till midnight. She's a horse."

Horse   (3) Any candidate in a particular race. To have a candidate in a particular race. "Hell, I've got no horse in that race, I don't care who wins."

Horse Race   The candidates matched up one against the other. The press, and the public, often seem much more interested in the horse race aspects of a campaign than any serious discussion of issues. "There is too much horse race polling in the media today. The media doesn't care about anything else, horse race results drive the story."

Horsepower   Strength, determination, ability to raise money. "She's got the horsepower; she'll do all right in that primary."

Hot Gas   Newly released press release from a candidate. "That hot gas is more of the same; when are they going to get a life?"

Hot Line   A political operative who makes up his or her own gossip. "Forget it, he's his own hot line. That never happened."

Hot Shit   A cool operator, a candidate who does the unexpected and pleasantly surprises his consultant. "I would never have figured Jim Erwin as a hot shit, but he shook that sardine packer lady's hand dripping in fish guts and kept on smiling. What a hot shit thing to do, him in his three-piece suit and all. Jim is all right."

House Is on Fire Meeting   Fund-raising term for a gathering where disaster is forecast unless tons of money are raised. Usually called on losing campaigns and underfunded ballot measure efforts.

James 'Jim' Howaniec   Mayor of Lewiston and Congressional candidate in the Democratic Second District primary in 1994. Finished 4th with 14% of the vote.

Howard 'Howdy' Dana Jr.   Currently a Justice of the Supreme Court of Maine. One of four Reagan delegates to the National Republican Convention of 1976, and early state chair of the Reagan/Bush campaign, he was appointed a director of the Legal Service Administration by President Reagan and was chief fund-raiser for his former law partner, Governor John "Jock" McKernan (See "The Brothers.")

David 'Dave' Huber   Late Republican State Senator from Falmouth and longtime chair of the appropriations committee. A class guy in the best sense. Husband of Sherry.

Sherry E. Huber   Republican representative from Falmouth. Ran for governor as an Independent in 1986 and got 15% of the vote. Previously ran for governor as a Republican in 1982 and finished second in the primary with 33% of the vote. She is still famous among insiders for her 1986 television commercials having something to do with population control, leading many to think she was running for office in Bangladesh rather than for governor of the state of Maine. Important Maine player for several decades. A longstanding and effective environmentalist, she was director of Maine Audubon Society. Later she headed up Mainewatch, a environmental and governmental think tank, and served on the board of The Nature Conservancy. Currently head of Maine Tree.

William B. Hughes   Independent candidate for governor who received 1,314 votes in 1974.

Hummer   (1) A hard, inside pitch designed to scare an opponent, usually a reference made by someone over 40. "We don't really need to but let's send a hummer right by Barringer so he stays passive the whole campaign."

Hummer   (2) An adoring, overly complimentary portrait of a candidate, usually by a young reporter, male or female. Usually a reference by someone under 40. "Did you see the hummer he gave Smith? It's enough to make you vomit."

The Hunt   The chase, the election. "We were in the hunt, gentlemen, until election day."

The Hunt Blew Up   A GOB saying for "things went wrong and we don't know why." "One minute she was sailing along in first place and then the next thing we knew, the hunt blew up." (See also "GOBs.")

The Hunt for a Dole October   Maine Republican's search for good news during the fall of 1996. "God, we need a hunt for a Dole October or we could lose the House and the Senate."

Hurl   To throw up, to be disgusted with. "Those commercials were so hokey, they made me hurl. Where do these DC guys get the gall to charge real money for such trash?"

Hurt Locker   To put an opponent at a disadvantage. "We put them in a hurt locker with that ad. God, it felt good to turn the tables on them."

Robert Huse   Executive secretary, Maine Democratic Party during Ed Muskie's 1958 Senatorial campaign, then executive assistant in Muskie Senate office 1959–1961.

Leroy Hussey   Finished 2nd in the Republican primary for governor in 1952, receiving 32.4% of the vote.

Hustings   Out where the voters are. "Get out of the headquarters and get on the hustings. You already have all the votes you're going to get from your own staff."

Hype   Excess praise. The press is often guilty of hype with a particular candidate, only to follow that with a blistering attack. Also used as a verb: to build up. "Can you believe the way they hyped the Bush visit?"

Hyperbole   The essential ingredient in political campaigns, whether candidate or ballot measure.

I

....

Never interrupt an enemy

when he is making a mistake.

NAPOLEON

....

I Am Not a Crook   Famous utterance of President Nixon concerning Watergate. This heartfelt cry for help was ignored by the scorps of the day, and today it has become consultant-speak for any candidate statement which on the face of it, appears irrational and self-destructive. "You want to say you never had sex with anyone under 16? Why don't you just go on TV and say 'I am not a crook'?"

I Could Be Wrong   Consultant-speak for "I absolutely, categorically am not wrong." "I could be wrong, but I don't think it's a good idea to tell voters you want to cut Social Security by 20%."

I Don't Think So   Political-speak for "Not on your life" or "Are you crazy?"

I Wouldn't Appoint Frank Coffin Dog Catcher   President Johnson's private explanation when Senator Ed Muskie pressed him about former

President Kennedy's earlier announcement that he intended to appoint Coffin as Ambassador to Panama. Two years later Johnson accepted Muskie's recommendation of Coffin for Maine's seat on the U.S. Circuit Court of Appeals in Boston.

Icarus   In Greek mythology, Icarus put on wings held together with wax in order to fly, and when he flew too close to the sun, the wax melted and he fell into the sea. Used in Maine politics to describe a person who leaves a safe Congressional seat to run for the Senate, only to fail. "Too bad, Tom Andrews pulled an Icarus, just like Dave Emery." Or, "Both Baldacci and Longley avoided pulling an Icarus in 1996."

Ice Queen vs. Motor Mouth   Davis Rawson's term for the 1994 Senate race between Olympia Snowe and Tom Andrews, calling it "The Dream Match." Turned out to be duller than that and a rout!

Identifier   The buried word in ballot measure language which tells the voter the best thing about the measure. "Put 'compromise' in as the identifier and we'll pick up 8% with that alone. Call the initiative a compromise and we'll win this sucker yet."

Idiosyncratic   A single non-representational opinion as contrasted with the law of large numbers. "So your yuppie friends don't like the commercials? Tough. That's just idiosyncratic. The statewide totals are 3–1 in favor of those elements." (See also "Law of Large Numbers.")

IEs   Independent expenditures in campaigns. A loophole in campaign financing laws which allows "independent" groups to produce and run ads against particular candidates and causes without these expenditures counting against the party limits as long as there is no coordination with the campaign.

If It Bleeds, It Leads   Dictum of TV news directors, which explains why so few political stories get to lead off a newscast.

If You've Got the Money, Honey, I've Got the Time   Consultant credo and theme song. Has a historical ring to it when used by Dr. Demento to answer Cardinal O'Connor's question as to whether Governor Mario Cuomo could be defeated. "Can he be beaten? If you've got the money, honey, I've got the time."

I'm Great. I Know It   Margaret Chase Smith's puckish, tongue-in-cheek comment after being eulogized by Maine's politicians and civic leaders on her 90th birthday. But you know, she really was. For those who only saw her late in her career and those who felt the wrath and spite of her or General Lewis, it may be hard to appreciate her place in Maine's political life. Certainly she was a consultant's nightmare, never hiring one. Certainly, it is a very viable hypothesis that with a single media consultant in 1972 she would have been able to defeat Bill Hathaway. When you think of where she started in the 1930's, without a college education, without powerful friends or patrons and yet she made herself into one of the most successful political figures of the 20th century, you have to call the feat "impressive." After 1940, when her husband died, she won four Congressional races in six months (two primaries and two general elections). In 1948, she fought three popular, well-connected Republicans, one of whom was a sitting governor, to win her party's nomination for the Senate; she beat all of them combined and won going away. Overall, she won 15 races and lost only 1! During the period under review, she won 9 and lost only 1. These are very impressive feats by anyone, in any political culture. Two recent biographies, Patricia L. Schmidt, *Margaret Chase Smith: Beyond Convention* (Orono: University of Maine Press, 1996) and Patricia Ward Wallace, *Politics of Conscience: A Biography of Margaret Chase Smith* (Westport: Praeger, 1995), capture much of her story, but neither seems truly to understand the magnitude of her electoral achievements nor the true nature of her courage in standing up to Senator Joe McCarthy at a time when even President Truman was afraid to challenge him.

I'm Happy, I'm Honored, I'm Humble   Congresswoman Margaret Chase Smith upon winning the 1948 Republican primary for U.S. Senate, defeating former Governor Sumner Sewall, Rev. Albion Beveredge and Governor Horace Hildreth, and setting the stage for her four terms in the Senate.

I'm on Deadline   Print reporter's gambit to get your comments quickly.

I'm On the Air in 20 Minutes   TV reporter's gambit to get your comments quickly.

I'm Sorry, I Blew It   Sounds of a candidate blaming her- or himself for an electoral defeat. Seldom heard in Maine politics.

I'm Still Drinking His Whiskey   White hunter talk used by political consultants to explain why they do not criticize some outrageous statement or action of one of their clients. Means "I'm still on his or her payroll." "Now he wants to close Maine Yankee? Hell, I'd say something, but I'm still drinking his whiskey."

I'm Talking to Them about That   Consultant-speak for "I haven't signed up that client, but I got there first." "Alan does more talking to them about that than any other consultant in Maine."

Image Enhancement   To improve the image of a candidate, a company or a cause. What keeps pollsters, ad agencies and public relations firms in business.

Imaginary Horribles   Name given to influence vectors which frighten voters to vote against a referendum question. Usually exaggerated consequences to prove the proposition "fear drives out favor." "In the ERA referendum the no side used the 'imaginary horrible' of gay and lesbian marriages to defeat it." (See also "Fear Drives Out Favor" and "FUD" as well as "Greater Good.")

Improve His/Her Performance   What every consultant hopes he or she can accomplish. Most fail, as a candidate's bad habits usually are deeply imbedded and only the most energetic want to change. "Her husband asked me why we didn't improve her performance. I told him she refused to practice."

In a Walk   Any campaign where the winner gets 60% or better. "Baldacci will beat Young in a walk; I don't care what the polls show now." (See also "Blowout.")

In Market   In a designated market area (DMA), sometimes a polling survey confined to that DMA. "We did cable and 600 GRPs and the numbers in market went up 20%." (See also "Outmarket.")

In Mortise   In a notch, cutout or box. Used in campaign advertising to show a person or figure at the end of a commercial where instructions are given to the voter such as "Vote Yes on One." "I want that Audubon gal in mortise in the first ending and that SAM guy in mortise in the second. I want the voters to see who's telling them to vote yes."

In or Out   Magic words having to do with a potential candidate. "Is she in or out?" A candidate who is "in" offers a packet of positive possibilities for the candidate, consultants and eventually, civilians. A candidate who is "out" is dead meat. At the start of the week, I had three in and one out. By the end of the week they were all dead meat. Talk about this being a cruel business."

In Play   Any demographic group still up for grabs as an election progresses. "The Francos are in play, go get them."

In Search of Clients   Political consultants' operational style. "We're always in search of clients, not truth."

In Search of Enemies   (1) Operational style of any ideological movement in Maine. "NOW and the NRA, what do they have in common? They're always in search of enemies."

In Search of Enemies   (2) Some consultants and most party workers actually do better running a campaign against someone than for someone else. "She's in search of enemies for the next cycle already."

In the Can   On film. "It's in the can; we got Mitchell with the little old lady. Talk about a testimonial!"

In the Clear   To be on TV while your opponent is not. Thought to be a very desirable position in which to be. "I tell you if we go up on October 1, we'll be in the clear."

In the Crib   In the bank, already gotten. Votes which will not shift. "Don't worry about the women outside the home; they're already in the crib. They aren't going anywhere the last week."

In the Hunt   In action, not dead yet. Consultant-speak for any situation of possible gain or positive outcome. "We're still in the hunt, ladies, let's keep on trucking."

In the Pucker Brush   Anywhere outside the urban centers of Maine, especially in the rural areas of Franklin, Somerset, Piscataquis, Hancock, Washington, Aroostook and Penobscot Counties. "Please don't send me back to the pucker brush; I'll do anything else. I can't take another one of those general stores and their soggy old subs."

In the Rotation   In the mix of television advertisements. "I put her in the rotation but only in the fringe time slots."

In the Tank   (1) Defeated, lost. "He was in the tank as soon as Olympia hit him with 2,000 GRPs." (See also "GRPs.")

In the Tank   (2) Very effective commercial of Greg Stevens which put presidential candidate Dukakis in a tank, making him look very foolish. "It's all over; did you see Dukakis in the tank?" (See also "Greg 'Zen Master' Stevens.")

In the Toilet   Over, done, finished. "They're all in the toilet, they just don't know it yet."

In the Vault   Consultant-speak for "truly between you and me," comments not for attribution. "Look, I know how she spent the weekend; I'm only telling you in the vault, though."

Incident in Managua   Shelling of the Managua airport by Contra rebels, September 9, 1983, just prior to the arrival by air of Senators Gary Hart and Bill Cohen. Quite rightly, Both Cohen and Hart, subsequently questioned both their motives and their aim.

Inclination Scale   Polling technique in which the respondent is asked to rank choices from first to last or to give each choice its own rank thereby telling the pollster which word picture or phrase is most appealing. "Look, if you want to get both the gun guys and the enviros, you have to put in "wildlife habitat" and "threatened and endangered species.""

Income Tax Indexing   A truly ironic phenomenon. In 1982, Charles Cragin, Republican candidate for governor, pushed to referendum a measure calling for income tax indexing. He campaigned hard and widely for it. In the general election, the ballot measure passed handily but Cragin lost badly to Joe Brennan.

Incoming   A bad hit on your candidate while you watch. "By the time the Hathaway people were yelling 'incoming,' their candidate was toast." (See also "Toast.")

Independent Democrat   Democrat running for office in a Republican district.

Independent Republican   Republican running for office in a Democratic district.

Independent Variable   That which makes a difference in the campaign. Consultants are prone to believing they are the independent variable. "Civilians think it was his personality which won it for him but the independent variable was the strategic plan we did for him. He had sense enough to stick to it no matter what the reporters said about him."

Independents   Often used interchangeably with "unenrolled," the correct term for those Mainers who are not in any political party. Descriptively, it is a catch-all word to cover many League of Women Voter types who carefully look at candidates and issues and always vote, as well as a mass of know and care-nothings who never vote. The Maine press has yet to distinguish between these two groups, each of which make up approximately 50% of the unenrolled voters in Maine.

Indian Fighter Joe   Joe Brennan, for his stand against giving the Passamaquoddy and Penobscot Indians the northern two-thirds of the state in

1978, thus helping him win the governorship. This occurred despite the best efforts of his longtime rival Ken Curtis to get him to support the politically correct but electorally disastrous (at the time) suggestion of settling with the tribes.

Influence Vectors   Information which gets voters to change their minds. Can be facts, factoids or "imaginary horribles." "In the telecommunications bond issue, the influence vector was keeping Maine school children competitive." (See also "Imaginary Horribles.")

Informed Ballot   A polling technique used when a candidate is not well known and some description of him or her is used to inform the voter before a choice is asked for. The voter is given a description of that candidate such as "an Afro-American who is a former FBI agent" in order to test the upside potential of that candidate. "Spencer looked lousy on the informed ballot section; I don't think he's going to give Brennan a run for his money."

Inoculate   To put on campaign advertising in order to mute a criticism or to take a position on which you know your opponent is going to attack you. "One of the best inoculation efforts I ever saw was when they inoculated Collins with those Social Security spots."

Inside Baseball   Political gossip or trivia of no interest to the general public. "John Day's column this week is strictly inside baseball; don't worry about it."

Inside Information   To political junkies what catnip is to cats. Most "inside information" is really political gossip and not exclusive at all, but it is worth listening to because it is usually ahead of the news reports.

Inside the Beltway   Refers to inside the beltway around Washington to denote politicians, bureaucrats, and media cut off from the average people and their concerns. "Inside the beltway, they think it matters what committee you chair."

Intensity   In polling, intensity refers to how strongly an opinion is held. "Opposing all abortions is not a widespread opinion in Maine; only about

12% of the voting population opposes all abortions, but there is a lot of intensity with that position. It is virtually impossible to drive the opinion below 12%."

Internationalist   Charge hurled by Robert Jones, Joe McCarthy-backed candidate against Margaret Chase Smith during the 1954 Republican primary for the U.S. Senate.

Irish Bully Boys   Franco term for the Irish who tend to dominate the Democratic Party at the expense of Franco-Americans. "Those Irish bully boys like our 'get out the vote' on election day but they don't give us the spots on the ticket we deserve." "Hold back the Biddeford vote; I want to see what the Irish bully boys get out of Portland first."

Is This a Great Country or What?   Consultant's paean any time she or he lands an important and/or lucrative client. "They're going with our firm; is this a great country or what?"

It Doesn't Get Any Better Than This   September 28, 1997. Loving wife. Book almost finished. Good swimming practice. Son in the business doing killer ads on the Turnpike. Daughter standing by with Jimmy B ready to protest against Brownie if needed. 25 wild turkeys in our field. First-rate polling from Government 111 class at Bowdoin. Call from the governor. Call to the SecDef's chief of staff. Damn, life here in Maine is good. Oh, *que ça dura.* Thank the Lord and pass those overnights.

It Wasn't Lost on This Coast   Quote attributed to Roger Mallar, who, upon hearing that the 1991 measure to widen the Maine Turnpike was defeated, indicated that the fault lay elsewhere. He was referring to the California-based consulting firm of Winner, Wagner, Mandabach, which advised the widening supporters and did their media. (See also "The Boys from California.")

It's Over   Erik Potholm on September 17 at 6:40 P.M. speaking about the Maine Turnpike referendum of 1997 after the final edit of his and Greg Stevens's ads featuring safety officials riding on the Maine Turnpike.

It's the Economy, Stupid   Clever epigram of James Carville during the 1992 presidential race from which flowed the strategy of always keeping the Clinton campaign focused on domestic concerns. Now in general use for any effort to keep a political campaign "on message." Can sound funny when used as in "It's the economy, stupid, talk only about drugs."

Dr. H. Rollins 'Rollie' Ives   Republican candidate for Congress in 1986, received 43% of the vote in a losing cause to Joe Brennan. Later Department of Human Services Commissioner under Governor Jock McKernan. Later still, a TV pundit. Strong supporter of Bob Monks.

Good judgment comes from

experience, and experience comes

from bad judgment.

BARRY LePATNER

Jack Shit   GOB name for something worthless, not worth worrying about. "One story in the weekly paper doesn't mean jack shit." It isn't actually clear why jack shit should be worth less than any other kind of shit, but in Maine this is apparently the case. (See also "Pisshole in the Snow.")

Peter Jackson   Former Associated Press Augusta bureau chief, with 18 years' experience covering Augusta and its denizens. Not much impressed him, which may sound like a good trait in a newsman, but he often came across as cynical even if he was fair. Some insiders say he was not inclined to dig too deeply into stories which didn't originate in the capitol (or on his floor at the statehouse). During his time at the AP it was alleged that if your candidate came up with a cure for cancer, the AP would give cancer equal space in the article. Now in Pennsylvania where he can be more justifiably cynical.

Jacksonians   Term for rural, Protestant Democrats in order to distinguish them from urban, Catholic Democrats. "Frank Coffin was really a Jacksonian, and that helped him in the general election of 1956; some Republicans thought he was one of them."

Charlie Jacobs   Former member of "last" executive council, former Muskie and Mitchell staffer in Maine and Washington.

Paul Jacques   Waterville state rep and strong advocate for sportsmen and women during an 18-year stint in the Maine House. Could sway the entire House to support more moose permits, but couldn't get cats licensed and leashed. A near demi-god to many GOBs. (See also "GOBs.")

Jammed Up   All-purpose political excuse meaning "I can't do it" when you really don't want to do it but don't have a real excuse. "The 4th of July parade in Leeds? I'm all jammed up."

John Jannace   Independent Senatorial candidate in 1978. From Gardiner and owner of Fairview Wines, he received 3% of the vote. Probably should have given away more free samples of his product.

Jar Head   Affectionate Republican name for Senate President (1994–1996) Jeffrey Butland (R-Cumberland), who, in a former life, was a U.S. Marine. "If I were in a foxhole, I'd want it to be with Jar Head."

Jenny Jones Filter   Pollsters are always searching for filter questions to divide respondents who will actually vote from those who will not. The Jenny Jones filter assumes that any person who has ever been on the Jenny Jones show has not ever voted and will never vote. This is somewhat different from the Ricki Lake filter, which assumes that any person who has been on the Ricki Lake show or ever watched the Ricki Lake show should never be allowed to vote. "Look at this soft data, can you believe these people. Too bad we can't use the Ricki Lake filter on them."

Come to Jesus Meeting   Fund-raising term for meetings which are called when fund-raising is going poorly and it is necessary to increase partipation by imparting a sense of urgency. "Nobody is making their quotas. It's time for a come to Jesus meeting."

Les Jeux Sont Faits   French for "the cards are down," meaning the election is over, even if the votes haven't yet been counted. "Friday night and les jeux sont faits. Cool."

Jihad   An ideological crusade. In consultant-speak, a group or candidate who cares more about making an ideological statement than in winning. "All they want is a jihad, count me out."

Jingle   (1) A telephone call, usually with no real purpose to it except to fish around for information. "Hell, give her a jingle and we'll see what they're doing."

Jingle   (2) Catchy phrase and/or tune to go with a commercial. "The jingle is better than the visuals on those Congressional ads."

Jink   BNAS pilot term for quick, evasive action. "Cohen was the best I ever saw. He'd give the crowd that something about the glass being half full or half empty, and then he was jinking away and they never knew where he ended up." (See also "BNAS.")

Joan of Arc   Ohio Senator Robert A. Taft on Margaret Chase Smith after she won the U.S. Senate seat in 1948. "Margaret Smith is the Joan of Arc of the Republican party, who may well lead us out of the morass of defeat."

Job or **To Job**   To bash unfairly. "The scorps often say, 'I didn't want to job her but it just came out that way.'"

Jock Lite   Democratic derogatory phrase for any Republican candidate who is good-looking, smooth and superficial. "He's no rocket scientist; he's just another Jock Lite." This is actually an odd piece of terminology since McKernan graduated from Dartmouth, certainly as good or better a school than that which most of the speakers attended.

Joe   Joseph Brennan, Portland state representative (1965–1971), Cumberland County District Attorney (1971–1972), State Senator (D-Portland) (1973–1974), Maine Attorney General (1975–1979), Governor (1979–1987), U.S. Congressman (1987–1991). One of the few players in Maine politics who is known to most everyone by his first name. A dedicated public servant and professional politician, Brennan ran for governor twice more, losing to Jock McKernan in 1990 and Angus King in 1994. His race for the U.S. Senate in 1996 surprised a number of Democrats, although it shouldn't have. He lost that race to Susan Collins. Still, he deserves a special place in any insider account since Joe Brennan was involved in more meaningful elections than just about anybody else in the post-war period and the loyalty of his followers (over 50% in a Democratic primary, 35% in a general election) is a polling marvel which did not change over a long period of time. (See also "Joseph 'Joe' Brennan.")

Joe's Mantra   Republican and non-Brennanista Democrat term for Joe Brennan's fascination with his origins on Munjoy Hill. According to them, running for office so many times over 30 years, Brennan must have told the story of his humble beginnings to every man, woman and child in Maine. Some Democratic activists claim to have heard his story over 100 times. Best placed in context by John Menario who, running for governor in 1986, said "Let's get one thing straight; I came from the tough side of the Portland tracks, not Joe." Another Brennan supporter observed, "Even after he was making $125,000 as a Congressman, Joe still had to tell his Munjoy Hill stories, they're his mantra."

Johnnie, You're Not Getting My Bud Lite   Refers to the famous Bud Lite commercial in which Johnnie tells his Dad, "I love you, man," and his father responds, "Johnnie, you're not getting my Bud Lite." Political way of saying "No, and I know what your scam is."

William 'BJ' Johnson   Channel 13 reporter and anchor. One of the last TV personalities who really understood print journalism. Became press secretary to Republican candidate for Governor Harry Richardson in 1974, case worker for Senator Bill Cohen and later, case worker for Democratic Congressman Tom Allen. Obviously talented and light on his feet.

Willis Johnson   AP reporter and author of the humorous and insightful *Year of the Longley*, an antic view of Maine's first Independent governor this century.

Jolly Green Giant   Some paper industry insiders' name for Jonathan Carter.

Cyril 'Cy' M. Joly Jr.   GOP state party chair in the late 1960's and early 1970's, and Republican mayor of Waterville. He was also National committeeman for most of the 1970's. Drafted to run for a third term as mayor in 1965, he lost by 16 votes to Democrat Malcolm Fortier. When some prominent Republicans found out that their absentee ballots had not been counted, they brought suit to have their votes added to Joly's total. The Maine Supreme Court correctly ruled that this could not be done because only a losing candidate and not a mere voter had standing to bring such an action. Joly choose not to do so, because he did not want to deal with an all-Democratic city council!

F. Woodman 'Woody' Jones   George Mitchell confidant and Democratic insider.

Harold Jones   Longtime Republican activist and fund-raiser. Spiritual godfather for Maine conservatives and state party chair.

Robert Jones   Former staffer and 1952 campaign manager for Senator Owen Brewster, he was handpicked by Wisconsin Senator Joe McCarthy who hoped Jones could upset his antagonist, Margaret Chase Smith, when she ran for reelection. He lost the Republican primary for U.S. Senate in 1954, receiving 16.7% of the vote.

The Judge   (1) Respectful nickname for Frank Coffin, one of the founders (with Ed "Big Ed" Muskie and Paul "Haze" Hazelton) of modern Democratic politics in Maine. Successfully elected to Congress in 1956, he lost to John Reed for governor in 1960. Later appointed a federal appellate judge in 1965.

The Judge   (2) What most people were calling George Mitchell after President Carter "ended" Mitchell's political career by accepting Senator

Muskie's suggestion to have him appointed to the federal judiciary. (See also "*The* Senator.")

Judgment Cycle   A consultant term for the time it takes the press, pundits and media to elevate, scrutinize and then discard a candidate. Usually, the press will not focus on a candidate for a while, then scrutinize his or her every real and imagined flaw and then pass judgment on him or her. The classic example is the pundit who talked about "The failed presidency of Bill Clinton" *before* his inauguration! "Stay out of that judgment cycle for as long as you can. The less the scorps know about you, the better. They'll puff you up and shoot you down within a week."

Jujitsu Ad   Ad which takes the negative energy from a candidate or political figure and turns it against the other side. The classic jujitsu ad in recent Maine politics was the Stop the Widening ad which turned the unpopularity of Governor McKernan against the turnpike-widening effort in 1991.

Junior Tuesday   In Maine, the Yankee Primary comes on "Junior Tuesday," which falls one week ahead of "Super Tuesday." "I heard Bob Dole say Junior Tuesday was really super to him in 1996."

Junkie   A political junkie is somebody who follows politics very closely and requires a constant stream of information, however irrelevant, of a political nature. A junkie avidly follows political trivia that a civilian would never even read. "She's a junkie all right, she reads Hanrahan and Diamon both, every week," or "What a junkie, he reads that political gossip column in the *Maine Sunday Telegram* and then calls around to see what else is new."

Jurassic Park   A very expensive TV commercial. "All we wanted was a 30-second spot and we got another Jurassic Park." (See also "Gone With the Wind.")

K

I looked around at the little fishes

present and said, "I'm the Kingfish."

HUEY LONG

K   A unit of measure for political consultants, $1,000 in 1996 dollars, as in "She gets 7K a month and she's well worth it." (See also "A Grand.")

K1, C2   Shorthand for a Republican national and Congressional attack strategy on the Democrats in the early 1950's: "Korea, Communism and Corruption."

Edward 'Ed' Kane   Prominent leader of the 1985 campaign against the low-level radioactive waste initiative.

John V. Keenan   The Democratic nominee for Congress from the 3rd CD in 1950, Keenan lost the general election to Frank Fellows, receiving 37.1% of the vote.

Keep on Trucking   Consultant-speak for "don't give up." "Forget the editorial, editorials aren't worth jack shit unless you put them in a 30 second. Just keep on trucking and things will work out."

Keeping the Store Open   Consultant-speak for hanging around a political campaign which is going down to defeat; distancing yourself from a losing effort in a nice way, as in "Hey, I'm just trying to keep the store open, I didn't order the merchandise."

Thomas 'Tom' Keily   Democratic pollster from Boston who did the polling for Joe Brennan in 1990, 1994 and 1996. Insiders believe that he accurately projected the difficulty Brennan would have in the 1994 race for governor as early as January 9, 1994.

Ronald Kellam   State Senator and Democratic candidate for Congress in 1962. Lost to Stan Tupper, gathering 40% of the vote.

Edward 'Ed' Kelleher   Former Democratic state rep from Bangor and chief of the Appropriations Committee. Insiders know him as a master at redistricting, for being an original Brennanista, and for his strong support of Bill Hathaway when he ran for Congress and U.S. Senate. Current public information officer for the Maine judiciary.

Peter S. Kelley   Democratic State Senator from Caribou, finished third in the four-way Democratic primary for governor in 1974 with 24% of the vote. Best remembered as "Kilowatt Kelley" for his association with the 1973 public power referendum, a cause that failed but which gave him strong name recognition in the 1974 primary.

Ken   (1) Democratic insider name for former Congressman, Republican governor (1987–1995) and current first husband, John McKernan. Democrats refer to him as the Ken in the Ken and Barbie dolls. Since he's handsome, a good athlete and smart, this name seems to many objective observers as sour grapes.

Ken   (2) Kenneth M. Curtis, Democratic governor and Congressional candidate. Elected governor in 1966, winning the Democratic primary with 55% of the vote and defeating John Reed in the general election with 53% of the vote. Reelected in 1970 after beating Plato Truman in the primary with 63% of the vote, he narrowly (50.1% to 49.9%) defeated Jim Erwin. Previously ran for Congress, winning the 1st District Democratic primary in 1964 with 65% of the vote but lost the general election with 49.9% of the vote. One of the few Maine political figures known by his first name. (See also "Joe.")

Kennedy Twist   Senator Margaret Chase Smith's name for President Kennedy after he became President and switched a number of policy positions. She called it "The Kennedy Twist . . . done in agony to a Cuban beat." As a result, Kennedy from then on released information about federal grants to the state of Maine through junior Senator Ed Muskie instead of through the entire Maine delegation headed by Smith.

Kevin Keogh   Republican state chair and candidate for Congress in Maine's First District primary in 1994. Received 18% of the vote. Later went back to being party chair and advising other candidates on how to run their campaigns.

David 'Dave' Kerry   Super field organizer and fundraiser in York County for many Democratic candidates over the years. Nice guy. Brother of John.

John M. Kerry   State Senator (D-Saco), beat three other candidates in the 1982 Democratic primary for Congress, then lost to Jock McKernan in the fall, getting 48% of the vote.

Key Precinct   Any town in Maine, such as Turner or Winthrop, which accurately predicts the outcome of statewide elections when run through "all against all" mathematical equations.

KFC   Kentucky Fried Chicken. The coin of the realm for "volunteers" and those trucked in to pack meetings, rallies and hearings. This art form is believed to have started with Bob Monks and his 1972 campaign against Margaret Chase Smith when he packed the Topsham Fair Grounds with KFC-rewarded people for a "rally" covered by the CBS Nightly News. "Smitty, we got the go-ahead for $200 worth of KFC; send Lil and her people to the hearing. And don't forget the walkie-talkies."

Angus Khan   Al Diamon nickname for Angus King. "You decide to make a political donation to that nice, albeit hypothetical, Angus Khan."

Kill the King   Short for "If you strike a king, kill him," meaning if you are going after a major political figure, you must be sure you really defeat him or her so they cannot take revenge. "Chuck flew up to Eagle Lake and struck the king. Amazingly enough, he later killed him."

Kill Two Red Birds with One Stone   Phrase of Charlotte Iserbyt, founder of the Maine Conservative Union (MCU) quoted in Willis Johnson's *Year of the Longley*. Used to describe how nice it would be to have Governor Jim Longley run against both Senator Bill Hathaway and Congressman Bill Cohen, both of whom were regarded as being too liberal by the MCU.

Killer   A very good campaign worker. "He was a killer; we just pointed him in the right direction."

Kilroy Was There   Expression referring to the ubiquitous June Callan Kilroy, Democratic stalwart. Few weddings, wakes or bar mitzvahs in Portland could be convened in her absence during a career which spanned the period from 1934 to 1974 when she lost her Maine State Senate seat to an energetic 28-year-old law student named Phil Merrill. George Mitchell's aunt (by marriage), she was a top vote getter in her 9 successful elections but insiders know her best for her singing the national anthem at Democratic State Conventions.

Angus King Sr.   One of the two truly self-made figures in post-war Maine politics (the other Jim Longley Sr.). Running for governor as an Independent in 1993, he started with less than 10% of the vote and refused to be discouraged by the outcomes of the Republican and Democratic primaries in 1994. Fighting an uphill battle to victory, he won a four-way race with 35% of the vote. A former aide to Senator Bill Hathaway and a very successful entrepreneur and author, he became one of the most popular governors in post–World War II Maine history by taking courageous stands on controversial issues. His success in politics turned out to be contrary to the advice of many consultants who ended up being forced to say, "The exception proves the rule."

King of Signs   Davey Redmond, longtime Democratic activist and candidate for governor in 1986. An original and still Brennanista, Redmond has long been famous in Maine politics for his statewide network of coaches and athletes, his many contacts in Portland and Biddeford, his advocacy of lawn signs as an antidote to any campaign problem, and his sale of a Maine island—at their request—to The Nature Conservancy. A player.

KISS   Keep It Simple Stupid. 1980's memo from Dick Jalkut, vice president of New England Telephone indicating his strategy in dealing with the PUC. Dick Jalkut also made sure that Bruce Reeves did not win the elected PUC referendum in 1981, winning 61% to 38%.

Kiss of Indifference   To be polite to a candidate but show no interest in his or her plans or activities. "Wherever Phil went in '95, he got the kiss of indifference."

George W. Kittredge   Republican candidate for Congress in 1966, received 23% of the vote in the 1st District primary, coming in second. George, a distinguished submarine commander, subsequently designed and manufactured one-man submarines.

Felicia Knight   Anchor and political reporter for Channel 13 in Portland. Began broadcasting in 1978 at WABI in Bangor and moved to WGME in 1988 as Bill Johnson's replacement. An excellent moderator of political debate who does not back down in the face of candidate bluster and often asks strong follow-up questions.

Knowing and Not Knowing   What makes a pollster's heart pound. To know what is happening or is going to happen before other people do can provide a tremendous rush of adrenaline and then a warm, comforting feeling of peace and tranquillity for having been right. At some point, the candidates and the causes fall away and the knowing is all that matters. Even a losing campaign can salvage something for the pollster if he or she calls it correctly. "At 5 P.M. on election day, it was no longer about Joe or Angus or Susan or Jonathan, it was about knowing and not knowing. I knew."

Kooks   From Richard Nixon's dictum that "30% of the electorate are kooks," meaning that if you add up the nuts of the right and the nuts of the left, you get 30% of the voters. While Maine people and pundits might think this figure high, it is probably only a little bit high. "Forget about those two groups. We have our 12% of the kooks and they have 14% and that's all she wrote." (See also "That's All She Wrote.")

Barbara 'Bar' Kovach   President of Research Communications, and accurate tracker of dozens of Maine ballot measure and candidate campaigns.

Peter Kovach   Longtime political activist, staffer and pulse taker for New England Telephone and later, NYNEX. Thought to be king of the car-phone users in the Pine Tree State.

Peter Kyros Jr.   Son of the Congressman and campaign aide to Senator Muskie in his Vice Presidential and Presidential campaigns.

Peter N. Kyros Sr.   Democratic Congressman from the 1st CD. Won the Democratic primary in 1966 with 60% of the vote, won the general election with 50.4% of the vote. Won the Democratic primary in 1968 with 75% of the vote and the general election with 56% of the vote. Ran again in 1970, getting 83% of the vote in the Democratic primary and 59% of the vote in the general election. Ran for re-election in 1972, defeating Brownie Carson in the Democratic primary (66%) and Bob Porteous in the general election (59%). Won the Democratic primary with 69% of the vote in 1974, only to lose to Dave Emery with 49% of the vote that fall. Peter Kyros is unique among Maine's major election winners for having primary opposition every time he ran for Congress. He also should be remembered as having been the first in the Maine Congressional delegation to accent a multiplicity of district offices.

L

I am a living legend in some people's

minds, my own being one.

RON MANN

LA The Lewiston-Auburn metroplex, a key swing area which often determines the outcome of statewide elections because they in turn determine the outcome of Androscoggin County. (See also "Andro.") This LA is much more important to the citizens of Maine than the other LA, which is much more often depicted on television.

La Mess Politically incorrect Anglo politician's term for the Franco-American Festival "Kermesse" held every year in Biddeford.

Labor Goons Unkind Republican nickname for the Maine AFL/CIO.

Lady in Red Susan Collins who, on the night she won the Republican primary for governor in 1994, wore a red dress. During that summer, polling calls indicated that many people in Maine only identified her as the "lady in red," thus enabling Angus King to round up many Republicans before Labor Day.

Lady with Brass Knuckles in Her Handbag   John Day's term for Senator Olympia Snowe and her tenacious fight to save Loring Air Force Base.

Stanley E. 'Tuffy' Laffin   Three-term (1975–1980) Republican representative to the Legislature from Westbrook and famous for his advocacy of the death penalty for capital crimes. He dramatized his support by declaring that he would volunteer "to pull the switch" if Maine would restore capital punishment. Died in 1996, leaving a less colorful political arena in Maine.

Alexander LaFleur   Two-term Maine Attorney General, he finished 3rd in the Republican primary for governor in 1956, receiving 19.6% of the vote. LaFleur inaugurated a tradtition followed by Jim Erwin, Joe Brennan and Jim Tierney of using the AG as a platform from which to seek the governorship.

Lloyd P. LaFountain   Democratic candidate for governor in 1974. Received 9% of the vote in the primary.

Curtis LaMay Attitude   Wanting to hit the other side with everything you have, even if it means getting heavy negative press. "I love the guy, he's got a Curtis LaMay attitude and it's only July 15."

Lamb Chop   Al Diamon's name for former Congressman Jim Longley.

Robin Lambert   Insider aide to State Senate Majority Leader Jerry Speers and 1990 Republican State Senate candidate, one of the first openly gay GOP legislative candidates even though that hurt him in the Republican primary. Vindicated by the Maine Won't Discriminate victory in 1995.

Lame   Poor, ineffective, a bad effort. "What a lame speech that was. A trained chimp could have given a better one."

Lame Duck   An officeholder who is not seeking reelection and who therefore has little power over his opponents or his supporters. "He's a lame duck; I'm not going to his fund-raiser, I don't care how much he owes."

Landline   A secure telephone line. Political types love to talk on car phones. Political consultants prefer landlines. "I think you'd better get to a landline, Congressman, before we talk about that."

Janet Langhart   Washington TV personality, and wife of William S. Cohen. Works any crowd with grace and style.

David Langzettel   Portland AP bureau chief in the 1950's.

Lap Dancing   Working closely with a candidate you don't like for money. "Lap dancing with him just wasn't worth it."

Lap Dog   A political actor who is seen as unduly obsequious. "Did you see him with the candidate during the general? What a lap dog he turned out to be."

Constance 'Connie' LaPointe   Campaign manager for Governor Joseph Brennan in 1978. Later his fianceé and wife. An effective political operative in her own right. During the 1996 Senatorial campaign, when asked what he had been doing since his defeat in 1994, Brennan proudly stated that he had both seen the Pope and gotten married.

Thomas 'Tom' LaPointe   Longtime Democratic activist and strategist with a specialty in dealing with the free media. Brother of Connie.

Don Larrabee   The longtime dean of the Maine press corps in Washington. Started reporting for the *Bangor Daily News* in 1947 and continued for 30 years. Also took over May Craig's coverage for the Gannett papers in 1966, giving him a monopoly over Washington coverage of Maine. Larrabee always tried to find something good to say about the political figures he was interviewing and about the state of Maine. Belonged to an earlier, kinder era of political journalism. Highly respected and an effective communicator. Sold his news bureau to his staff in 1978 and began a 12-year tour of duty as Washington representative for the Maine governor's office. Wrote the interesting *It's News to Me* about his press experiences.

Late Money   Political money which comes into the campaign late in October after it can be effectively used. "When Emery ran for the U.S. Senate, there was a ton of late money, but by then he had lost."

Latency   In polling, refers to the upside potential for getting a particular issue into the public's consciousness. "There was powerful latency in the issue of the 200-mile fishing limit even though few people had ever heard of it when it was first developed. It became a very popular issue in Maine after having very minute beginnings."

Louis Lausier   Won the Democratic primary for governor in 1948 but lost the general election, receiving 34.4% of the vote.

Law of Diminishing Returns   Sometimes in politics, things don't get better as time goes on. Plato Truman getting 38.5% of the vote in the Democratic primary in 1966 was the best he would ever do in his long and tumultuous political career.

Law of Large Numbers   Mathematical law which says that the predictive value of a large sample is better than a small sample. In politics, this means that the 600 people you sample on a statewide basis have more predictive value than the five people the candidate talked to that morning who didn't like his ad. "Relax, Tom, the law of large numbers says your ad will do great in the Portland DMA." (See also "DMAs.")

Law of Unintended Consequences   When somebody wants something in politics, gets in and then discovers he or she would have been better off without the wish coming true. "Phil Merrill wanted Cohen out of the race. Cohen got out but Joe came in. Net, net, net, it was not a pretty picture for Phil. Ah, the law of unintended consequences."

Mark W. Lawrence   Maine Senate President (1997–) and important Democratic operative in York County. Hardworking and respected. But may need more passion on the stump if he is to reach his full electoral potential when Tom Allen decides to run for governor or senator.

Oram R. Lawry   Republican candidate for Maine's First District in 1982, lost to Jock McKernan, gathering 22% of the vote.

Lazarus   Insider Democratic name for Joe Brennan after he rose out of a year's seclusion to run for the U.S. Senate in 1996. "I saw Lazarus campaigning in the Old Port. He was reborn, I tell you. Looked 10 years younger and light years happier. He's really a good guy."

LCP Scale   Scorp rating system. Some reporters and columnists are regarded as generally liberal, some generally conservative and some as highly personal, that is, if they like you they write great things about you and if they don't they never can find anything good to say. "It's a good idea when you bring a new press person on board to run them through the LCP scale on all the scorps, otherwise they may get disillusioned and take it personally."

League of Women Voters Types   Refers to voters who claim they are more interested in issues than personalities and in positive messages rather than negative messages. MPBN to the contrary, to political consultants, this is not a very important political typology in Maine politics.

Mal Leary   Reporter and commentator for the Maine Public Broadcasting Network. Consistent, fair and accessible, Mal Leary has done very good political reporting—with polls to match—for over two decades . Balanced, objective, and spinnable but only if you have decent material. One of the very best reporters in the state in any medium. Great sense of history.

Shep Lee   Mega car dealer and Democratic fund-raiser par excellence. A close confidant of Senators Muskie and Mitchell and longtime Democratic insider and money man. A major Democratic player on the Maine scene for over four decades.

He Left Us a Better World   John Cole's summation of the political life of Edmund S. Muskie. Insiders agree. Muskie was one of the Titans of Maine politics since the end of World War II.

Legs   Having staying power, continuing to be a positive force for a long time. "Boy, did that commercial have legs, they used it for 12 weeks."

Porter D. 'Port' Leighton   Republican legislator from Harrison. Third choice of Howdy Dana for head of the Reagan election campaign in Maine. Parlayed that into a job with the GSA and then decided to run for governor. Did so in 1986, getting 31% of the vote against Jock McKernan in the Republican primary. Great sense of humor, if poor sense of timing. Subsequently moved from Harrison to Eastport, just ahead of salmon farming. Became mayor of Eastport.

Lionel A. 'Lal' Lemieux   Political reporter and editorial writer, *Lewiston Evening Journal* during the 1950's and 1960's.

Jerald Leonard   Democratic candidate for Senate in 1996, received 1% of the vote.

Ralph Lerner and Lowe   Ralph Lowe, a former song-and-dance man who became a TV anchor in Bangor and later was Governor Longley's communications coordinator. "Here comes Ralph Lerner and Lowe; what tap dance does the governor have him doing today?"

Alton Lessard   Lawyer and active Democrat in Lewiston; law partner of John Clifford and Thomas Delahanty (1954 Second District Congressional candidate, later Public Utilities Commission member, Maine judge and justice), Democratic Party state chairman.

Let Me Get This Straight   Consultant-speak introduction to bashing a candidate's idea or one coming from his or her brother-in-law. "Let me get this straight, you want to go where you want to go and say what you want to say? And you expect to get elected?"

Let Me Say This about That   Famous expression of John F. Kennedy. Used to give a candidate time to think up an answer. "Let me say this about that. (Pause) It may well be a state issue."

Let Skindivers Harvest Lobsters   Not-so-brilliant proposal to ensure one's electoral defeat in coastal Maine. First-and-only recorded use was by Republican Robert Porteous running against Democratic Congressman Peter Kyros in 1972. Kyros did not break a sweat in his reelection bid.

Let's Do Lunch   Let's *not* do lunch or "Don't call me, I'll call you." "You want to do policy papers for the Senator? Sure, let's do lunch."

Let's Rock and Roll   "Let's do something; that seems like a good thing to do. I like a photo op with the Olympic contingent; let's rock and roll."

Letters Over Signs   Most insiders would rather have a good letter to the editor from their field operation than a few lawn signs put up and plan their campaigns accordingly. "I don't care if they always put out signs in Lewiston; remember, letters over signs."

Juliana 'Julie' L'Heureux   Author of the influential newspaper column "Les Franco-Americains" in the *Portland Press Herald*. Very good on ethnic politics in Maine and a super source. One of the leaders of the Maine Citizens for Jobs and Safety in 1997. Head of CHANS.

License to Print Money   A golden political opportunity. "His campaign was just a license to print money, and the media guy acted accordingly."

License to Steal   Consultant-speak for a good opportunity. "Billy, it's a license to steal. The Dems take Lewiston for granted; let's get in there and take the election from them before they know what's happening."

Anna Lidman   Longtime Democratic operative in Iowa and Texas, later finance director for Maine Won't Discriminate and Citizens for Jobs and Safety, one of the best fund-raisers in the state, especially in terms of follow-up.

Lie and Die   Consultant advice to any and all candidates except where sex scandals are concerned. "It's very simple, you jerk, lie and die." Of course, sometimes you die anyway but at least you feel good about telling the truth as you expire.

Lie Key   Any question embedded in a poll which tries to determine if the respondent is telling the truth. "Yeah, the lie key got her; she said she voted in every election, but she couldn't give us the governor's name and only one of the senators."

Life List   Short for "Life Is Too Short List." Consultant's and (sometimes) candidate's list of people whose messages shall never be returned "because life is too short." "He's on my life list, I won't be calling him back."

Jack 'Big Jack' Linnell   Former mayor of Auburn and Republican Party chairman, one of the original supporters of Bill Cohen, Olympia Snowe, Jock McKernan and other moderate Republicans. Spent a long and important evening at the Pisces Club in Washington, D.C., with Bill and Diane Cohen trying to get then Congressman Cohen to come back to Maine and run for governor in 1978. Only succeeded in convincing Diane of the benefits of being the First Lady of Maine. With Big Jack's support, Cohen ran successfully for the U.S. Senate in 1978. Big Jack is also justly famous as a longtime player on the Maine political scene and infamous for selling Republican Party headquarters and its prime location opposite the Blaine House.

Sumner Lipman   Republican representative from Augusta who finished second in the primary for governor in 1994 with 19.9% of the vote.

Lisbon Street   One of the major streets in Lewiston, home of many clubs where drinking is the order of the night and of the day. A good place to test new candidates and their ability to relate to real voters. "I sent him to Lisbon Street one Saturday night and he was a wreck for a week afterwards. This is going to be a long campaign."

Lit Drop   Short for "literature drop." Refers to the practice of leaving campaign literature at the doors of citizens or on their cars while they are at church (if it is a Right to Life lit drop). "We always rely on lit drops the last weekend." Lit drops often make candidates and cause leaders feel good because they can see concrete activity, but pollsters can rarely track any measurable results.

Litmus Test   A position by which an interest group judges candidates. "Their litmus test was some arcane vote on foreign aid to Somalia. Give me a break."

Little Canada   Ward 6 in Lewiston. Heavily Franco area which is a good predictor of Franco-American voting patterns statewide.

The Little Lady   Republican male taunt of Margaret Chase Smith when she decided to run for the U.S. Senate in 1948 against a former and a sitting governor. "The little lady has simply stepped out of her class." The "Little Lady" beat them and was the first woman ever elected to the U.S. Senate totally in her own right!

Little Lord Fauntleroy   Name given to Frank Coffin by his Democratic primary opponent in 1956, Roger Dube.

Little Money, Little Fun   Credo of Professor C. P. Potholm who tells his students, "In politics you should make a little money and have a little fun, otherwise it isn't worth doing. Life is too short to be miserable." Think about it for a moment, why should TV stations be the only ones to make money from political campaigns?

The Littlest Gunslinger   Mike Harkins of the political consulting firm known as The Agency. Mike is now head of the Delaware Port Authority. Amusing and insightful political consultant for Bill Cohen in his initial 1972 campaign for Congress. Lost his briefcase in 1974 during the Republican gubernatorial primary. Said briefcase held Harry Richardson's strategic game plan which became widely known when it was "given" to John Day. Harkins is said to still want his briefcase back from Day. Harkins also consulted on the gubernatorial campaign of Linwood Palmer in 1978.

Living Well Is the Best Revenge   Wisdom in life as well as politics. Consultant's satori.

LL   Short for L. L. Bean, the icon of Maine business and an important trend-setter for outdoor issues and causes. "L. L. likes harmony in the woods; they won't go for that shot."

Load   A poor candidate, one who is heavy to "carry." "What a load; all he wants to do is blow off about his dumb ideas on welfare reform."

Lobster Boy   Extremely effective, but apparently irritating, 30-second spot which helped to win the so-called Gay Rights Referendum in 1995. Attacked by editorial writers, pundits and even portions of the "Maine Won't Discriminate" coalition as "confusing," the ad nevertheless delivered a no vote in the coastal counties of Sagadahoc, Lincoln, Knox, Waldo and Hancock where the no vote had been behind 2–1 before the spot aired.

Local Yokels   National Democratic and Republican consultant-speak for Maine political consultants. "I don't even know where this Arooostick or Aroostook County is and I don't care; let the local yokels worry about it—wherever it is."

Robert 'Bob' Loeb   Bowdoin College class of 1974 graduate who brought the idea of a statewide walk to the attention of Dr. Demento in 1972. Dan Walker walked to the governorship in his home state of Illinois.

The Logs Are Closed   For most TV stations, Friday noon is the time when their station logs close for the weekend. Therefore, campaigns often try to sneak in a negative commercial just before that time so that all weekend long their negatives run while the other camp can do little about it. "We got our zinger in before the logs closed. They won't know what hit them. They'll go crazy all weekend."

Loki   Norse god of mischief. Patron saint of Dr. Demento. "I don't know why I did that, I think Loki made me do it."

Long March   John Day's term for Bill Cohen's odyssey from Gilead, Maine, where he began his 600-mile walk across Maine in his bid for Congress in 1972 to his position as Secretary of Defense in 1997.

Long Story Short   "We won" or "We lost."

Long War   A campaign term for a long struggle with lots of activity during the summer. "Maine Yankee and Turnpike Widening I were long wars." (See also "Short War.")

James 'Jim' Longley Jr.   Winner of Republican First District Congressional primary in 1994 with 43% of the vote, won the general election with 51%. Lost to Tom Allen in a 1996 reelection bid.

James 'Jim' Longley Sr.   Independent candidate for governor in 1974. Won with 39% of the vote, defeating George Mitchell and Jim Erwin by putting together an unusual political alliance of urban Franco Democrats and rural Republicans. (See also "Longley's Legionnaires.") Self-made and a one-of-a-kind political force, Longley spawned a host of would be imitators and Maine gubanatorial races were clogged up by Independents for 25 years after his run. Father of James Jr. and Susan Longley. (See also "First Family.")

Longley's Legionnaires   Followers of Maine's 1974 Independent governor. "Here come Longley's Legionnaires again."

Looking Good, Billy Ray   Dan Aykroyd line from "Trading Places," means "We've won" or "We pulled it off." "At 7 P.M. on election night, I heard Dr. D say to Angus, 'Looking Good, Billy Ray.' Then I knew we were home free."

Loose Cannon   Any candidate, spokesperson, or political operative who is "doing their own thing" and not under the control of the campaign or the officeholder. "Staff people, afraid of losing their jobs, are seldom loose cannons."

Loring   Loring Air Force Base in Limestone, Maine, cornerstone of the Aroostook County economy since 1950. Although outmoded, the base was kept open by the political pull of Senators Muskie, Cohen, and Mitchell. When Tom Andrews rather courageously and rather gratuitously called for the closure of this base as being in the best interests of the United States, he was roundly criticized by many citizens living north of Bangor. Is now used as political shorthand to mean a policy statement made without regard to political fallout. "Don't pull another Loring." (See also "Political Fallout.") Still, Tom Andrews can have the final sense of satisfaction because the base was closed as unnecessary. At the same time, no Maine political figure of the 1970's and 1980's was ever elected to statewide office without calling for the continued operation of the base.

A Lot of People Feel   Consultant-speak for "I feel." "Senator, a lot of people feel you should go to that event."

Ralph Lovell   Republican candidate for Congress in 1966, received 8% of the vote in the Republican primary for the 1st District.

Low Ball   To deliberately downplay your own prospects in a campaign or referendum. "We low balled it and the scorps bought it, even though we're up five points."

Low Maintenance   A candidate who doesn't require a lot of consultant hand holding. "Angus would only call once or twice a week; he's a low-maintenance guy."

Donald G. Lowry   Democratic candidate for Congress. Received 4% of the vote in the 1976 First District primary.

Loyalty Begets Loyalty   A good credo for both consultants and politicians to both remember.

Luckiest Man in Maine Politics   (1) John H. Reed. He was nominated by the Republican caucus in 1959 by one vote as their candidate for Senate President. By the end of that year, Reed became governor upon the death of Clinton Clauson. On the coattails of a strong Republican ticket of Vice President Nixon and Senator Margaret Chase Smith, Reed defeated Second District Congressman Frank Coffin for the right to fill out the remainder of what was supposed to have been Maine's first four-year term as governor. Reed then beat Maynard Dolloff by a mere 500 votes in 1962 for his first full four-year term. A fluke of partisanship made Reed chairman of the National Governor's Conference in 1965. The job normally rotated between a Republican and a Democrat and it had been the turn of the Republicans (who were in the minority) but instead of letting the Republican choice, Presidential candidate George Romney, take the position, the Democrats insisted on the Republicans picking the more obscure Reed.

In this position, Reed helped shepherd through a resolution supporting President Johnson's Vietnam War policy. When Reed lost his attempt at a second full four-year term in 1966 to Maine Secretary of State Ken Curtis, Johnson appointed Reed to the newly formed National Transportation Safety Board. When the Republicans took over two years later, Reed became its chair until 1976 when he was appointed Ambassador to Sri Lanka. Insiders thought his luck had run out with the election of Jimmy Carter, but he was restored to the Sri Lanka post when Republican Ronald Reagan became President in 1981. Governor Reed remains a very gracious and grateful participant in politics.

Luckiest Man in Maine Politics   (2) The second is clearly George Mitchell who, after blowing a huge lead and losing the governorship by poor campaigning in 1974, was appointed U.S. Senator when Ed Muskie became Secretary of State in 1980 after the failed mission to rescue American hostages in Teheran. Mitchell went on to become Majority Leader of the Senate, retiring just before the Republicans got control of that body. Believed to be choosing between the U.S. Supreme Court and Commissioner of Baseball, Mitchell actually settled for a job trying to get the IRA to the peace table! Perhaps his string had run out, at least temporarily. In addition to being a diplomat, he now teaches at several colleges in Florida and is a partner of Preti, Flaherty and Beliveau, where he has maintained his Maine connections.

Luckiest Woman in Maine Politics   Perhaps less clear than in the male category, but a strong case can be made for Olympia Snowe, who was finessed out of a Senate race by Dave Emery's early entry in 1982 only to see Emery crushed by George Mitchell. Then, facing defeat for Congress in 1992, she was aided by the intervention of the Green Party, which drained off votes from her opponent, Pat McGowan. When Mitchell retired, she was handed the perfect opponent in Tom Andrews by Mitchell and President Clinton. Still, she made the very most of her opportunities and never gave in, being one of the harder-working candidates in recent Maine history.

Lucky Me! . . .   Words believed by Republican insiders to have been spoken by Joe Brennan upon hearing the announcement that Senator William S. Cohen was retiring.

Lucky Me! . . . oh Shit, Joe Wouldn't . . .   Words believed by Republican insiders to have been spoken by Phil Merrill upon hearing the announcement that Senator William S. Cohen was retiring. Merrill was already running for the Senate seat.

Lumber Lords   Al Diamon's shorthand for the major paper companies of Maine, although sometimes—often in the same column—he calls them "lumber barons." Ah, class warfare. "The lumber lords wanted to defeat the Greens on their own terms."

Lumper   A pollster who likes to lump demographic categories together to make more respondents fall into fewer categories. For example, instead of having, say, 12 different categories for income, a lumper will have only 4 or 5. This is in contrast to a pollster who likes to have fewer voters in more categories. "Tubby is a splitter, Potholm's a lumper."

Lunch   To destroy, beat badly, from "to have him/her for lunch." "Olympia lunched Andrews, no question about it." This is very different from the Hollywood "Let's do lunch" which is a much more polite kiss off. (See also "Let's Do Lunch.")

Lunch Break   Channel 6 (WCSH) noontime talk show with Jim Crocker. Insiders love the show because although Crocker is opinionated, he lets political guests run wild and set their own agendas and it is easy to pack the telephone lines with set-up questions for your candidate.

Lunk   Ken, one of the three Cianchette brothers.

Willis Lyford   Activist press secretary for Governor Jock McKernan and Bob Monks when he ran for the U.S. Senate in 1996.

Jed 'Jethro' Lyons   Bowdoin graduate class of 1974, the field man against whom all subsequent field people are measured in Maine politics. Worked on Cohen for Congress in 1972.

M

....

Moderation

is the reason

of politics.

LEON GAMBETTA

....

M&M Crowd   Nickname of Al Diamon for the McKernan operatives who gave lip service to Susan Collins as Republican nominee for governor in 1994, but who were "actually working behind the scenes for Independent Angus King." These people formed the basic campaign team for Bob Monks when he ran for the U.S. Senate in 1996. (See also "McKernanistas.")

M and M   Ticket splitters delight in the general election of 1954. "Vote M and M, Margaret and Muskie." Many did and both won, Muskie becoming the first Democratic governor since the 1930's.

Ma Meres   Peter Burr's term for Franco-American women who work in the home. The term literally means "my mothers" and is thus a corruption of the French-Canadian colloquialism for grandmothers, Les Mémères.

One of the most important voting targets in Maine politics due to their love of community and their ability to communicate among themselves. Very important to ballot measure campaigns. "Hang in there, the ma meres are going to win it for us again."

Maagwa   Legendary leader of the Hurons who decided that the Europeans must be stopped and their traitor allies the Mohicans along with them. In Maine politics, Maagwa stands for those who wish to do evil to others before evil is done to them. "Strike first. That's what Maagwa would say." (See also "Do Unto Others What They Would Do Unto You, But Do It First.")

Joseph 'Joe' Mackey   Consultant and former chief lobbyist for Maine State Employees Association.

Kenneth P. 'Ken' MacLeod   Republican Senate President (1969–1974) and candidate for Congress in 1964. Ken beat Herbert Silsby with 62% of the vote in the Republican primary in the 2nd CD but lost to Bill Hathaway in the general election, getting 38% of the vote. Influential President of the Senate and early supporter of Bill Cohen and Harry Richardson. (See also "Harry the Horse.")

Glenn MacNaughton   Second Congressional District candidate in 1994. Received 25% in the Republican primary.

Madam Speaker   Elizabeth Mitchell (D-Vassalboro) who made history December 4, 1996 when she became the first woman Speaker of the House in Maine history. It had taken 176 years.

Magazines   With their low overall reach and difficulty in confining messages to target regions, magazines are seldom used in political campaigns. For good reasons.

Maggie   Affectionate nickname for Senator Margaret Chase Smith, but a name which she herself despised.

Magic Moment   A memorable vignette which captures the ebb and flow of a political campaign. "Bob Monks jumping out into the audience during his press conference was a magic moment."

Henry Alexander 'Hank' Magnuson Jr.   WCSH radio and TV reporter who really knew politics inside and out. Became director of public relations for the Maine Republican State Committee in 1965 and late editorial director (1965–1973) of Channel 13 news.

Maine Audubon Society   With 7,000 members (1996) this environmental group is the second largest in Maine and has the most believable name to the average Maine voter, hence making it a valuable partner as an "authority figure." It is thus seen as having accomplished a lot at the ballot box, especially when partnering with SAM. Maine Audubon has taken the lead in forest management questions. Thomas Urquhart is the current executive director. Maine Audubon has also done a lot with environmental education issues. (See "Authority Figure" and "SAM.")

Maine Coast Heritage Trust   Led by Jay Espy, this 2,000-member environmental group has major accomplishments to its credit in preserving Maine's priceless coastal heritage. Although Maine Coast Heritage Trust rarely ventures directly into the political arena, it is very effective in working with local land trusts, public agencies and interested landowners to protect scenic open space and in helping to set the political agenda on land acquisition.

Maine Impact Coalition   Conservative political action group in the 1980's formed by Linda Bean (then Linda Bean-Jones). Also known as MICPAC.

Maine People's Alliance   Although this organization claims 16,000 members (1996), its true political influence in Maine to date is minimal and blunted by its predictability. Really not a player on the Maine political scene. Steve Campbell has called its leaders "hypocrites" for attacking Republican campaign contributions and ignoring those to Democrats.

Maine Political Yearbook   Annual publication in the 1960's which reviewed political news of the year, highlighted Maine historical articles—

and raised so much money for the Republican party that often the major canidates barely needed to raise much in the way of additional funds.

Maine Times   First published in 1968 and bearing the stamp of publisher Peter Cox and editor John Cole, this weekly newspaper became a staple for political insiders. At its height in the 1970's, its circulation was probably as high as 20,000 copies a week. Did a great deal to focus public, at least upscale public opinion, onto the environmental issues confronting Maine. By the 1990's, had become too predictable to be very effective. Consultants of every stripe privately praise it for creating a lot of business on the environmental and corporate image-enhancement fronts even if they have never agreed with its editorials. By stirring up trouble, the paper has probably made more money for political consultants than any other newspaper in the state. A major profit center for the political subculture, and in that regard, a true mover and shaker!

Maine Won't Discriminate   A nice thought and, after $1.5 million spent in 1995, a statement made believable by the Maine electorate.

Louis S. 'Sandy' Maisel   Colby College professor of political science and television pundit. Ran for Congress in 1978 and received 17% of the vote in the Democratic primary. A pundit of note with a fine sense of humor and a great deal of knowledge, not just about Maine politics but about national activity as well.

Andrea Maker   Classy player on forestry issues. A mainstay of the Compact I and Compact II efforts. Respected.

Make Megabucks, Spend Megabucks   Consultant dream lifestyle. "I see you have a super new car, John; make megabucks, spend megabucks. Ain't politics grand?"

Make the Unpopular Popular   The task of truly good consultants. "Anybody can win with a Mitchell or a Cohen; it's making the unpopular popular that sets you apart in this business."

Male Bonding Shows   Campaign shorthand for TV programs catering primarily to males such as football. "Anywhere they show Bud Lite commercials will get us the male bonding crowd."

Mall Intercepts   Research methodology in which people in malls are shown products or sample ballots and are engaged in discussions to gather impressions about a product, a cause or a candidate. "I never like to use mall intercepts; they can produce such irrelevant material and the time-limit constraints are enormous." (See also "Time-Limit Constraints.")

Roger 'Rog' Mallar   Also known as "Mr. Fix-it" (Davis Rawson), and "The Lone Arranger" (also Rawson), head of the Department of Transportation under Governors Curtis, Longley and Brennan. Roger is a Republican who can obviously think like a Democrat and act like an Independent when required, and is a player in his own right based on his direction of two major referenda campaigns: the 1981 Elected PUC effort and the 1991 referendum on the Maine Turnpike campaign and his chairing of the 1983 Reapportionment Commission. (See also "It Wasn't Lost on This Coast.") Valuable asset. Now president of Mallar Associates.

John J. Maloney   Won the Democratic primary for the 2nd CD Congressional seat in 1950, but lost the general election, receiving 42.3% of the vote.

Mama Baldacci's   Bangor restaurant where political heavyweights and lightweights gather. Where John Baldacci learned politics and cooking while his father argued politics with Ruby Cohen, father of Bill.

The Man 'the Man the People Found' Found   Another insider term for "The Littlest Gunslinger," Mike Harkins of The Agency who was the media and political consultant of Bill Cohen's 1972 Congressional campaign.

The Man the People Found   Campaign slogan developed for Bill Cohen in his initial race for Congress in 1972. Shows the value of political consultants. (Also broadened by Democratic insiders to "The Man the People Found . . . and Dead River Paid For.")

Paul Mandabach   Partner of Winner/Wagner and Mandabach of California who was the lead consultant on the 1983 Save Maine Yankee III effort and the opposition to the Stop the Widening campaign of 1991. Knowledgeable and effective.

Manolo   Any aide to an elected official who is obsequious and fawning to that official. "Here comes Manolo again, probably going to wipe down the toilet seat for the Congresswoman."

Mantra   Any politician's basic stump speech or verbal talisman. Repeated over and over, it becomes part of the political culture. " 'The best welfare program is a job' is a favorite mantra of Maine politicians." (See also "Joe's Mantra.")

Gordon Manuel   Longtime reporter and anchor for Channel 5 in Bangor, subsequently a spokesperson for Great Northern Paper and Bowater. Best remembered—according to himself—for his on-air prediction that Bill Cohen would run against Ed Muskie in 1976. Political insiders remember him for the courage of making such a prediction as opposed to the error of it. Well liked and has a good sense of humor. One of the few TV personalities who could laugh at himself and mean it.

Guy A. Marcotte   Former mayor of Biddeford and Democratic candidate for Congress in 1978, got 26% of the vote in the primary, losing to John Quinn. Later a member of Governor Brennan's cabinet.

Robert Marden   Waterville State Senator and President of the Maine Senate (1963–1965). Important Republican player in central Maine for much of the period under review. In 1964, drafted the resolution which pledged Maine's delegates to Margaret Chase Smith in the 1964 Republican Presidential convention.

Margin of Error   The statistical degree by which a poll can be off. Usually this is stated as a percentage such as plus or minus 5% with the seldom heeded caveat "at the 95th level of confidence." This means that in reality, the margin of error it is likely to obtain in 95 cases out of a hundred, but that in the other 5 cases, it will be off by substantially more. Needless to say, pollsters downplay this second part of the equation and almost never indicate that even this suspicious margin of error obtains only when there are two choices. In a four-way gubernatorial race, for example, the actual margin of error may be twice as high.

Market Decisions   Polling firm of South Portland. Long headed by Evan Richert who now is director of the Maine State Planning Office. Richert purchased the firm from Peter Davis in 1978 but sold his share in 1995 to take that position with the state. Current president is Barbara Nash. Tends to do omnibus polls, some results of which appear in the press and usually get a lot of play.

Market Research Unlimited   South Portland research company with the best facilities for focus groups around. Run by Fran Mavodones, Market Research Unlimited has been the site where all sorts of election outcomes have been gamed and predicted long before they actually take place. A very nice lady.

Market Strategies   Republican polling firm out of Washington and Detroit. Principle Maine operative is Alex Gage, who insiders believe has an excellent sense of the numbers.

Marois   Key watering hole for politicians and would-be politicians on Lewiston's famous Lisbon Street.

John Martin   (D-Eagle Lake) Longtime Speaker of the Maine House and intrepid fighter against term limits. Also known as "The Earl of Eagle Lake." John Martin must loom large in any history of Maine politics during the period under review. Indeed, he is perhaps the most important figure in the modern history of the Legislature and by extension, the laws it passed. Yet in terms of *this* book, and its focus on statewide and Congressional electoral politics, it is difficult to find as much *direct* impact of his activity. In other words, his concentration on the Legislature and the Democratic Party undoubtedly led indirectly to the existence of many qualified and talented Democrats waiting in the Legislature to enter that arena. In the arena itself, his direct impact is far less discernible. Never having left the smaller worlds of Eagle Lake and Augusta to run for higher office, Martin left the broader state canvas of electoral politics to others. He always worked behind the scenes, though, and tried to make sure the

Democrats had a strong ticket which would help his party keep control of the Legislature. For example, he helped recruit Pat McGowan to run for Congress, and he advised Libby Mitchell when she ran for the U.S. Senate. And he was close to both Ed Muskie and George Mitchell.

Marion Martin   A founder of the National Federation of Women's Republican Clubs of America in 1938 and an important supporter of Margaret Chase Smith. Longtime commissioner of Labor and Industry in Maine and political appointee of Republican Presidents.

Martin Bormann Syndrome   Person closest to the candidate usually has the last word in determining the outcome of a policy or campaign debate, no matter how much or how little that person really knows about the campaign.

Martinized   Being relegated to legislative Siberia by Speaker of the Maine House, John Martin (D-Eagle Lake). Usually was proscribed by the Speaker when a House member forgot to genuflect deeply enough when the Speaker passed by. "Fred? He's history. He's been Martinized. You won't see him with his committee anymore."

Mary Hartman   Staff nickname for Mary Herman, wife of Angus King, and an influential strategist in her own right. Mary often has good political instincts and insights.

Masking Questions   Questions at the beginning of a poll designed to provide camouflage for the real purposes of its subsequent questions.

Masshole   GOB name for many residents of the Bay State who have the temerity to come to Maine and tell them what to do. Actually, some fine Maine politicians, such as Tom Andrews and Bill Hathaway, have come from Massachusetts, but come to think of it, they have not always done well with the GOBs, at least not those north of Augusta. "That Masshole doesn't know one end of a gun from the other." (See also "GOBs.")

Mating Ritual   The ritualized meeting of candidate and person he or she wants to support him or her. Also called "Mating Dance." The trick is to get that support without giving anything away in return. Not all mating rituals are consummated. "It was an awkward mating ritual watching Bush seek Cohen's help, but nothing like Jock trying the same thing."

Eugene Mawhinney   Highly regarded political science professor at the University of Maine and teacher of many of Maine's political figures. Also, director of Boy's State.

Lewis G. Maxwell   Democratic candidate from Franklin County for Congress in 1972 in the 2nd CD, lost in the primary with 21% of the vote.

May Fly   GOB term for a short-time phenomenon. "He started out strong in the primary but he turned out to be another May fly."

Mary Mayhew   1990 campaign manager for Pat McGowan for Congress and advisor to John Baldacci during his 1994 campaign. Later founded Mayhew Government Relations. Now a partner in Hawkes and Mayhew.

Mary McAleney   Campaign manager for Phil Merrill for governor in 1978 and for Joe Brennan for governor in 1990. Also a staffer for Senator George Mitchell.

McCabe and Duval   Portland advertising agency with political experience, winning a number of highway bond issues and the important 1995 Telecommunications Bond. Chief political operative is Christopher "Chris" Duval.

J. Horace McClure   Finished second in the Republican primary for the 1st CD in 1954, receiving 15.3% of the vote.

Dale McCormick   Democratic State Senator from Hallowell, and before that Monmouth. Maine's first openly gay State Senator, Dale subsequently ran for Congress in 1996 and narrowly lost in the Democratic primary to Tom Allen. Elected state treasurer by the Legislature for 1997.

John S. 'Jack' McCormick   Right to Life candidate for the Republican nomination for Congress in the 1st District in 1990. Received 38% of the vote.

Peter McDonald   Democratic nominee for U.S. Senate in 1946, he lost the general election, receiving 36.5% of the vote to Ralph "Senator from Pan Am" O. Brewster.

McDonald's Account   A low-paying consultancy, one where you could make more money if you worked hourly at McDonald's. "I'm embarrassed to tell you it worked out to be another McDonald's account."

Pat McGowan   Ran twice for Congress against Olympia Snowe (in 1990 and 1992). Got 49% of the vote against her in 1990 and might well have defeated her in 1992 if it had not been for the Green Party, which siphoned off a number of votes which would most likely have gone to him. A major Democratic player for many years and a prime mover behind the 1985 $35 million bond issue for Maine land. Subsequently New England head of the Small Business Administration under the Clinton White House.

James 'Jim' McGregor   Press secretary for Jim Longley Sr. and later spokesperson for Bath Iron Works.

Clifford G. 'Cliff' McIntire   Republican Congressman from Maine's old 3rd District from 1951–1963. Won in 1958 with 56% of the vote. Won in 1960 with 64% of the vote. Ran for U.S. Senate in 1964, losing to Ed Muskie with 33% of the vote.

John R. 'Jock' McKernan Jr.   Republican legislator from Bangor, also ran for Congress and governor. In 1982, he won the Republican primary in the 1st CD with 77% of the vote, and the general election with 50.3% (over John Kerry). Beat Barry Hobbins in 1984 with 63% of the vote. Defeated Porter Leighton in the 1986 Republican primary for governor with 68% of the vote and then beat Jim Tierney and two Independents in the general election, getting 40% of the vote. Subsequently re-elected in 1990 (over Joe Brennan) with 46% of the vote. Never defeated in Big Board politics. In fact, although he retired with somewhat low approval ratings, after Olympia Snowe and Bill Cohen and tied with Ed Muskie, he is the third most successful electoral political figure of several generations with 7 wins and 0 losses. Thus, by the criteria of this work, he deserves another, more positive appraisal. (See also "Big Board Politics" and "Warriors.")

Robert 'Bobby' McKernan   Brother to Jock but a political player in his own right. Campaign manager for Bob Monks when he ran against Ed Muskie, and political strategist for Linwood Palmer when he ran against Joe Brennan. Bobby now works for Smith and Haroff, the media firm which helped bring the people of Maine Olympia Snowe, Bill Cohen and Jock McKernan, but not Bob Monks. Very close to John Day. A player.

McKernanistas   Hard-core followers of Congressman and Governor Jock McKernan. According to some Democrats, McKernanistas believe that less government is better, that public appearances are more important than governance, and that Joe Brennan is a direct descendant of Boss Tweed. A more objective view of them would accent their loyalty to Jock McKernan and faith in the quality of his leadership. (See also "Brennanistas.")

Richard 'Dick' McMahon   Waterville city treasurer who was Ed Muskie's campaign manager during Muskie's 1954 successful run for governor. Later a member of the Maine Public Utilities Commission.

James A. McVicar   Two-time Democratic nominee for Congress from the 1st CD, losing general elections in 1948, and in 1952, receiving 37.5% and 38.4% of the vote, respectively.

Vaughn Meader   The best impersonator of President John F. Kennedy. From Hallowell. Lenny Bruce once cracked that two graves were dug in Arlington: one for Kennedy and one for Meader. Goes by the name of Abbot Vaughn Meader now.

Meat Wagon   Consultant's term for the campaign which pays him or her. "It was a hell of a meat wagon while it lasted."

Media sChmedia   Tom Hanrahan's short-lived weekly column in the *Casco Bay Weekly*. Well named and widely read (for the brief period in 1996 it appeared) despite its weird title. Insiders loved it.

John E. 'Mr. Menario' Menario   Portland city manager for nine years and impressive campaign manager for Save Maine Yankee in 1980 and 1982. Menario then ran for governor as an Independent in 1986 and urged people to shut down the plant! He got 15% of the vote but had an enjoyable campaign. A successful entrepreneur with his Governmental Services consulting group, John eventually found true happiness as Senior Executive Vice-President and Chief Operating Officer at People's Heritage Bank. Great sense of humor and good political perspective. Classy guy.

Carlton E. Mendell   Democratic candidate for Congress in 1966, receiving 9% of the vote in the 1st District primary.

Gary F. Merrill   Republican candidate for Congress in 1968 in the 1st CD. Finished third with 16% of the vote. Although long active in Democratic politics, Merrill chose to run in the Republican primary where even his considerable acting skills could not carry the day.

Leslie Merrill   Engaging and effective behind-the-scenes operative for a number of political campaigns including Duke Dutremble for Congress (1994) and Citizens for a Healthy Economy and Forest (1996). (See also *"The* Duke" and "CHFE.")

Philip L. 'Phil' Merrill   Colby grad and Democratic activist, former executive director of the Maine State Employees Association, and frequent candidate. Finished second in the 1978 Democratic primary for governor, getting 36% of the vote although he had earlier been elected governor of Dirigo Boy's State in 1963. Ran for Congress in 1982, finishing ahead of Plato Truman with 21% of the vote in the 1st District Democratic primary won by John Kerry. Later campaign manager for Joe Brennan in 1994 and candidate for the U.S. Senate in 1996 until Bill Cohen dropped out and Joe Brennan dropped in. An insider's insider.

Merrymeeting Bridge   The name for the Brunswick-Topsham bypass bridge which should have been called the "Senator George Mitchell Memorial Bridge" because without him, federal funds would never have been appropriated for it. A good example of where a politician did a lot of real, solid, deal-making work and got little credit for it.

Jean Meserve   Host of MPBN's weekly show called "Legi-state" that covered the news from Augusta in the late 1980's. Talented reporter and good interviewer with a great sense of humor. Jean went on to become a reporter and anchor for ABC and CNN. Still comes back to her Maine sources on state stories of national interest.

Message Development   Creating the central themes of the campaign, an effort made to position your candidate to support popular issues and oppose unpopular ones and deciding which ones to highlight in your campaign. "He's a real pain to work with but he is very good at message development."

Message Team   The group working with the candidate on developing a coherent message for the campaign. Usually a wild mix of competing egos and truly bizarre ideas. "You call that a message team? I call it a zoo."

John Michael   Independent candidate for Congress in Maine's 2nd CD in 1994, he got 8% of the vote. Spearheaded term limits drive as well as the "litmus test on term limits" for ballots.

Charles 'Charlie' Micoleau   Longtime Democratic operative of note. Campaign director for the Democratic State Committee in 1960. Active in the Curtis for governor campaign in 1970 and the Mitchell for governor in 1974. Ran Muskie's pseudo campaign against Bill Cohen in 1975 and oversaw Muskie's real campaign against Bob Monks in 1976. He served as counsel for the Mitchell for U.S. Senate campaign in 1984. Also served as Muskie's administrative assistant. Now a partner in the law firm of Curtis, Thaxter, Stevens, Broder, and Micoleau.

Micromanager   A candidate who is trying to be his or her own campaign manager. "She's a real problem, micromanaging everything."

Midnight Run   Clandestine movement of Tom Daffron, Erik Dodds Potholm, and Paul Curcio from Washington, D.C., to Portland, Maine, in the middle of the night in order to film and produce the final commercial for the Collins campaign in the Republican primary for U.S. Senate in 1996. The spot was not completed until 5 A.M. but it was on the air by noon. Widely credited with keeping a positive message up on the air at the time of the monumental mudslinging between Bob Monks and John Hathaway. "The midnight run, that's real inside baseball."

Milk   Short for Mother's Milk, campaign cash. Money for a campaign. "Milk, milk, we need more milk. I don't care who milks the cow but we have to have more milk."

Milking Rattlesnakes Is Hard Work   Consultant's lament concerning cheap and ungrateful candidates. "Sure I get paid a lot, but milking rattlesnakes is hard work."

Sharon Miller   Finance director for Jock McKernan when he first ran for Congress and campaign manager when he ran a second time. Campaign manager and chief of staff for Governor Jock McKernan (1986 to 1994) and campaign manager for Olympia Snowe (1994). She also advised Bob Monks in his 1996 run for the U.S. Senate. Founded Cape Communications Group, "a grass roots political consulting firm." A player.

Miller Time   Consultant-speak for "We've won." "We were sitting there saying it was Miller Time and the polls hadn't even closed. Those guys from Congoleum thought we were nuts, but Peter whipped them into shape, had them getting him junk food all night long. Miller Time was five hours long that night."

Miller's Restaurant   Famous political watering hole in Bangor. Sonny Miller, its owner, is close to Cohen, Mitchell, Baldacci and other assorted pols.

Dora Ann Mills   Former Democratic national committeewoman and now head of the Maine Health Bureau. Articulate spokesperson for the health of Maine people. A Bowdoin graduate, she is believed to be the only person on the planet to have studied under both Dr. Demento and Mother Teresa and to have gotten an A from each of them.

Janet Mills   Brennanista loyalist and former district attorney for Androscoggin, Franklin and Oxford Counties. Ran for Congress in Maine's second Congressional district in 1994, losing in the primary to John Baldacci and getting 17.7% of the vote. (See also "Tough As Any Man and Twice As Smart.")

Paul Mills   Insiders know Paul as one of the most knowledgeable historians, raconteurs and analysts of the Maine political scene. An important TV pundit with a truly fabulous sense of, and love for, Maine political history. Should write a book about Maine politics!

Peter Mills Jr.   Insiders regard this Republican State Senator from Skowhegan as a very viable gubernatorial candidate once Governor King retires. Some scorps feel "he is too damn smart to be governor."

Peter Mills Sr.   Father of Janet, Paul, Dora and Peter, maverick Republician, U.S. Attorney and prominent State Senator. An early supporter of Margaret Chase Smith, insiders know him for his habit of riding a motorcycle from Farmington to Portland long before Governor King made Harley Davidsons the mode of transportation for political figures.

Mind Dump   A truly foul expression which has found its way into the political lexicon from the nether reaches of the advertising and public relations subculture. Means a strategy session which continues to be what civilized people call it. I refuse to honor this phrase with even a pseudo quote!

Mini-Max   Term from game theory describing a situation in which one player wins something big and another player wins something smaller but still wins something. Politics almost always has a mini-max outcome in that the defeated candidate eventually gets a state or national government job if he or she wants one. (See also "Zero-Sum.")

Mister High Road   John Day's ironic nickname for Tom Allen, Democratic candidate for Congress for letting the AFL/CIO use very negative and false ads against his opponent Jim Longley while claiming he was not using negative ads but taking the high road.

Mister Matchbook   Harold Silverman (R-Calais) who ran against Olympia Snowe in 1980 as a Democrat and handed out matchbooks as his campaign memento. He got 21% of the vote.

Mister Mean   Senator Phil Gramm of Texas, justly thrashed in the early Republican Presidential primaries of 1996. " 'Mister Mean' got whacked and boy am I happy."

Mister Potato Head   Nickname for Governor John Reed from Fort Fairfield in Aroostook County, who, as ambassador to Sri Lanka, tried to get his newfound constituents to eat potatoes instead of rice. (See also "Luckiest Man in Maine Politics" and "John Reed.")

Mrs. Right to Life   Sandy Faucher, head of the Maine chapter of the National Right to Life Committee and upholder of the faith of the unborn. "Mrs. Right to Life is at it again; she took after poor Dave Emery this time, stirred up that John McCormick fellow to run against him in the primary."

Elizabeth 'Libby' Mitchell   Longtime Democratic legislator from Vassalboro. Ran for the U.S. Senate against Bill Cohen in 1984, getting 26% of the vote. In 1990, she ran for Congress and finished third in the Democratic primary in the 1st District with 17% of the vote. Following the 1996 elections, she was chosen by the majority Democrats to be the first female Speaker of the House in Maine history. In 1997, she served with her daughter Elizabeth, a state representative from Portland.

George Mitchell   Bowdoin grad and longtime Democratic activist and leader. Considered one of the four "Titans" of Maine politics in the post–World War II period. Ran for governor in 1974, losing to Jim Longley Sr. with 36% of the vote, after winning the four-way Democratic primary with 37% of the vote. Appointed to the U.S. Senate by Governor Brennan in 1980; defeated Dave Emery in 1982 with 61% of the vote. Reelected in 1988 with 81% of the vote. Majority leader of the Senate from 1988 to 1994, making him the highest ranking Maine politician since House Speaker "Czar Reed" at the turn of the century. Retired in 1994. Mitchell now serves on a number of boards (including Disney) and is affiliated with Verner, Liipfert, Bernhard, McPherson and Hand, a law firm in Washington; and Preti, Flaherty, Beliveau and Pachios, another in Augusta.

James E. 'Jim' Mitchell   Democratic candidate for Congress in 1976, finished second in the Democratic primary with 19% of the vote. Husband of Libby Mitchell.

James F. 'Jim' Mitchell   Democratic candidate for Congress in 1994 from Bangor. Finished second to John Baldacci with 22% of the vote. Nephew of George Mitchell and, like Jock McKernan, an alumnus of Dartmouth. Now a lobbyist in Augusta and a partner in the Public Affairs Group. Has done various highway bonds successfully. No relation to the other Jim or Libby.

Mix   For those fortunate enough to have more than one commercial, the blend of one with the other(s) is something of an art. "I like her mix, hard and soft, something for the seniors and the businessmen."

MM   Short for "Mother's Milk," which is short for "Money is the mother's milk of politics." In Maine, as elsewhere, mother's milk can buy you a lot of things in politics, including love, but it cannot always buy you victory. But you have to have it. "She's gone after the MM, it's a big-time fundraiser with the docs. Hope she isn't too disappointed; they hate to part with MM unless it's for their own IRAs."

Mogul of Moguls   Davis Rawson's moniker for Les Otten of Sunday River ski resort. Otten, a major Republican fund-raiser, nearly ran for the U.S. Senate in 1996, stepping aside only to buy an additional six mountains.

Money and Momentum   Wonderfully ironic statement by Senator Richard Lugar who, when asked before the Maine Republican Primary in 1996 how long he was going to stay in the race, said, "As long as I have the money and the momentum." After "Junior Tuesday," he had neither. Nor did he have any delegates. From anywhere. Since it was widely believed that he ran for President in 1996 only because he was slighted in 1988 (when George Bush, prompted by his media guru Roger Ailes, picked Senator Dan Quayle instead of Lugar), Lugar's forlorn campaign seemed to, once again, underscore the genius of Roger Ailes. (See also "Junior Tuesday.")

Money Talks, Bullshit Walks   Not! At least not in Maine politics. For every rich person who spends a lot of his or her own money to get elected and wins (such as Angus King), there are four or five who lose, often decisively, as if the money were actually a handicap. Think of Bob Monks (3), Neil Rolde (2), Linda Bean (2), Bill Troubh (1), or Dick Spencer (2).

Monkeys Grooming   Consultants sitting around helping each other out, often at considerable cost to the client. "It was amazing; Chris wanted to do a sample of 500 and George said, no, we'd better do 600 and then when George wanted to send out 100,000 pieces of mail, Chris said, no, we'd better do 200,000. Two monkeys grooming."

Monkeys Work There?   Sarcastic question asked in campaigns when something goes wrong. "When I got the spot back from the editing house, my first thought was, monkeys work there?"

Robert A. G. 'Bob' Monks   Cape Elizabeth Republican. Ran for the U.S. Senate in 1972, getting 33% of the vote in the Republican primary against Margaret Chase Smith. Captured the Republican nomination for Senate in 1976 with 83% of the vote over Plato Truman, losing to Ed Muskie in the general election 60% to 40%. Ran again for the U.S. Senate in 1996, finishing third in the Republican primary to Susan Collins and John Hathaway and getting 13% of the vote. Bob Monks actually made a lot of contributions to Maine politics and the Republican Party. It would be too bad if all people remembered were his three losses instead of what he did to make modern Republican politics better. Monks was a major force behind the elimination of the straight ticket voting "Big Box." And his early support, financial and otherwise, of Bill Cohen, Olympia Snowe and Jock McKernan helped to make them all viable candidates. It is difficult to see how the post-1972 Republican party would have had the winners it did in the succeeding two decades without his involvement. Deserves a more positive position in the history of Maine politics than he currently enjoys. Very generous and intelligent person, just a bad candidate for the Maine arena.

Monksmobile   Giant Winnebago used by Bob Monks to tour Maine during the 1996 Republican primary for U.S. Senate. (See also "The Pimpmobile.")

More Beloved There Than Here   (1) Former Attorney General James Tierney who was twice rejected by Maine voters, once for governor in a four-way race in 1986 and following that in the Democratic primary for Congress in 1990. Later found happiness advising the good citizens of Bulgaria about democratic politics. "Interestingly enough, after Mr. Tierney went to Bulgaria to teach them about democracy, they returned the former Communists to power." Now a major player involved in the national anti-tobacco lawsuits.

More Beloved There Than Here   (2) Rick Barton, former Congressional candidate who lost to Dave Emery in 1976 and who later found happiness advising the rotund Presidential candidate in Haiti, Marc Bazin, who lost to Jean Betrand Aristide in 1990.

More Beloved There Than Here   (3) Alan Caron, Democratic strategist and communications director for Joe Brennan in 1994, he was later sent by the Democrats to Siberia in order to teach the Siberians democratic politics.

More Beloved There Than Here   (4) Tom Andrews, having lost his Senate bid to Olympia Snowe, was then sent first to Kampuchea and then to Yemen to advise those who would listen about how to organize Democratic politics. Fortunately Tom listened to Dr. D, who suggested that he not push his luck and attempt to do the same thing in Peru with the Shining Path.

More Mud, Faster   Consultant's sage advice when a campaign turns negative. No matter who starts it, it is the volume of mud which determines the outcome. "I don't care who started it; more mud, faster, is all that counts now."

The More You Show, the More You Sell   The rationale behind candidates working crowds and consultants making many pitches. "I hate to go to those stupid fairs, but the more you show, the more you sell."

Charles 'Charlie' Moreshead   Longtime Republican activist and state party chair in the 1970's. Loves intrigue as much as anybody in politics and with Severin Beliveau, Alex Ray, John Day and Dr. Demento as friends, he has enjoyed more than his fair share. A conservative before being conservative was cool, he led the fight for Ronald Reagan when most Maine Republicans thought Nelson Rockefeller was *the* man. Longtime supporter of Joe Brennan as well.

Morgo the Magnificent   AKA "Morgo the Magician." Professor Richard Morgan of Bowdoin College, whose TV commercial questioning the need for an Equal Rights Amendment singlehandedly turned Maine people from a positive to a negative vote on that issue in 1983. This feat earned him the magician's wand because it was done in the face of opposition from Senators Mitchell and Cohen, Congresspeople Snowe and McKernan, and Governor Brennan. It also prompted the Bowdoin faculty to consider a rule prohibiting professors of that august institution from appearing on television in any commercials in the future regardless of their personal position. Fortunately for Bowdoin College—and the First Amendment— that rule did not pass. Morgan has been a most prominent and articulate spokesperson for Maine's intellectual conservatives during the past two decades.

Morning in America   Any warm and fuzzy spots designed to make voters feel good about themselves and thus the candidate who brings them such a fine feeling. Initially they referred to the national commercials of Ronald Reagan in 1984 but now the term has more generic meaning. Any spot which accents positive emotion and feeling good over issue specifics. "Forget issues, give them Morning in America stuff."

Morph   To change one image into another on television where one face blends into another and then another. In political terms, to change a candidate's image by highlighting one issue over another or stressing some new aspect of the candidate's personality in order to appeal to different segments of the public. "I think they took Duke up to the trout pool at L.L. Bean's and morphed him into an outdoorsman." "Joe Slade White morphed Tom Andrews into a friend of business, what a hoot!"

Richard 'Dick' Morrell   Former state rep and State Senator (R-Brunswick), early and consistant supporter of moderate Republicans such as Bill Cohen, Olympia Snowe, Jock McKernan, Dave Emery and Susan Collins.

Election night 1978: Chris Potholm and Senator Bill Cohen

Election night 1994: Chris Potholm and Governor and Mrs. Angus King

THE TITANS:
THE FOUR
WHO HAD A MAJOR
NATIONAL IMPACT

Margaret Chase Smith

George Mitchell

Ed Muskie

Bill Cohen

THE UNDEFEATED ACES:
THOSE WITH AT LEAST
FIVE VICTORIES
WITHOUT A LOSS

Olympia Snowe, 9–0

Bill Cohen, 7–0

Ed Muskie, 6–0, with Mrs. Muskie

Jock McKernan, 6–0

PHOTO COURTESY OF *TIMES RECORD*

Stan Tupper, 5–0

PHOTO BY HARRIS & EWING, COURTESY OF THE LIBRARY OF CONGRESS

Charles Nelson, 5–0

ACES WITH AT
LEAST ONE LOSS

Robert Hale, 11–1

Margaret Chase Smith, 9–1

Peter Kyros, 9–1

Fred Payne, 6–1

Cliff McIntire, 6–1

Ken Curtis, 5–1

Bill Hathaway, 7–2

SPECIAL MENTION

PHOTO BY FRANK CONNORS, COURTESY OF *TIMES RECORD*

Dave Emery, 5–2, as true to himself and his
Maine roots as the day he entered politics

PHOTO COURTESY OF *TIMES RECORD*

Joe Brennan, 7–4, who, winning or losing,
commanded the stage for twenty-five years

Jim Longley Sr., 1–0, Independent governor

Angus King Jr., 1–0, Independent governor

Frank Coffin, 3–1, helped to
institutionalize the Muskie revolution

Bob Monks, 0–3, helped to institutionalize the Cohen counter-revolution

Richard 'Dick' Morris   New York consultant of national fame. Once tried to sign on the Charlie Cragin for governor team in 1981 but was vetoed by Tom Daffron as "too difficult to control." With hindsight, it is possible to see Tom as wise beyond his years, even at that early stage. Later Morris resurfaced in 1984 in connection with the Elizabeth Mitchell for Senate race but was likewise unsuccessful in landing the account. Morris's revenge on Maine was elevating Trent Lott to national prominence along with Bill Clinton. (See also "Thomas 'Tom' Daffron," "He Was Honest With Me," and "Triangulation.")

Moscow Maggie   Senator Joe McCarthy's supporters' name for Senator Margaret Chase Smith after she visited the Soviet Union following her 1954 election.

Moses in Nylons   Westbrook Pegler's name for Senator Margaret Chase Smith after she denounced the tactics of Senator Joe McCarthy in June, 1950.

Mouse   Affectionate nickname for Millie Monks, wife of Bob Monks, who ran three times as a candidate for U.S. Senate, and a splendid, classy lady in her own right. "I don't think I could have elected Monks to anything he ran for, but I could have elected Mouse to almost everything. What a great lady."

Moved Numbers   Changed the polling results. The best thing you can say about any TV or radio spot. "That spot moved the numbers. It was pure crap but it moved numbers."

Moxie   A soft drink of Maine origin but now brewed in South Carolina, judged "truly foul" by many political insiders but beloved by "real" sportsmen such as George Smith. Even today, signs for the drink can be found in Lisbon Falls, home of the annual Moxie Day parade. Also means a candidate has courage to try something. "Senator, it would take a lot of moxie to make that statement, but if anyone can do it, you can."

MSEA   Maine State Employees Association, the largest union within Maine state government. Usually supports Democratic candidates, especially for governor, but found Joe Brennan as tough as any Republican when they wanted pay raises.

MTA   Maine Turnpike Authority, one of the few quasi-governmental agencies which makes money. The target of much criticism for its efforts to widen the turnpike in 1991 and 1997. Many insiders believe the road is one of the best run in the state considering the huge volume of traffic it handles yearly.

Mud   (1) Negative comments tossed at your opponent. "More mud, faster, he's getting away."

Mud   (2) A news story which is a draw with neither side getting its messages across enough to dominate the story. "Are you kidding me? It's mud, beautiful mud. You guys held Brownie and Dick to mud. Way to go."

Mud Slinging   To attack an opponent unfairly. To attack with dubious charges and half truths. "Some supporters of my opponent have resorted to mud slinging in a desperate attempt to stave off defeat." Sometimes, though, candidates, especially incumbents, charge that their opponents are "mud slinging" when they are in fact raising legitimate policy or voting record differences. "It is not mud-slinging to read my opponents' voting positions from the Congressional Record."

Mugwumps   As used by Bonnie Washuk of the *Lewiston Sun Journal,* someone who is a ticket splitter, the voters of Maine as Independents. First used in 1884 to describe the Republicans who refused to support the Presidential candidate of their party, James Blaine of Maine. "In 1996, the Mugwumps voted for Clinton, Collins and Baldacci."

Murder on Spouses   Any and all campaigns. "They're all murder on spouses no matter how you conduct them. Campaigns are not great for marriages, no matter how strong they are when the campaign starts."

Murderers   Negative Right-to-Lifer term for Pro-Choice candidates.

Victoria Murphy   Democratic Party chair during Joe Brennan's run for governor in 1994 and U.S. Senate in 1996, Tom Andrews run for the U.S.

Senate in 1994, John Baldacci's runs for Congress in 1994 and 1996 and Tom Allen's run for Congress in 1996. Wife of Pan Atlantic polling president Patrick Murphy.

Musical Chairs   Scramble for position when a candidate drops out unexpectedly. "Cohen and Mitchell caused quite a game of musical chairs." (See also "St. Vitus Dance.")

Edmund S. 'Ed' Muskie   One of the Titans of Maine politics. Founder and energizer of the modern Democratic Party. A graduate of Bates. Elected governor in 1954, elected senator in 1958 with 60% of the vote. Reelected U.S. Senator in 1964, defeating Clifford McIntire with 66% of the vote, reelected in 1970 beating Neil Bishop with 62% of the vote and again in 1976, beating Bob Monks with 60% of the vote. Resigned in 1980 to become Jimmy Carter's second Secretary of State. (See also "The Titans.") A towering figure in the post-war politics of the Pine Tree State.

'President Muskie.' Don't You Feel Better Already?   Slogan for Senator Ed Muskie when he ran for President in 1972.

My Staff Made Me Do It   Lament of all candidates and office holders when there is a mistake made on the campaign trail. "I wanted to come to your event but I had to attend some other function. My staff made me do it."

My Way/Highway   Consultant shorthand for "my way or the highway." In reality, most consultants are happy to be on someone's payroll during the election cycle and very few ever say "My way or the highway" for fear of losing the account. Fewer still would ever say it to the client and mean it. Strangely perhaps, those who do say it—and mean it—are prized.

N

Never say never.

OLD ADAGE

Greg Nadeau Longtime Democratic activist, campaign manager for Dennis Dutremble in 1994, and legislative assistant to Governor Angus King. Nadeau also managed Libby Mitchell's Senate race in 1984. Nice guy and obviously very nimble on his feet. A player and very knowledge-able about practical politics. Cute fellow, always upbeat.

Name ID The basic recognition a candidate has. Out of a hundred peo-ple, how many recognize the name of a candidate? Recognition is always easier than recall, the ability to name a candidate or office holder without prompting. Getting name ID up is the goal of candidates running for office and explains why they often do seemingly foolish things to get their name in the paper. "His name ID is low but he plans to get a lot of ink in the coming weeks." (See also "Getting Ink.")

Narrowcast To go after particular viewer segments, usually by cable TV. Narrowcast is used in contrast to broadcast, where you are going after the general population.

Nasty Boy   Political insider's compliment for whoever ends up doing the dirty work in a campaign. "They loved the guy; he was their nasty boy that whole cycle."

National Abortion Rights Action League (NARAL)   Not very important in Maine politics where it is often confused with the narwhal, a whale with only one horn. No relation to Cetacea Productions, a Maine media firm.

The National Conservative Political Action Committee (NCPAC)   Forever making lists of candidates in Maine to be defeated.

NATO   A non-performer in politics, as in "Nothing Accomplished, Talk Only." "He's very much a NATO character; don't bother to invite him."

Natural Resources Council of Maine (NRCM)   Interestingly enough, NRCM was initially formed in the 1950's by Gus 'Doc' Garcelon and environmentally conscious Republicans. A large, active environmental group now claiming (1996) 6,000 members, many of whom are actually from Maine. Has the best press contacts among environmental groups. Among environmental insiders, however, it is not always viewed as a team player. Led now by Everett "Brownie" Carson and under his leadership has been a continuing political player, usually favoring Democratic canidates, especially liberals. NRCM was an early pioneer in the fight for clean air and water in Maine. NRCM has, in recent years, been seen to act somewhat rigid and cantankerous in battles over the widening of the Maine Turnpike and "parts per trillion of dioxin" in the state's rivers as the Green Party and Sierra Club have squeezed it from the left. This organization has proven to be a huge boon for consultants of almost every stripe. NRCM spokespeople retain the capacity to raise the blood pressure levels of many, many business people.

Nature Abhors a Vacuum   Frank Coffin's stated reason why he became chairman of the Democratic State Committee in 1954, and why he ran for Congress in 1956 when he defeated James Reid in Maine's 2nd Congressional District.

George Neavoll   Fair minded and engaging editorial page editor of the *Portland Press Herald*. Insiders regard him as liberal and most likely to endorse Democrats but objective in his news coverage philosophy. A fine gentleman of the old school. Has a very much appreciated concern with, and love for, Maine and its natural history. Insiders love his editorial essays on the wildlife of Maine.

Negative Ads (NEGs)   Contrast ads run by your opponent. Nothing gets Jim Brunelle, former editorial writer and now columnist for the Gannett papers, more exorcised than negative ads. Usually a negative ad's success is measured in the changing head-to-head numbers and in the extent to which Brunelle gets excited about them. Brunelle seldom likes ads which work, but has made a career out of criticizing them. "Jim is negative on NEGs again; it's like a broken record. He doesn't realize there are good NEGs and bad NEGs."

Negatives on Negatives   Negative ads about one's opponent, charging him or her with going negative. "McKernan beat Brennan to the punch in the negatives on negatives race and it paid off big time later on. Collins used almost the same footage in '96."

Charles P. Nelson   Four-term Republican Congressman from Maine's old 2nd Congressional District. He served from 1949 through 1957, winning one primary and four general elections, retiring undefeated.

Neo-Nazis   Democratic name for arch-conservative Republicans, often found along the border with New Hampshire in western York County.

Nest of Born Agains   Polling slang for a key precinct which always goes for candidates who are extremly conservative on social issues. Believed to have originated with Peter Burr. "Discount it, we just got a nest of born agains; it won't mean anything in the law of large numbers." (See also "Peter Burr" and "Law of Large Numbers.")

Nets   The television networks. "It drives me wild when a candidate only believes they have won when the nets say they have. Hell, we know by 2

P.M. and the nets are often the last to know. Sometimes for fun we call them up and call the race for the noon news. Drives them crazy."

Alfred E. Neuman   A disparaging expression used to denote any candidate who appears in a frivolous or silly situation. The expression is taken from the cartoon protagonist of *Mad* magazine which among other things, has run Neuman as a fictional candidate for President every four years since 1956. "Did you see Alfred E. Neuman on the 11 P.M. news last night?"

Never Explain, Never Complain   Consultant's credo, at least the best of them. "What happened to that campaign? Never explain, never complain."

Never Say Never   John Martin to Bob Dyke.

Never Throw Away Your Brennan Signs   Charles O'Leary, president of the Maine AFL/CIO. A tribute to the longevity of Joe Brennan and his impact on the Maine political culture.

Campbell 'Cam' Nevin   Publisher of the daily *Times Record* in Brunswick and nurturer of John Cole, the editor of the *Times Record*'s first issue, and Peter Cox, its early managing editor before both went off in 1968 to bring out the *Maine Times*. The *Times Record* is believed by insiders to be more likely to endorse Democrats than Republicans.

New Auburn   Most heavily Franco district in Auburn. Good predictor of, and check on, Lewiston voting.

New Dealer   Senator Owen Brewster's derogatory term for Margaret Chase Smith when she ran for the U.S. Senate in 1948.

News Cycle   The flow of news a 6 A.M., 12 noon, 5 P.M. and 11 P.M. In Maine, the most important part of the news cycle is getting on the early evening news. Since the TV stations have pushed that time back from 6 P.M. to 5 P.M., candidates have changed their schedules to accommodate the earlier start time of the news. Also, since the TV stations now have an hour to an hour and a half of air time to fill, candidates can get on and talk for longer periods of time.

The Peppery Little Newshen with the Quaint Little Hats   Senator Margaret Chase Smith's term for reporter May Craig who, she felt, had been taking credit for being Smith's mentor when she first arrived in Washington. May Craig also was accused of not being sufficiently enthusiastic about Margaret's run for the U.S. Senate in 1948.

Newt   Newt Gingrich, Speaker of the U.S. House of Representatives (since January, 1995) and author of the "Contract for America." Perhaps the most despised politician during the 1996 election cycle and the target of Democratic candidates no matter what office they were running for. "As selectman of Corinth, I will fight against Newt from the moment I take office."

Newt Ninny   Democratic name for Rep. Jim Longley for his support of the Contract for America. "Newt Ninny, that's all he is."

Newt North   Davis Rawson's term for former Senator Dana Hanley (R-South Paris) for his conservative views.

Newtoid   Al Diamon phrase for any slavish follower of Newt Gingrich. "Jim Longley was a fluke to begin with but becoming a Newtoid sealed his fate early."

David 'Dave' Nichols   Phi Beta Kappa Bates graduate who was Jim Longley Sr.'s first judicial appointee to the Maine Superior Court and later to the Maine Supreme Judicial Court. Chairman of the Republican Party from 1960 to 1964 and national committeeman from 1964 to 1968. Republicans never lost a major state race while he was chairman of the party.

Donald 'Don' Nicoll   Executive secretary, Maine Democratic Party (1954–1956), administrative assistant to Congressman Frank Coffin and later Senator Ed Muskie when Nicoll succeeded John Donovan who had left Muskie's staff to join the Labor Department. Important Democratic player for two decades. Now chair of the Board of Visitors of the Senator

Edmund S. Muskie School of Public Affairs at the University of Southern Maine.

NIMBY   Not in my backyard. Good working model for voters having a say on clear-cutting, prisons, halfway houses, boat-launching ramps, etc. "He's still a NIMBY after all these years."

NIMTOF   Not in my term of office. "With regard to gay rights, he was a NIMTOF guy."

No Balls   GOB term meaning to be afraid of doing something, to back out (See also "Cuomo.") In Texas and other Western states this can roughly be translated into "All Head, No Horns."

No Brainer   A campaign decision so simple a civilian could make it. "Skip the press conference with the Maine Militia? It was a no brainer."

No Can Do   I won't do it. Even if I could do it, I wouldn't. "Drive to Kennebunk tonight to do what in the studio? No can do."

No Good Deed Goes Unpunished   Even when you do something for someone in politics, they do not always reciprocate in the way you had hoped—or planned. "Think of Phil Merrill; he served as Joe Brennan's campaign manager in 1994 and then, when nobody wanted to run against Cohen, he took up the task. As soon as Cohen dropped out, Joe jumped in. No good deed goes unpunished."

No Heavy Lifting   Political phrase meaning no hard work, usually in a situation where the consultant is making money. "She's getting a couple of K a month and there's no heavy lifting involved."

No Message There   A candidate in trouble because his or her candidacy has no theme except to stay in office if they are an incumbent or to get into office if they are not. "The second time Longley ran, there was no message there."

No, No and No   Consultant answer to question, how did you vote on the bond issues whose committees didn't hire you? "Highways, parks and airports? No, no and no."

No Nuke of the North   Anti-nuclear bumper strip from the referenda of 1980 and 1981.

No Other Life   A perennial candidate, someone lost outside the world of politics, someone who acts half-dead in civilian life. "He had to run, he has no other life."

No Problem   A political phrase which often means "We have a problem." Often that problem is a big one. "The abuse story? It's no problem."

No Vice President   Jim Brunelle's suggestion that Presidential candidates leave the whole business of naming Vice Presidents *until after the election.*

Nondenial Denial   When a candidate or staffer doesn't want to take the blame for something, but wants to appear that way without lying. " 'I would never do anything to hurt you' is a classic nondenial denial when uttered, instead of the more truthful 'No, I didn't tell the press you screwed up.' "

Noodle   Advertising and political consulting term for thinking about a problem and hopefully coming up with a solution. "Ok, so our candidate has been accused of cheating in college. Let's noodle this through; what kind of spin can we give on it?"

Not a Pretty Sight   William Coogan, professor of government at the University of Southern Maine, commenting on the conscience of former Senator George Mitchell after he signed on in 1997 to represent the major U.S. tobacco companies.

Nothing But Net   A nice job, no problems, a clear shot at one's opponent. "That column was nothing but net; he never even saw it coming and it's untraceable."

Nothing Fails Like Success   Consultant's credo that past success usually contains in it the seeds for future failure. Best Maine example is that of Margaret Chase Smith and General Bill Lewis's reliance on grass-roots organization and generalized image to win elections. These tactics worked very well for much of her, career but overreliance on them probably cost her the election of 1972. "Nothing fails like success; remember Margaret."

Now There's a Choice   Ross Perot for President slogan in 1992. Insiders believed it was *some* choice.

Nugget   Naval aviation term for a virgin or new pilot. "She was a nugget when Bobby signed her up but she learned fast." (See also "Cherry.")

Numb As a Hake   Coastal expression for a really stupid person. "Of course he did; he's numb as a hake, I told you that before we hired him."

Numbers   Polling numbers. Usually the most important numbers in any campaign. "Their own numbers have him dropping like a stone."

Floyd T. Nute   Augusta UPI bureau chief in the 1950's and later news secretary for Governor Muskie.

The Nuts Aren't Jumping Ship This Time   Al Diamon's explanation as to why Republican Susan Collins did so much better running for the U.S. Senate in 1996 than she did running for governor in 1994.

Fred Nutter   Influential editorial personality of Channel 6 whose dour countenance and tough words often dooms costly bond issues. If you are against those bond issues, he is "a great American." If you are for those bond issues, he is "the grump" often glowering at the mere notion of spending tax-payer money. Nutter's career spans nearly 40 years, having been a city hall reporter, a Statehouse reporter and news director at WCSH. Once, while a disc jockey on WPOR, he interviewed Margaret Chase Smith when she was in New Hampshire running for President in 1964. A big foe of political correctness. Nutter is most ebullient when announcing the coming of the senior games every September. His editorial emissions are known among some insiders as "Freditorials." All in all, he is currently the most important on-air personality in terms of political issues. (See also "Fluffer" for one scorp's view of Fred.)

O

....

I used to say that politics was the

second oldest profession, and I have

come to know that it bears a great

similarity to the first.

RONALD REAGAN

....

Jadine R. O'Brien   Democratic candidate for Congress in 1974 in Maine's 1st CD. Lost to Peter Kyros with 31% of the vote. Now a lobbyist for Blue Cross-Blue Shield. Insiders remember that her 1974 campaign was the first in Maine in which a female candidate was referred to (at her own insistence) in news stories by her last name standing alone. Previous etiquette required a title such as "Mrs.," "Ms." or "Senator," etc., even though newspaper style books had never required this for male candidates.

Joy O'Brien   Longtime Democratic activist, who, along with Pat Eltman, is known to insiders as "Wonder Woman." Daughter of Jadine, Joy is now Secretary of the Senate. (See also "Wonder Woman.")

October Panic   The state of mind which comes over a losing campaign late in the game. It is thought that many campaigns make serious mistakes during this period. Actually, players and consultants know the real mistakes in a campaign are almost always made far earlier. "I don't worry about October panic, I worry about hiring the wrong campaign manager in the first place."

Odd Adornments   Awards given to Senator Margaret Chase Smith after her "Declaration of Conscience" speech on June 1, 1950. These included being called one of the "Ten Best Tailored Women of the World," "Best Tailored Woman in Government" and one of the "Six Best Dressed Little Women (under five feet five inches)."

Odd Couple   Any strange pairing for political advantage of the moment. "I thought the National Right to Life members' support of King made for the odd couple of 1994; why they disliked Collins that much was never clear to me."

Peter O'Donnell   Former mayor of Portland and strong supporter of gay rights. Subsequently became director of Portland West, now regional director of Maine Department of Mental Health. One of the nicest people in Maine politics.

Off and Running Guy   A consultant who moves fast on a new account and hits the ground running. "Havey likes off and running guys. He likes to jump all over a project and if you don't come in Saturdays, he says don't bother coming in on Sunday."

Off-the-Call   Consultant-speak for "we'll settle that later when we're not on this conference call." "Don't worry about that, Congressman, we'll handle it off-the-call."

Off-the-Record   In politics, there really is no such thing and good consultants always try to make their clients understand that. "Forget what Campbell or Day says, there ain't nothing really off-the-record when it comes to the head-to-head stuff."

Oh My God   A truly magic moment. A unique event. "Oh my God, he gave an interview in the Old Port and told everybody he was going to finish third. I've never seen that before." (See also "Magic Moment.")

Franklin 'Frank' O'Hara   Longtime Democratic activist and Brennanista. One of the principals in Market Decisions and now Planning Decisions. Now a columnist for the *Maine Times*.

OJ   Nickname for Congresswoman and later Senator Olympia J. Snowe. Understandably, this nickname was used more often before the O.J. Simpson trial than after.

Okey-Dokey   Davis Rawson's name for Willis Lyford, press secretary for Governor Jock McKernan and campaign spinmeister for Bob Monks in 1996 when he ran for the U.S. Senate.

Old Joe   Al Diamon's name for Joe Brennan in his column of October 12, 1996, predicting the coming victory of Joe in the U.S. Senate race.

The Old Lady   Not-so-affectionate name for Senator Margaret Chase Smith.

Old Rope   Semi-mythical person who was in charge of open dumps before recycling. Collector of trash and hunter of rats, Old Rope is famous for his sign on election day: "Am Sick. Go Home. Old Rope." Many candidates, especially for local office, often use the town dump or recycling center as a good place to meet voters. Sometimes they even help you sort your trash. "Hang out with Old Rope and you'll get some terrific insights into politics as well as life."

Charles 'Chick' O'Leary   Longtime head of the Maine AFL/CIO. In Maine, the AFL/CIO generally rises and falls with the Democratic tide and is not an independent variable in most races. Chick grew up with Bill Cohen; the two of them played basketball in Chick's driveway as boys.

John O'Leary   Democratic candidate for Congress in Maine's First Congressional District in 1982. Finished second in the primary with 36% of the vote. Former mayor of Portland.

James C. 'Big Jim' Oliver   Oliver has the distinction of being the only Maine political figure in modern times to have served as a Republican in Congress (1937–1943) and then as a Democrat (1959–1961). A Bowdoin grad, he served in both World Wars. As a three-term former Congressman, he gave credibility and stature to the Democratic ticket after he switched parties. He was the Democratic nominee for governor in 1952 (the last time before Muskie) and for the 1st Congressional District seat in 1954, 1956 and 1958. His loss in 1956 was by less than 100 votes. Oliver was also a mentor to Ken Curtis who became his aide fresh out of law school. He then lost to Peter Garland in the general election of 1960, getting 46% of the vote.

John Oliver   Former head of Maine State Employees Association and now head of public affairs for L.L. Bean. John is an inside player of note and always has his finger on the political pulse of the state.

Edward S. 'Ted' O'Meara   Cohen and Collins staffer and former Republican State Party chairman. Ran for Congress in Maine's 1st District in 1988, defeated Linda Bean-Jones with 52% of the vote in the Republican primary, then lost to Joe Brennan in the general, getting 36% of the vote. Later formed McDonald/O'Meara Communications and, with Rick Barton, led the successful "No More Than Four" term limits referendum. In 1997, Ted became director of communications for the *Portland Press Herald* and the *Maine Sunday Telegram.*

On Deadline   Newspaper phrase for reporters who have to write their story by a certain time. Reporters often leave the message they are "on deadline" in order to get political figures to call them back as soon as possible. Sometimes they are really on deadline. "He's always on deadline; you can get back to him tomorrow."

On Message   Staying on your best themes. "John Hathaway was very good at being on message most of the time."

On the Ground   In Maine. What Washington consultants want to know about during a campaign. "What's it like on the ground today? We're coming up to shoot this weekend."

On the Horn   On the telephone. "Daff spends so much time on the horn, I don't know when he has a chance to go to the bathroom."

One-Hit Wonder   A consultant who has had only one successful client or a single elected official. "For a long time, Muskie was his only success; he was one of those one-hit wonders."

The Only Good Advice Is That for Which You Pay   Dr. Demento's favorite saying which is self-explanatory except to some foolish candidates or cause seekers. "Your husband told you what? Are you kidding? Remember, the only good advice is that for which you pay." (See also "Advice Is Worth What It Costs" and "The Best Advice Is That for Which You Pay.")

The Only State Institution Run by the Inmates   The Maine Legislature as seen by its critics.

Operation Burma Shave   Governor McKernan's 1990 re-election ploy of having a series of road signs with positive messages about his administration. For some reason, this campaign technique has never been copied since, despite the governor's narrow victory.

The Opportunity State   Governor Jock McKernan's 1986 description of Maine.

Opposition Research   Polite name for digging up dirt on a candidate. "What do you mean it's going to cost us $10,000 for opposition research? He hasn't done enough interesting stuff in his whole life to be worth 10 K." (See also "K.") In Maine, opposition research is not regarded as the same thing as hiring a private investigator although some would argue that it is.

Order of the Wilted Rose   Columnist George Dixon's name for those reporters such as May Craig who had received the enmity of Senator Margaret Chase Smith. It was also applied to members of the Maine delegation, other Republicans and just about anybody who disagreed with the senior Senator.

John Orestis   Democratic fund-raiser and political operative of note and former mayor of Lewiston.

Dan Osgood   Of Video Productions in South Portland, Dan actually directed many of the commercials in Maine which have come out under many of the state's ad agencies' imprints during the 1980's.

Other Side of the River   The eastern side of the Kennebec River in Augusta, and in particular that part of the eastern side occupied by the Augusta Mental Health Institution (AMHI). Most often used in a context such as: "We sent our legislator to Augusta but he spent most of his time on the other side of the river" or "We'd get better laws if we let those folks on the other side of the river run the Legislature."

Other Than That   From the sick joke whose punchline is "Other than that, Mrs. Lincoln, how did you like the play?" In Maine politics it is often used for any excessively negative comment from a candidate. "You say the spot sucks, makes you look like you were dead? Other than that, Congressman, how did you like it?"

Out of Play   Off limits to the campaign. "Damn it, I told you my wife and my girlfriend were both out of play. Neither one of them are going out on the stump. I don't want them doing separate schedules, and I certainly don't want them doing schedules together."

Outdoor   Short for outdoor advertising, i.e., billboards. No longer in use in Maine, they were last used in a major way by George Mitchell when he ran unsuccessfully for governor in 1974. "Outdoor? It's a lost art form, thank God."

Outmarket   Beyond a particular designated market area (DMA). "We bought the hell out of the Bangor DMA but nothing happened in the outmarket." (See also "In Market.")

Overdog   The favorite in any political race. "No more of this underdog stuff; I want an overdog and one with big bucks."

Overnight   A long time in politics. "We've got overnight to do the spot, let's get going."

Overnight Rushes   Raw footage of the candidate in action. "Don't show her the overnight rushes; she'll throw out all those scenes she doesn't like before we get them into the commercial."

Overnights   Overnight polling numbers from tracking surveys. A rolling estimate of shifting political fortunes, they can sometimes display gut-wrenching movement from night to night. This is why the grid outcome system is a preferred methodology with its framework for analysis. "My God, the overnights have Billy dropping like a stone. Let's get some perspective on this; I do not believe he has lost 10 points in York County since we looked there last. Peter's numbers are holding steady." (See also "Grid/Outcome System.")

Ray 'Bucky' Owen   Commissioner of Inland Fisheries and Wildlife under Jock McKernan and Angus King. Selection of the GOBs (see also "GOBs.") A sometime player in referenda circles, he lost narrowly on the Fish Hatchery Bond issue of 1994.

P

Public men must expect public abuse.

GENERAL LEONARD WOOD

PAC   Political action committee, a legal entity which can give more money to candidates and causes than allowed for individuals. Instituted as a reform in the aftermath of Watergate, PACs have become a very powerful and much attacked political institution for what is perceived as their corrosive impact on the political process. "Senator George Mitchell currently holds the record for PAC contributions in a single election cycle in Maine."

PAC Man   Republican insider name for George Mitchell who, calling for campaign finance reform, set an indoor Maine record for PAC contributions. "Oil PAC Man" was the Democratic rejoiner when Libby Mitchell pointed to Bill Cohen's fund-raising in 1984.

Harold C. 'Hal' Pachios   Democratic candidate for Congress in 1980, received 31% of the vote against David Emery. One of George Mitchell's closest friends, he is now a partner of Preti, Flaherty, Beliveau, and Pachios. A longtime Democratic activist, Hal was organizing California in the Muskie-for-President effort when that collapsed. Insiders wonder how history might have been different if Muskie had made it as far as the California primary.

Pack Journalism   Most scorps pay the most attention to what other reporters are saying and generally go with the conventional wisdom. They would rather be wrong and in the majority than right by taking a big risk. Most reporters do not usually break major stories unless those stories are handed to them. "According to the pack journalism of the day, there was no way McGowan was going to get close to Olympia but he did."

Pack the Conference   Set up a press conference in a small room and fill it with supporters of your candidate or cause.

Pack the Hall   Fill an auditorium with supporters of your candidate or cause.

Pack the Lines   Have supporters of your candidate or cause jam the lines of a talk show. "Abbot didn't like it when we packed the lines. MPBN didn't like it either."

Paid Media   As opposed to "free media" which is new time that radio, TV and newspapers give to a candidate, paid media is the time purchased by the campaign. Because paid advertising is the only aspect that a campaign and the candidate can control totally, it is one of the most important ingredients in any campaign effort.

Albert Paige   Teamsters Union leader in Maine during the 1950's and 1960's; active Democrat in Auburn and Androscoggin County; important labor union leader in the Democratic Party during 1950's–1960's period.

Pair-Wise Comparisons   Polling technique for testing two alternatives— such as ballot measures—side by side. "We found out that the 'Governor's Compromise' was twice as good as the 'Governor's Compact.' "

Pal   In politics, the opposite of pal. A negative. "Don't try that, Pal, or we'll roll over you and your candidate."

Carol Palesky   Leader of a property tax referendum campaign which wants to cap property tax rates throughout Maine.

Linwood E. Palmer   Christmas tree farmer from Nobleboro and Republican candidate for governor. Won the Republican primary in 1978 with 48% of the vote, lost in the general election to Joe Brennan, getting 34% of the vote.

Pan Atlantic Consulting   Portland-based consulting firm headed by Patrick Murphy. Has a polling division, Strategic Marketing Services (SMS). Close to Democrats, including Murphy's wife, Victoria, also a principal in the firm. Victoria was Democratic Party chair during the 1994 and 1996 election cycles. Pan Atlantic does a variety of polling for firms and groups, often using "ominbus" polls where clients have one or more questions answered on a statewide basis along with those of others. (See also "Strategic Marketing Services.")

Paper Industry Information Office (PIIO)   Often referred to as P110 (as in P One Ten). Tries to bring together the paper companies and others in the forest products industry in order to have political clout. Helped with the forestry referendum of 1996. Sometimes it was referred to by people in the environmental movement as "P000" for its lack of effectiveness in stopping the Natural Resources Council of Maine from always putting it on the defensive. Now renamed the Maine Pulp and Paper Association.

Dan Paradee   Press secretary for the Senate President and candidate for Congress in 1994, Duke Dutremble; later press spokesperson for the Maine Turnpike Authority.

Paradox of Consultants   All consultants want to make money advising their clients. (See also "The Only Good Advice Is That for Which You Pay.") And most cultivate the image of the professional gunslinger (see also "Teach It Round or Teach It Flat" and "I'm Still Drinking His Whiskey.") Yet many consultants long for the loyalty which comes from a long association with a particular candidate. "She's doing that for nothing? The only way I can make sense out of it is the paradox of consultants."

Pardon Papers   Davis Rawson's name for the assortment of charges that Brennan political "cronies" acted improperly during the last months of his administration. These acts allegedly included the pardoning of political supporters, and hurt Brennan's chances against McKernan in the 1990 election. Yet to this day there is no evidence that Brennan acted improperly or unlike other governors in granting pardons.

Party Builders   Political figures who spend a lot of time, energy, and effort to recruit new and varied people for their party. In the last three decades, there have been only three real party builders in Maine, all Democrats: Senator Ed Muskie, Speaker John Martin and Secretary of State Rodney Quinn. No Republican has come close to their efforts.

Party of Lincoln   Republicans. A somewhat ironic phrase given the party's difficulty in attracting Afro-American voters. "If it's the party of Lincoln, why is Jack Kemp the only one reaching out to African-Americans?"

A Pay Phone in Every House   Effective slogan used against the "Measured Service" proposal of New England Telephone during the 1986 referendum to ban per-call charges for local telephone calls.

Payback   Consultant-speak for revenge. "Of course, I worked for his opponent. It was payback."

Anthony 'Tony' Payne   Republican candidate for Congress in 1992, lost to Linda Bean, getting 33% of the vote.

Daniel 'Dan' Payne   Head of Payne and Company, Democratic media firm from Boston, initial media firm for Dukakis for President, Kunin for governor and the campaigns of other mainline Democrat candidates. Subsequently media firm for the Angus King, Independent-for-governor effort in 1994 and was a major contributor to that enterprise.

Frederick G. 'Fred' Payne   Two-time Republican governor of Maine, elected in 1948 with 65.6% of the vote, and re-elected in 1950 with 60.5% of the vote. Elected to the U.S. Senate in 1952, receiving 58.7% of the vote. Defeated in a re-election bid in 1958, receiving 39.2% of the vote.

PC Polling   To do polling in a politically correct way even if the questions asked in this fashion are less helpful. For example, the most important demographic break in Maine politics is between women who work at home and women who work outside the home. There is usually no significant difference between men who work at home and men who work outside the home, so the most sensible Sex/Occupation break is "Male, Female/Home and Female/Out" but often clients will try to insist on only two breaks, male and female (two categories, too simplistic) or male/in, male/out; female in/female out (four categories, unnecessarily complicated). "They think this is a League of Women Voters exercise; they want PC polling from start to finish."

Peasants with Shit on Their Shoes   Political and media consultant's word picture for amateurs who try to get their clients to do strange things. "I tell you, the peasants with shit on their shoes are at it again; she's going to make another mistake."

Allen 'Al' Pease   Important Democratic player and right-hand man to Governor Ken Curtis. Professor at the University of Maine and Democratic Party chair. Assisted Curtis with his TV and radio efforts.

Violet 'Vi' Pease   Important Democratic activist and party chair during the Curtis era. Credited with recruiting a lot of good candidates for the Legislature.

Peg   Davis Rawson's term for a campaign or candidate's central message. "His campaign has no peg, he's going in 16 different directions."

Edward L. Penley   Political reporter and editorial writer for the *Lewiston Daily Sun*; editorial writer and editor, Gannett Newspapers in the 1950's and 1960's.

The People's Choice   What most candidates claim to be, many think they are and few really are. "He thinks he's the people's choice; what a joke, he's never done an honest day's work in his life."

People's Republic of Arrowsic   Name given to voters of Arrowsic for their espousal of more liberal/radical candidates and causes in the 1970's and 1980's. An opposite predictor of statewide outcomes for many elections during that time, Arrowsic always voted against Dave Emery even when he got 60% of the vote, and voted to shut down Maine Yankee three times when the rest of the state voted to keep it open in 1980, 1982, and 1984.

People with Spirit Names   Democratic insider term for very liberal Democrats, the kind who voted for Jerry Brown for President in 1972.

James B. Perkins   Finished second in the Republican primary for the 2nd Congressional District in 1948, receiving 23.1% of the vote.

Permanent Underclass   People who have been on welfare five years or more. Seen as a campaign issue by Republicans and as a pool of potential voters by Democrats. "Views about the permanent underclass tell you a lot about the different parties."

Perotistas   Followers of Ross Perot. "Some of the Perotistas are willing to follow Buchanan, but his stand on abortion bothers them."

Nancy Perry   Longtime (18 years in 1997) political reporter for the *Portland Press Herald* and *Maine Sunday Telegram*. Nancy is a good reporter and is usually objective, fair and balanced. Will make the calls necessary to get the story. Protects her sources very well. On occasion, she seems to have a point of view which structures the way her political stories get written. This of course irritates consultants who have other causes and other candidates. Some McKernanistas, for example, claim she was always a closet Brennanista. Spinnable.

Edward 'Ed' Pert   President of Young Democrats at the University of Maine; executive secretary, Maine Democratic Party; Clerk of the House, Maine House of Representatives.

Pet Rock   A particularly dumb candidate. "He's my pet rock but he's paying 5K a month for babysitting." (See also "K.")

Allen Philbrick   Anti-nuclear activist and co-founder of the Green Party in 1984.

Phone Sex   Soothing words from a consultant after a candidate has screwed up big time. "After the debates I had to give him 20 minutes of phone sex. He thought it was all over."

Photo Op   Short for photo opportunity, a chance to have a candidate appear on the campaign trail in a setting which will have a good chance of making the evening TV news or the morning newspapers. "I know there's no point in it other than a photo op, but book it."

Pied Piper Syndrome   When the election is over and won, candidates and causes sometimes resist paying off campaign debts. "It's the Pied Piper thing again. We got NYNEX 64% of the vote and they think we should have held the last weekend of TV." (See also "The Rats Are Out of the City.")

Richard H. 'Dick' Pierce   Former Republican State Senator from Waterville. Ran for governor in 1982, and received 29% in the Republican primary, good for third place. Insiders know him as a very astute political strategist with a great sense of humor. Called "Señor Wences" by Cohen operatives Tom Daffron and Bob Tyrer when he headed up Cohen's succesful 1978 senatorial bid. A player.

Joseph 'Joe' Pietroski   Extremely effective fund-raiser for Dave Emery's 1982 Senate campaign, raising over $1.1 million. Now executive director of the Maine Banker's Association.

Pimpmobile   Huge yellow car driven by Cohen for Senate 1978 campaign manager Senator Richard Pierce (R-Waterville). Cohen staffers enjoyed riding through various metro areas of the state waving to the populace from its air-conditioned interior. Replaced in the motor car hall of fame by the huge 1972 white Caddy (with license plate "Too Long") driven by Phil Merrill as he ran for the U.S. Senate in 1996, dropping out after Joe Brennan jumped in. Picture of said caddy appeared in the first edition of *George*, gaining Phil even more, this time national fame.

Pimps   Governor Longley's name for the members of the Maine Legislature.

Pine, Power and Politics   Political science professor and author Duane Lockard's chapter title for Maine in his book *New England State Politics*, referring to the historical hold of the paper and power companies on the GOP and the Maine Senate.

Pinhead   Ross Perot. Or, as Jon Doyle so aptly put it, "a small, and noisy, pointy headed insufferable type from the only state where they ever lost a war to the Mexicans." (See also "Jon 'Clogs' Doyle.")

Pisces Club   Site of William S. Cohen's 1974 decision not to run for governor. Famous for its fish tank containing a shark (a very small sand shark), it was a political hangout owned by Tungson Park. (See "Jack 'Big Jack' Linnell.")

Piss off the Pope   GOB expression denoting deep dissatisfaction. Often used in politics to express anger at a staffer. "He's enough to piss off the Pope; he got lost taking the Congresswoman to the airport."

Piss on the Fire   From the good old boy saying "Piss on the fire, call off the dogs, this hunt's over." In Maine politics, it means that for better or for worse, this operation is finished. Can be positive as in "Piss on the Fire" ("We've won") or negative as in "Piss on the Fire" ("We've lost") depending on the context.

Pisshole in the Snow   GOB term of contempt for a person, activity, or action, as in "That press release isn't worth a pisshole in the snow" or "His being in the governor's race won't amount to a pisshole in the snow." (See also "Jack Shit.")

Pitch   Make a presentation to a client. "Boy, we made a great pitch but that Congressman from Cleveland was a real jerk. Most of the those self-made millionaires are."

Pixie Dust   To say a magic phrase to turn something marginally illegal into something marginally legal, as in "I'll sprinkle some pixie dust on this Congressional phone so you can use it as a campaign phone. OK?" Best example of this does not come from Maine but from President Clinton's re-election bid in 1996 when both he and Vice President Gore apparently used a ton of pixie dust to operate a huge fund-raising operation from the White House.

The Place to Watch   English translation of the Abnaki word *Skowhegan*, home of Margaret Chase Smith when she was a Congresswoman and Senator. "Ike has to go to the place to watch, don't ask me why."

Plaid Shirt   Nickname for Lamar Alexander, Republican candidate for President, who wore a red flannel shirt as a political gimmick to show he was a regular guy. Better known for his statement, after having come in third, that the first-place finisher, Bob Dole, should drop out so that Alexander could contest the number-two finisher, Pat Buchanan! He faded from the national political debate shortly thereafter but made it very difficult for Maine residents who like to wear flannel shirts for comfort rather than for a political statement.

Jerome 'Jerry' Plante   Democratic field opeative from the 1970's and close confidant of Peter Kyros. Insiders remember fondly his old style grass roots interests and his zest for partisan battles.

A Player   Someone who counts in politics. As used in this lexicon, a player is someone who has played a major part in both candidate and ballot measure politics in Maine for more than a decade (5 election cycles). For consultants, the best thing which can be said about anyone in Maine politics is that he or she is a player.

Player-Scorp   A reporter who, while claiming and perhaps even trying to be "neutral," nevertheless gets involved in politics by taking sides in candidate elections by writing enough, and powerfully enough, to influence the outcome. In Maine journalism today, there are really only two scorps with both the power and the inclination to be intrusive players on a regular basis as oppposed to strictly reporters. John Day is one. Steve

Campbell is the other. If they favor your candidate, you think they are great reporters. If they are on the side of your opponent, you think they are lousy reporters.

Mr. Plywood   Jim Ward, head of Portland volunteers for Cohen in 1978. Requested—and received—something on the order of $5,000 for plywood to be used on lawn signs in the area. Even longtime Democrats who consider themselves masters of that art form admitted they had never seen anything like it. "Mr. Plywood wants $2,000 more for signs; what are they building down there, an airplane hangar?"

Pod   Television technique of using two 30-second spots back to back with another spot in between. Thought to be more effective than one 60-second spot due to the short attention span of the Maine TV-watching public. "I like using pods; I think you get better recall on your themes when you do."

The Poet Warrior   *Sun Journal's* Christopher Williams's title for Bill Cohen after he became Secretary of Defense.

Pogie Man   GOB name for Governor McKernans as they blamed him for the decline in bluefish fishing along the coast due to his letting the Russians have the rights to take vast numbers of that species of bait fish in the late 1980's. "I don't care that Pogie Man shut down the government but I do care he let those Russkies spoil our fishing."

Points   Percentage points in a political race. "We picked up 10 points on that exchange of ads; we'll take that for the rest of the campaign. Our guy is now up by 15." Also gross rating points in a TV buy. "We need 500 more points this weekend." (See also "GRPs.")

Points Behind   (1) How far you are behind in an election.

Points Behind   (2) How many gross rating points you have behind a TV commercial.

Pol   Short for politician but means someone who really cares about all the inside baseball of politics and for whom politics is the main focus in life. "She's a pol's pol. I love her."

Political Cemetery   A place where defeated candidates sometimes go when the public and/or consultants think they are dead. Unlike real cemeteries, some candidates can in fact come back from the political cemetery. "No question about it, he was in the political cemetery a year ago and now he's walking about and taking solid nourishment. I saw him on TV the other night campaigning in the Old Port. He looked great!"

Political Embarrassment   A candidate feeling embarrassed about one of his or her positions or tactics. Hard to think of any Maine examples, for political embarrassment is not a staple of politics.

Political Fallout   The negative aftermath of a policy statement or action which the candidate makes or does without thinking. "He really got some fallout after he took on the NRA without meaning to."

Political Groupie   Someone who hangs around with politicians and treats them like rock stars. Often seeking sex with the candidate or office holder, they sometimes settle for sex with a staffer.

Political Terrorists   Representative Barry Hobbins's (D-Saco) and Tony Buxton's term for the Maine State Employees Association members when they threatened to picket the Democrats' Jefferson-Jackson Dinner in the early 1980's.

Politically Correct   To consultants, this usually means something that Democrats are forced to do in their primaries. "I couldn't take it anymore; there were so many politically correct things to do, I gave it up. I dropped out of the race."

Politically Incorrect   Usually means something electorally correct. "Let them attack the NRA in rural York County; it's politically incorrect."

Politics Is the People's Business, the Most Important American Business There Is   Quote from Adlai Stevenson. This sentiment is something scorps should remember at all times and write about once in a while.

Politics Makes Strange Bedfellows   (1) Traditionally refers to odd alliances of seemingly different groups making common cause for a political purpose. "It's always a hoot to see NOW and the Christian Right getting together to oppose pornography. Politics really makes strange bedfellows."

Politics Makes Strange Bedfellows   (2) Campaign sex.

Politics on the Half Shell   Reporter, editor, and columnist Davis Rawson's political column in the *Kennebec Journal* (and *Waterville Sentinel*). Rawson, a Bowdoin College graduate, writes some of the funniest and most insightful pieces about the foibles of Maine politicians. His jibes at politicians are usually done with good humor and good grace. Likes blue-collar candidates and was, for many years, a not-so-closet Brennanista. Spinnable.

Politics Should Be the Part-Time Profession of Every Citizen   Quote from President Dwight D. Eisenhower. A basic belief of the author of this work.

Polls Are a Creation of the Devil   Davis Rawson's paean to the profession which put my children through college! He did go on to admit that "It's fun to ask." It truly is.

Poll Driven   One who follows polls slavishly. "He's as bad as Clinton, poll driven from beginning to end."

Pontificate   To make public pronouncements assuming the public is interested in your view. "It's truly amazing that he pontificates on anything that comes up. He must think people value his opinion. *Quel dommage!*"

Popeye Tactic   Columnist Don Hansen's description of Margaret Chase Smith's tactic the last time she ran for Senator in 1972. "I yam what I yam." She lost. What is often overlooked, however, is that if she had said

"I yam what I yam" on TV, she would most likely have been re-elected. Hathaway spent over $150,000 on TV and she spent next to nothing.

Poppy   President George Herbert Walker Bush of Kennebunkport, Maine, and Houston, Texas.

Pork, Pork, Pork   In Maine, bond issues for highways often attract other funding for railroads, bridges, airports and cargo ports. The result is a package of projects which is attractive to many voters who might vote against the individual projects. "Did you see that $60 million mess? It was pork, pork, pork and then some."

L. Robert 'Bob' Porteous Jr.   Portland department store owner and Republican candidate for Congress in Maine's 1st District in 1972. Won the primary with 78% of the vote, lost the general election to incumbent Peter Kyros with 40%.

Portland Press Herald   Along with the *Bangor Daily News*, the most important daily newspaper in the state and the one with the largest daily circulation as of 1997 (72,000 + to 69,000 + for the *Bangor Daily*). Its Sunday edition, the *Maine Sunday Telegram*, has over 120,000. Insiders generally expect endorsement of Democratic candidates from the *Portland Press Herald* and *Sunday Telegram*, and Republican candidates from the *Bangor Daily* although both endorse other candidates.

Post Campaign Letdown   All true political junkies know the horrible feeling of emptiness which comes when an election cycle is over. While it is sometimes possible to string out the high from an election victory for a few days, the depression which inevitably follows from the end of the game is the post-campaign letdown. "I hate December. I'm never over my post-campaign letdown until January at the earliest."

Post Man   As in "dumb as a post," not a very bright candidate. "Let the post man go to the debate, he doesn't know any better."

Jackie Potter   Campaign manager for Tom Allen, 1996.

Pound the Piss Out Of   GOB term for hurting someone badly. Although it has never been clear out of what the piss is to be pounded, it does sound like a dreadful procedure. "We're pounding the piss out of him in the Second District."

Pour on the Syrup   In ballot measure campaigns, to send out comforting messages and avoid negative ones. "There are only two weeks to go on the Telecom campaign; pour on the syrup."

Big Pout   Davis Rawson's term for Ted O'Meara's 1988 Republican primary campaign against Linda Bean Jones. Republican voters may have liked it since they chose him over Linda Bean, but general election voters did not, choosing Joe Brennan in the fall.

Take a Powder   To disappear, quit on a campaign. "He took a powder again; I told you we couldn't count on him. He's really a civilian at heart." (See also "Civilian.")

Power Player   The elite of Maine politics, there are probably fewer than 25 true power players in the state based on longevity of action, impact of their choices, and ongoing influence over the course of politics, both candidate and ballot measure. These range from Dave Nichols to Mert Henry, from Severin Beliveau to Chuck Cianchette and George Smith to Bob Tyrer and Tom Daffron to Larry Benoit.

Power Position   Head of any conference table. Home habitat of the Alpha Wolf. "Always grab the power position, especially if there is a CEO or two in the room. They'll pick up on the symbolism very quickly." (See also "Alpha Wolf.")

Powerhouse   A major player on the Maine political scene. "Like him or not, Severin is a powerhouse."

Charles 'Charlie' Pray   Democratic State Senator (1975–1992) and Senate President (1984–1992) from Millinocket and longtime activist. A favorite target of Republicans for many years but kept in office for a long time by GOBs.

Press Shutdown   Insiders' reference to the process by which the working press—which candidates and causes try to "educate" during a campaign basically stop processing information except the head-to-head race about a week from election day, and it is useless to try to spin them about anything except the horse race. "Forget it, you could come up with a cure for cancer and those guys wouldn't pay any attention, it's press shutdown time."

Preti, Flaherty, Beliveau, and Pachios   Prominent Democratic law firm which often performs the functions of the Democratic State Committee, even before George Mitchell joined the firm in 1997. Four of its present members have served as Democratic Party chair.

Prime   TV hours between 8 and 11 P.M. Often very expensive for the net payoff to political advertising at this time.

Prince of Darkness   What every male political consultant would like to have as his nickname because it would be very good for business.

Princess of Darkness   What every female political consultant would like to have as her nickname because it would be very good for business.

Print   Newspapers. The largest in terms of approximate circulation are the *Maine Sunday Telegram* (120,000+), and the daily *Bangor Daily News* (69,000+) and the *Portland Press Herald* (72,000+) followed by the *Sun Journal* (40,000+) which has a Sunday edition of 43,000. As print readership has declined, the importance of TV news has grown, but to political insiders, print reporting is still regarded as very important. "We've got to get some print to back up our TV."

Print Drives Electronic   Claim by print reporters that their stories lead TV assignment editors to make their assignments based on what they read. Sometimes true.

Amy Pritchard   Campaign manager for the Maine Won't Discriminate effort in 1995. Savey and effective. Now works for the DCCC (Democratic Congressional Campaign Committee) in Washington.

Pro Aborts   Positive Right to Lifer term for pro-choice candidates.

Pro Choice   Later career positions of Joe Brennan, George Mitchell and Dave Emery.

Pro Life   Early positions of Joe Brennan, George Mitchell and Dave Emery. The first two made an easy transition to "pro choice"; Emery got caught in mid-move.

Production Assistants (PAs)   Despite their lowly status in a TV newsroom, some of the most important figures in that operation since they are often the ones who have read the newspaper for the day and who often set the assignments for the reporters until the news directors show up. Surprisingly enough, many PAs are often volunteers or interns.

Progressive   A word which in Maine politics may have lost all meaning since Alan Caron and Dick Barringer managed to apply it to "Good Old Joe" Brennan in 1994. (See also "Richard 'Dick' Barringer" and "Alan Caron.")

PSA   Public service announcement. "The trick is to do a commercial which sneaks up on you like a PSA."

Pseudo Event   Campaign event staged to get media attention. "We don't have to have a real rally, just make it look like one for a half hour, get the coverage and close it down." Also used by historian Daniel J. Boorstin to describe what each poll is: "a self-fulfilling prophecy in media motivation."

Pseudo Organization   An effort to create the illusion of a grass-roots campaign where none really exists. By hiring talented "field people," and using volunteers selectively, it is possible to make the press and your opponents think your support is more widespread than it really is. Increasingly, with more and more candidates relying on television, and the Democratic and Republican parties in Maine declining in numbers and authority, the creation and use of pseudo organizations is becoming more widespread.

Pseudo Voter   Someone in a shopping center who says he or she is a voter, signs your petition and then turns out not to be registered to vote. "He really got burned with pseudo voters in the Maine Mall drive."

Psy War   Short for psychological warfare, trying to get under the skin of your opponents. "Put that piece in Campbell's column, we'll see how they play psy war when they are on the receiving end."

Psychic Rewards   Non-material rewards which come from participating in politics. These include a sense of belonging, the pleasure of participation, the feeling of accomplishment, and of being part of something larger and more important than self.

Psychographics   Categories of voters based on lifestyle and psychological patterns which help pollsters and TV placement personnel fit the candidate's message to those most likely to receive it favorably. "The Yuppies love educational talk, give it to them."

The Public Arena Is My Classroom Now   Former University of Maine at Farmington professor turned Green Party candidate and ballot measure warrior Jonathan Carter, 1997.

Pucker Brush   GOB term for territory beyond the major cities of Maine. "Get him out in the pucker brush and we'll teach him a thing or two about assault rifles."

Puffball Shot   A weak spot by an opponent. "What a puffball shot; you have to look hard to even find the negatives in it. I think we scared them off the meat with our last blast."

Pull the Trigger   To start a poll. Pollsters do not like polls which are passed around from person to person and committee to committee before being put into the field. They like polls out in the field, getting responses. "Get the final ok anyway you can, I want to pull the trigger this weekend."

Pulled Quote   An opponent's quotation taken out of context. "Look at the pulled quote, put 1000 GRPs behind it and everybody will believe that's his true position."

Pumpkin Man   State representative Richard Spencer (D-Standish), who ran for Congress in 1978 and lost in the Democratic primary, lost again in the Democratic primary for State Senate in 1994 and then ran for the U.S. Senate in 1996. An early investor in "Tom's of Maine" natural health care products, Spencer started out running for the Maine House in 1974 by carving his name on pumpkins and giving them away to voters. This tactic has never been tested on a statewide basis in Maine.

Pundit   Someone who offers a political opinion thinking he or she knows what he or she is talking about. Often he or she does not but that is what makes this a great political system! Civilians often do not discern one from the other. Being a small state, Maine has a relatively small number of political pundits, many of whom come from its colleges and universities. Some Maine professorial collegiate political pundits include Richard Barringer and Oliver H. Woshinsky of the University of Southern Maine, Tony Corrado, Sandy Maisel and Cal McKenzie of Colby, Doug Hodgkin of Bates, Chris Potholm and Janet Martin of Bowdoin, and Ken Hayes of the University of Maine.

Punkons   Irish-American term for rich Republicans, the factory owners of old and any contemporary Republican fund-raisers. "We must fight the punkons in every primary and every general election."

Punt   To fail to support campaign staff. Failure to make a tough decision by passing it off to others. "She just punted to all of us; let us take the rap for her decision."

John Purcell   Republican candidate for Congress in the First District in 1992, got 20% of the vote, finishing behind Linda Bean and Tony Payne.

Push 'Em Out the Door   Get the candidate out and campaigning. "Who cares about his views on all those subjects; push 'em out the door."

Push Poll   A candidate-sponsored effort designed to get voters to vote against another candidate by using the tactic of a pseudo poll in which the caller pretends to be calling for a neutral polling firm and interjects questions which cast the opponent in a negative light. "Did you know that

Congressman Bob Gains wants to eliminate Social Security?" Most professional pollsters regard this type of push poll as an illegitimate campaign tool since it is really campaigning under the guise of survey research.

Push Questions   Polling questions designed to test the efficacy of certain facts. "If you knew that one candidate favored gun control and that one opposed gun control, which candidate would you be likely to favor?" This is the heart of polling when it comes to building a winning coalition and profile. These questions are regarded as legitimate, even indispensable, by most political pollsters.

Roger A. Putnam   A powerful political force at Verrill Dana. Republican Party chair 1964–1967. Influential mover and shaker behind the scenes in Republican Party circles. Early and staunch supporter of Charles Cragin and Jock McKernan, fellow Verrill Dana lawyers. A player.

PVS   Project Vote Smart. Yet another candidate rating system developed by yet another group of elitists who think they know what the voters should have. Headed by those all-time super pols, Jimmy Carter and Jerry Ford. "PVS? Don't even bother to send back the forms."

Pygmy Head   A candidate who thinks he or she knows a lot about politics but who is actually deficient in even the basics. "She wanted to campaign in all 491 towns in Maine. What a pygmy head; it would take her 3 years."

I was quoted

out of context.

CANDIDATE AND CONSULTANT LAMENT

The Quarterback Insider's name for Jack Kemp, Republican Congressman who has quite a following among Maine Republicans as a conservative with a heart. Actually, Kemp is really famous with consultants for the indecisive way in which he approaches running for President or even endorsing the bids of others. "The Quarterback is at it again." Still, he managed to stumble onto the national ticket in 1996. Although he was much heralded at the time by Republicans, he really only got Dole out of San Diego alive and did little to help the ticket thereafter.

Queen Bee Congressman Stan Tupper's nickname for Margaret Chase Smith.

Queen City (1) Name given to Bangor in the 19th century by logging crews who had been in the woods all winter long.

Queen City (2) Name given to Portland in 1995 by opponents of gay rights legislation.

Queen of the Hill   Olympia Snowe, the most successful electoral politician for major office in Maine political history during the past 50 years with nine major wins and no losses. "I found out Olympia was the winningest candidate in recent history; she's the Queen of the Hill."

Quid Pro Quo   You do something for me, I do something for you. Makes consultants feel like major players when they get one. "It's a quid pro quo, Governor; you give the speech the way I wrote it and you don't have to do those two fairs in the afternoon."

A Quiet Woman   General Bill Lewis's name for Senator Margaret Chase Smith as stated in her autobiographical *Declaration of Conscience*: "The purpose of this book is to recount several of the more significant statements of a Quiet Woman; to set forth why she made such statements, what led up to them, what resulted from them—as repercussions, reprisals, recognition, headaches, heart-aches, humiliation, or honors."

Francis 'Fran' Quinn   Longtime Associated Press reporter based in Augusta. Nobody's fool. Tries to be fairminded but can be somewhat jaded about politics and seldom leaves the Statehouse on a campaign story. Some Democrats regard him as a good conduit for Democratic material coming out of the Statehouse. Difficult to spin, unless he is on deadline. Covering the Legislature year in and year out seems to have taken its toll in terms of his enthusiasm for breaking political stories which is, to an outsider at least, understandable.

John Quinn   Ran for Congress in 1978 and won a four-way Democratic primary with 31% of the vote. Then got 35% of the vote against David Emery.

Rodney 'Rod' Quinn   Democratic Secretary of State from 1979 to 1989. A funloving but highly partisan and effective political actor who spent much of his time party-building and developing candidates. A player and one of the reasons the Democrats always had so many good candidates running at all levels during this era. Loved to buy the affection of others with low-number license plates. "If Rod had had his way, there would have only been one party in the Maine legislature. But he would have smiled as he made it happen."

Quoddy   Depression-era scheme to harness the huge tides in the Bay of Fundy in order to generate electricity. Long after the project was declared unfeasible by knowledgeable engineers, Maine politicians spoke of it in glowing terms. "We can harness the tides and light up the state from one end to the other with Quoddy."

R

A rising tide

lifts all boats.

JOHN F. KENNEDY

Radioactive   A topic, issue or personal problem which is too hot to handle. Can also refer to a campaign personage who upstages the candidate and is thus unwelcome on the campaign trail. "Look, it's radioactive, you can't really explain incest. Just stay away from it. Don't be a hero."

Ragamuffin   Insider's name for Robert Augustus Gardner Monks, three-time candidate for the U.S. Senate against Smith, Muskie and Collins. Ragamuffin is rarely mentioned by news hawks without the prefix "Cape Elizabeth millionaire."

Raise Megabucks, Spend Megabucks   Consultant's idea of a dream campaign. "I was with Mitchell on the Wyman election. Raise megabucks, spend megabucks, the poor guy never got off the canvas. I think we kept him under 20%."

Kay 'Her Royal Kayness' Rand   Regal and witty campaign manager for Angus King during his 1994 gubernatorial campaign. In a previous life she was legislative liaison for the Maine Municipal Association and policy director of the Maine Business Alliance. Subsequently named director of legislative policy for Governor King, 1995– . (See also "Central Planner.") A very important, knowledgeable player who developed into one of the better candidate campaign managers since World War II.

Theodore 'Ted' Rand   Republican candidate for Congress in the First District primary in 1994. He received 14% of the vote.

Orville 'Tex' Ranger   Republican activist who never met a conservative he didn't like, and who once indicated that Rush Limbaugh was too moderate for his taste. Insiders know him for "Ranger's Rule." (See also "Ranger's Rule.")

Ranger's Rule   Named for Orville "Tex" Ranger who stated his first law of politics as "You don't have to be smart to be in politics." (See also "Orville 'Tex' Ranger.")

Gunder Rasmussen   Finished fourth in the 1948 Republican primary for the 1st CD, receiving 3.2% of the vote.

Rasputin   John Day of the *Bangor Daily News*, known for his malevolent visage, complete with black beard, his hatred of Bolsheviks and their fellow travelers, and his sharp, often stabbing pen. We often forget that before Rasputin was killed by the Czar's entourage, he sent many to their political deaths. Not a closet Brennanista. Spinnable in little doses, usually has a point of view by the time he calls.

Ratings   What television stations live and die by since their advertising rates are directly related to their ratings as generated by Nielsen and Arbitron. "Fox's ratings are lower but I think they deliver better demographics if you want the 18–25-year-old cohort for your candidate." A program's rating is the percentage of households actually watching TV at a given time. Lower rated shows and stations command lower rates than higher rated ones. Sometimes bargains can be gotten for special programs geared to special interest groups. "Fox has a great program for sportsmen and it comes cheap because of its low ratings with the general public. Buy all you can, Dice Man."

The Rats Are Out of the City   Phrase meaning the dirty job is done, the task is accomplished. Often a consultant's lament, as in "Boy, once the rats were out of the city they started questioning all the money we spent." (See also "Milking Rattlesnakes Is Hard Work.")

Rat's Ass   GOB term for someone who is utterly worthless. "He's not worth a rat's ass." (See "Pisshole in the Snow" and "Jack Shit.")

Rats with Wings   Seagulls. Known for their inclination to hang around town dumps and fast food joints, seagulls are essential for any commercials on the Maine coast. "I want lots of rats with wings in that spot; they're a lot easier to sell than Maine Yankee."

Raw Data   Polling data unbalanced by gender, ethnicity, or any other demographic factor. "Even the raw data has you guys ahead, Tom, just relax."

Davis Rawson   Former writer for the *Bangor Daily News, Portland Press Herald, Kennebec Journal* and now editor of the *Central Maine Sentinel* and author of some of the most amusing political columns, "The Maine View" and "Politics on the Half Shell." Davis is usually pretty even-handed in dishing out both ridicule and praise and is always enjoyable to read. Husband of Nancy Perry, a reporter for the *Maine Sunday Telegram* and *Portland Press Herald* in her own right. The biggest problem with Rawson from our point of view is that he spends too much of his time and talent covering the Legislature and not enough covering the races for Congress and Senate. Has one of the best senses of humor among Maine political reporters. Spinnable.

Alex Ray   Former executive director of the Republican Party and now president of Chesapeake Media. Has great fondness for Maine. His efforts include winning the 1974 primary for Jim Erwin, and a close second for Sumner Lipman in the 1994 gubernatorial primary. Although his candidates have yet to win the governorship in Maine, Alex has won the Maine lottery. Would like to handle the "King for President" campaign.

Reach   A radio or TV station's audience, its "reach" to the listening or viewing public. "Sure it's got a lot of reach, but it's still too expensive."

Read the Numbers   Interpret a poll. "She could read the numbers better than anybody I ever saw."

Ready Money   Money which is available at the start or near the start of a campaign. This is very important to campaign consultants because this is the money they can count on, both for the campaign and for themselves. "He's got a lot of ready money and that makes all the difference in the world to me."

Real Voters   People who actually vote on election day as opposed to those who tell you they will vote on election day. "Finding real voters isn't as easy as it looks; lots of folks will lie right to your face and tell you they are registered to vote and that they are going to vote."

Real Woman   As in Are You a Real Woman or a Sandra Day O'Connor? Liberal Democratic woman question asked of Republican women. In these circles, apparently, it is thought difficult to be both a "real" woman and a Republican.

Recount City   A close election. "That governor's race looks like recount city to me."

Red Alert   Term used to get through to any campaign manager or any candidate. Since it conjures up powerful images of disaster and scandal, the caller will always get through. "Tell Larry it's a red alert. Period."

Red Legs   Black ducks, the GOB totem waterfowl, which come down from Canada usually after the hunting season has closed. "The election will be over before the red legs get here. I hope they get here before the hunting season is over.

David E. 'Davey' Redmond   Charter member of the Brennanistas. One of Brennan's closest and most loyal friends over the years and his chief of staff when Brennan was governor. Ran for governor on his own in 1986; finished fourth in the Democratic primary with 15% of the vote. (See also "King of Signs.") Democratic player of note for many years. One of the most engaging political actors on the Maine political scene (and behind it as well). Great sense of humor and history.

Carlton Day Reed   Democratic candidate for governor in 1966, getting 25% of the vote in the primary and finishing behind Ken Curtis. In 1965 he became the first Democratic President of the Maine State Senate in 54 years. A principal of Reed and Reed Construction.

John Reed   Republican President of the Maine Senate who became governor upon the death of Clinton Clauson in 1959. Elected governor in his own right in 1960 with 52.7% of the vote against Frank Coffin. Unopposed in the Republican primary of 1962, he beat Maynard Dolloff in the general election with 50.1% of the vote. In 1966, he defeated Jim Erwin in the Republican primary with 59% of the vote but was defeated by Ken Curtis in the general election, getting 47% of the vote. Congressman Dave Emery and Congressman Bill Cohen helped him get appointed Ambassador to Sri Lanka in 1976–1977 before that country exploded in civil war. Set sail for Sri Lanka with a year's supply of Maine baked beans. Has one of the loudest voices and best memory of any Maine politician. Lots of charm and lots of longevity. (See "Luckiest Man in Maine Politics," "Reed the Ribbon Cutter," and "Studmuffin.")

Reed the Ribbon Cutter   While governor, John Reed attended so many ceremonies he was known as "Reed the Ribbon Cutter."

Bruce Reeves   Democratic State Senator (D-Pittston), chairman of "Citizens for Utility Rate Reform" and, as a State Senator, leader of the unsuccessful fight to popularly elect the Public Utilities Commission in 1981. Also ran for Congress in 1976, getting 12% of the vote in the Democratic primary. Later a consultant for Portland West.

Reform Party   Ross Perot's creation, in Maine headed by Steve Bost, Orono State Senator who in a classic imitation of an overused art form, "reformed" the classic Maine walk and bicycled across Maine instead of walking in the tradition of Cohen, Emery, and Snowe. He ended up dropping out of the U.S. Senate race in 1996, but unlike Ross, he did not get back into the race. Instead, Bost went back to the Democratic fold, and endorsed Joe Brennan for U.S. Senate.

The Most Refreshing Figure in the American Campaign Is Ed Muskie of Maine   James Reston writing about the Presidential election of 1948.

The Regular Slugs   Name for Maine press corps attributed to McKernan press secretary Willis Lyford. (See also "Scorps.")

James L. Reid   Won the Republican primary for the 2nd CD in 1956 but lost the general election, receiving 46.6% of the vote.

Barbara Reinertsen   Former WABI-TV reporter, and then press secretary for Congressman Joe Brennan and spokesperson when he ran for governor in 1990. Now works for the United Way as director of campaign and communications for the United Way of Mid Coast Maine.

John 'The Brink' Rensenbrink   Bowdoin College professor of government, anti-nuclear and citizen activist and founder of the Maine Green Party in 1984. Rensenbrink, long a Democrat, felt that the party had abandoned its principles and became no different than the Republican party. First meeting of Maine Greens was in January, 1984, making it the first in the United States. Ran for the Senate in 1996 as a Green, getting 4% of the vote. (See "Duopoly.")

Republican Lite   Republican term of derision for President Bill Clinton. "There goes Republican Lite again, stealing another one of our programs."

Republican State Committee   An auk masquerading as an elephant.

Republicans for Muskie   Surprisingly successful effort by Neil Bishop, Republican candidate for governor who lost to Burton Cross in the 1952 Republican primary and then went on to help legitimize Ed Muskie as a candidate for governor in 1954. At that time in Maine, only 90,000 out of

480,000 voters were Democrats. Bishop had received 35,000 votes in the 1952 Republican primary and helped sell Muskie to the Republicans two years later. In fact, Muskie's margin of victory over Cross was only 22,000 votes. Ironically, Bishop was later to run against Muskie for the U.S. Senate in 1970.

Restore: The North Woods   One of New England's tiniest and often most extreme-sounding environmental groups, claiming 300 members (1996). Restore often sounds as if it has no idea that hunting and commercial forestry have been integral parts of Maine, and Maine politics, since the 17th century. No other group can drive GOB blood pressure up more readily or higher. Major factor in geting the government to protect native Atlantic Salmon runs.

Retail Politics   Getting votes one at a time using traditional methods such as handshakes and street tours or by going door to door. "I've got splinters in both hands from putting up those damn lawn signs. To hell with retail politics."

Revenge   Supposedly a staple of politics, but as Jim Brunelle has so wisely observed, "Revenge is like chocolate—sweet, impossible to resist and leaving you with a lot of heavy freight to carry around in the long run." Brilliant satori.

Paul Reynolds   Longtime editor of the *Bangor Daily News*. Republican and conservative-leaning on many issues, his editorial pages drove many Democratic insiders wild.

Harrison L. 'Harry' Richardson   Republican State Senator from Cumberland. Ran for governor in 1974, finishing second in the Republican primary with 38% of the vote to Jim Erwin's 39%. (See also "Horse.") As Republican Majority Leader of the House, Richardson was a prime mover in helping the GOP establish environmental leadership in the 1970's.

Riding the Rap   Consultant saying meaning the price for political foolishness, as "You got him into the Congressional race; now ride the rap and shut up."

John D. Rigazio   Democratic candidate for Congress in the 1st CD in 1970, getting 16% of the vote in the primary.

Right!   Ironic phrase meaning "wrong." "I hear you signed on with him." "Right! What have you been smoking?"

Rip-Shit   GOB term for very angry. "The candidate is rip-shit; that meeting in Lincoln was last week and we drove all that way for nothing."

Risk/Reward Ratio   Political calculus of the risks of a possible strategy compared with the possible rewards of that strategy. "The risk/reward ratio was high in calling a special session of the Legislature, but the governor had no choice, as he saw things."

RNC   Republican National Committee. Famous for sending people from Washington to tell people living in Maine how to appeal to Maine voters. Rich Bond and Charlie Black come to mind immediately. Charlie Black's last national effort was for Phil Gramm.

Road Kill   A dead candidate, one who is doomed. "He was road kill by October 15, but nobody would tell him."

Roadblock   Buying enough TV time on enough stations so that every person in Maine sees your commercial at least 10 times. "Sunday Sales was going down to defeat until Rett went with a roadblock."

David G. Roberts   Democratic candidate for Congress in 1960. Lost to Cliff McIntire, getting 36% of the vote in Maine's 3rd District.

Will Robinson   Unsung hero of various Maine campaigns from the Washington media firm of McWilliams, Cosgrove, and Robinson. Worked on the original media which elected Tom Andrews Congressman in 1992 (but avoided Tom's losing Senate race in 1994), did the media for the successful campaign against the widening of the Maine turnpike in 1991, and for the Maine Won't Discriminate effort in 1995.

Robo Candidate   Any candidate who does not crumble in the face of major attacks, who persists when the going gets very bad and it looks like defeat is imminent. Bill Clinton during the New Hampshire primary of 1992 is one of the best national examples. Most lesser candidates would have caved in under the relentless pressure. Dave Emery running for the U.S. Senate in 1982 is one of the best Maine examples. Assaulted by friend and foe alike after George Mitchell made up a 26% deficit to charge ahead, Emery never quit and although defeated, kept his head up high.

Likewise, in 1996, John Hathaway took media hits about his alleged involvement with an underage babysitter which would have knocked out another candidate. "I saw Hathaway on WCSH; he was the ultimate robo candidate, he didn't even break a sweat."

Nelson Rockefeller Award   The annual Nelson Rockefeller Award was given to the individual who had "demonstrated the characteristics of courage, integrity and leadership exemplified by the former Vice President, Nelson A. Rockefeller, a Maine native." It was supposed to recognize individual achievement but accent the outreach and unity of the party. The award was first given in 1979 to Mary Adams for her grass roots effort to repeal the state Uniform Property Tax. Delivered at a dinner with the special guest of honor Henry Kissinger, the award was very controversial, and far from promoting party unity seemed to sunder it. State Senate President Joe "Snort" Sewall and State Senator Ben Katz (author of the state Uniform Property Tax) walked out of the ceremony and Linwood Palmer, former House minority leader, objected in the press because Adams had supported an Independent candidate for governor, Buddy Frankland, against Palmer in 1978. Several years later, the award quietly ceased to exist, perhaps in recognition that party politics are always fractious. (See also "Mary Adams," "Eagle Award," and "HAK.")

Frank C. Rodway   Republican candidate for Congress in 1966, received 7% of the vote in the 1st District primary. Head of the Maine Maritime Academy in 1963–1964, Governor Reed's efforts to oust him as it head was one of the more celebrated controversies of Reed's administration. Jud Strunk even penned a song about it to the tune "Give My Regards to Broadway" which included the lyrics "Give my regards to Rodway, remember me to old Castine."

Neil Rolde   Democratic state representative from York, finished third in the Democratic primary in the 1st CD in 1976 with 18% of the vote. Later ran unsuccessfully against Bill Cohen for U.S. Senate in 1990, getting 38% of the vote. Major fund-raiser for the Democrats. Author of the beautiful *An Illustrated History of Maine* with illustration editor Charles Calhoun.

Roman Catholic Church   The most powerful religious organization in Maine politics today, having had discernible impacts on such diverse campaigns as the Equal Rights Amendment, the Pornography Referendum and the Maine Won't Discriminate effort.

Douglas Rooks   Formerly editorial page editor of the *Kennebec Journal*, he is currently editor of the *Maine Times*. Insiders know him for writing very complicated and convoluted editorials. "I think the *Maine Times* endorsed our position but I'm not really sure. Nothing we can use on TV anyway."

Rorschach Test   In politics, any commercial into which voters can read all sorts of positive qualities which they then transfer to the candidate. "Super job; it's a Rorschach test for all GOBs." (See also "GOBs.")

Route Jumper   Someone who can play a variety of roles in a campaign. "She turned out to be the best route jumper I ever saw. She did press one day and opposition research the next."

Rud   Maine phrase for "road." "I never vote against ruds; that makes the sand and gravel boys mad." (See also "Sand and Gravel Boys.")

Rumpelstiltskin   Patron saint of political consultants for his ability to turn straw into gold. "Is this a great country or what? Every one of us a Rumpelstiltskin."

Running Dog   Unquestioning follower of a candidate or cause. "Will you look at that, 5 running dogs in an entourage of 6. That's a record, even for a Senator."

Rush   (1) What candidates get when people clap for them; what consultants feel when they sign up strong, well-heeled candidates, and what pollsters feel when they know how people are going to vote before they actually do.

Rush   (2) Rush Limbaugh, the man whom the Democrats in Maine hate almost as much as Newt Gingrich.

Doris Russell   Longtime Republican national committeewoman from Castine. Usually supported moderate Republican candidates. An early Bush supporter in 1978–79.

S

I can't be no saint. I'm a politician.

SENATOR AUGIE SANGIAMINO
IN *THE SUNDAY MACARONI CLUB* BY STEVE LOPEZ

Herman Sahagian   Lost the Republican primary for U.S. Senate in 1958, receiving 16.4% of the vote.

St. Vitus Dance   A political frenzy. "Mitchell retiring produced the biggest St. Vitus Dance in Maine since World War II."

Saliency   In polling, this refers to the relevance of a particular opinion, i.e., what can be done with it. "Everybody's favorite issue is jobs, but the saliency of that issue is very low. Everybody is for jobs and nobody is against jobs in Maine, so it's not a very useful issue in any particular campaign."

SAM   The Sportsmen's Alliance of Maine, one of the most important interest groups in Maine politics. In 1994, for example, no candidate who was not endorsed by SAM won a major office, and all winners had been supported by this collection of hunters, trappers, gun enthusiasts, and fishermen. Also provided a good deal of the margin of victory of Susan

Collins over Joe Brennan in the 1996 senatorial race. (See "Hook and Bullet Crowd.")

Sample Ballot   Polling technique in which the candidates and their party affiliations are listed as the voter would see them in the polling booth. "We can't get her up by more than 6% on the sample ballot, I think we are losing ground since the last time we looked."

Jean Sampson   Close advisor and volunteer assistant to Frank Coffin in his Congressional and gubernatorial campaigns.

Sand and Gravel Crowd   The companies and individuals who are in construction, particularly those in road and bridge construction. Major donors and tough clients who expect 65% or more on their bond issues.

Sand Hill   Franco ward in Augusta. Good predictor of Waterville, as well as Augusta, outcomes. Over the years, it has shown the willingness of Franco Americans to accept Republican candidates. "Sand Hill says it's Snowe over Andrews. By a lot."

Sandbag   To set up someone on your own campaign staff in order to embarrass them with the candidate or the campaign manager. Sometimes done by withholding information. At other times, it is done by leaking a negative piece of information to the press. "Damn it, stop sandbagging me. I know you told her it was my idea to run that operation at the convention."

Dwight Sargent   Editorial writer and editor, *Portland Press Herald*, in the 1950's and 1960's.

Who'd Want to Be in the Papers on a Saturday?   Insiders regard Friday as the best day to try to get into the daily newspapers because if done properly, the story will hit heavily on Friday and bounce all weekend long, perhaps even being picked up in the Sunday paper recaps. But stories which drop on Saturday get lost, and both readership and intensity of interest are lower. "They're holding the press conference when? Who'd want to be in the papers on a Saturday?"

Aldric Saucier   Independent candidate for U.S. Senate in 1996, received 3% of the vote.

Robert 'Bob' Saunders   Political reporter in the 1980's for the *Journal Tribune*. Insiders credit him with inaugurating that paper's serious, sustained political coverage from a local perspective. Now an editorial writer.

James 'Jimmy' Sawyer   Democratic Party state chairman from Castine from 1952–1954; appointed Frank Coffin chair of the 1954 Pre-Convention Platform Committee—an important move in the development of the 1954 campaign which brought Ed Muskie to power.

Say It Ain't So, George   *Maine Times* editor Douglas Rooks on learning that George Mitchell was representing the tobacco companies in their struggle with the attorney generals of 23 states.

Scared Off the Meat   Driven away from a prize by a competitor. "Brennan was absolutely brilliant; he scared Baldacci off the meat, finessed him right out of the Senate race in 1996."

Political Schizophrenia   What Dave Emery said George Mitchell had when he ran against him in the U.S. Senate race of 1982. Emery declared at the Republican convention: "He has a split political personality, a political schizophrenia, by promising to be all things to all people."

Edward Schlick   Executive secretary, Maine Democratic Party, public relations consultant; continuing party activist.

Michael 'Mike' Schoonjans   Biddeford Democratic Party activist in York County and important labor union leader in 1950's–1960's.

Scientific Scheduling   An attempt on the part of political consultants and campaign managers to bring order to the chaos of the candidate's time. Done by a formula in which the number of days available for campaigning are strictly divided by the number of swing or attainable voters by county or city. "We tried scientific scheduling but it only worked for two weeks before the candidate began accepting invitations willy nilly again."

Adrian Scolten   Democratic nominee for the U.S. Senate in 1948, Scolten lost after receiving 28.7% of the vote. He subsequently lost Democratic primaries in the 1st CD in 1950, '52, and '56, receiving 29.2%, 37.6%, and 19%, respectively.

Scorps   Short for scorpions, name given to the press by James Carville's character "Richard" in *Primary Colors*, Joe Klein's novel about Bill Clinton's run for and to the White House. Klein, a *Newsweek* reporter, when asked if he were "Anonymous," lied and said "no" until unmasked by the *Washington Post*. Still, this name for reporters is worth the price of the book. "Watch out for the scorps, they've all read Rawson's column."

Scrapper   Davis Rawson's name for Charles "Charlie" Cragin who ran for governor in 1982, losing to Joe Brennan. "Say what you want, he's still a scrapper."

Screed   Bullshit. "Did you hear his presentation to the governor? I've never heard such screed."

Screen   Filter question designed to get or exclude groups during the polling process. "We ran a tight set of screens on voting patterns to make sure we got only most likely voters."

Screener   Script designed to get a certain demographic or psychographic mix into a focus group. "I want a screener that lets in only undecided voters in the Senate race. I don't care whether they are Republicans, Democrats or Independents."

Screw-the-Dues Guys   Davis Rawson's term for candidates and operatives who refuse to spend time working their way up through the party apparatus. "They're the guys who want to jump right in and start wailing away. They're the screw-the-dues guys. They all think they're JFK."

Scribes   Old-fashioned, basically positive name for reporters. "Look at all the scribes on the fourth floor; it looks very messy." (See also "Scorps.")

Fred C. Scribner Jr.   Portland lawyer and longtime Republican national committeeman. Very active in Maine Presidential politics, supporting Wilkie, Dewey, Eisenhower, Nixon (1960 only) and Rockefeller. As General Counsel for the Treasury Department, then Assistant Secretary and Undersecretary of the Treasury under Eisenhower, he was the highest Maine Republican in the executive branch of the Federal government until William S. Cohen became Secretary of Defense in 1997. Insiders know Scribner as one of those who advised Nixon not to contest his 1960 loss to Jack Kennedy.

Rodney 'Rod' Scribner   State auditor and Brennan Commissioner of Finance. Democratic activist.

Seance   Political consultant term for a long, inconclusive campaign meeting. "Not only was it a seance, I didn't even get the go ahead for the commercials."

SecDef   Secretary of Defense. William S. Cohen is Maine's only SecDef ever.

The Second Floor   The second floor of the Maine Statehouse where the governor's office is. This floor holds the decaying flags of the Maine Civil War units, numerous portraits of dead politicians, and the governor's office, which sits near an outside door allowing the governor to escape from the Legislature as quickly as is required.

Second Recess   Campaign phrase for the silly personality clashes and snits you encounter on the campaign trail and which remind you of the ones you used to encounter in the fourth grade during recess. "Joe's still mad at you? I'm sure things will be better by second recess."

Secret Meeting   Meetings held before campaigns actually get started, when people and consultants are choosing up sides and trying to finesse some candidates into the race and some out. In this early, dream-like state, it is possible to imagine almost any candidate as being successful "if only" you can keep someone else out of the race. "Sure, we've got a good start here tonight but just remember they're having their secret meeting too, probably this weekend if not before."

Secret Supporter   Not really a supporter. In a contested primary situation, many political types tell different candidates they are for them so that whoever wins will think they had their support. But they refuse to let their names be put on the campaign letterhead. "She is the all-time champ at being a secret supporter. She was on three primary guys' lists."

See Ya   Angus King's farewell line to any and everybody. Thought by some Democratic political insiders as an effort to sound like a "real person."

See You on the Water   Originally this phrase came from coastal Maine among lobstermen and commercial fishermen. Means "I'll see you out there where things are pure and simple and all these outsiders aren't around." Now has a political insider meaning as "We won't discuss it now in front of the client, we'll discuss it later." "Hell, don't worry about the fees, I'll see you on the water."

Segmentation Analysis   Probably the most important service provided by polling. Takes the electorate and breaks it up into manageable demographic and psychographic units to show a candidate or cause how to build a winning coalition by including various groups. In Maine, for example, if you can appeal to voters who have a high opinion of Audubon Society and to those who have a high opinion of the Sportsman's Alliance of Maine, you will have a winning combination on wildlife issues. In 1992, Audubon and SAM got 72% for a constitutional amendment putting hunting and fishing license revenues off limits for the general fund.

Segue   The transition from one phase of a campaign to the next. A very important and often overlooked aspect to campaigning except when it goes wrong. For example, most Republicans have to appeal to the right wing of their party during a primary and then move to the middle of the electoral spectrum in the general election. Most Democrats have to appeal to the left wing of their party during a primary and then move to the middle of the electoral spectrum in a general election. The segues in between these two stages tell a lot about how a campaign is going. "Did you see that segue? It was fabulous; one day she was a left-wing loony and the next she was mainstream."

Self-Fulfilling Prophecy   Doing something in politics which guarantees things will turn out the way you say they will. "For a long time it was a self-fulfilling prophecy, Republicans said they wouldn't do well in Lewiston so they never went there and thus they never did well there. Bill Cohen changed all that in 1972."

Selling   What politics is all about, whether it is a candidate, an idea, a program or a ballot measure. "Selling is the name of the game in this referendum. I don't want any pretty pictures without people in them. We're selling state parks."

The Senator   "*Your*" senator as opposed to the other 99 senators. Also can refer to "The Senator Motel" in Augusta where a great deal of the state's business is conducted from 5 P.M. to 2 A.M. and beyond.

The **Senator**   Most fervently said by Democratic insiders about Senator Ed Muskie.

The Senator from California   Democratic insider name for W. S. Cohen for his alleged love of Beverly Hills and the people who inhabit zip codes such as 90210.

The Senator from the Five and Ten Cent Store   Margaret Chase Smith as portrayed by the *Saturday Evening Post* in 1948 after her upset victory in the Republican Senatorial primary. This article and her subsequent national campaigning for Tom Dewey established Smith as a national political figure and helped set her image as a self-made heroine.

Send More Milk   Send more money. "Those TV stations won't put us on the air just because they like us; send more milk."

A Setting Sun Casteth Little Light   A retiring politician who has diminishing clout. "I don't see who will go to the fund-raiser, a setting sun casteth little light and generates less cash."

Joseph 'Joe' Sewall   Republican State Senator from Old Town and President of the Senate from 1975 through 1982, Joe Sewell is the political godfather to most of the successful statewide politicians in the Republican party. Bill Cohen, Jock McKernan and Olympia Snowe all owe enormous debts to him. Indeed, it is difficult to imagine any of the three attaining their initial electoral goals without his financial, psychological and mentoring assistance the *Portland Press Herald's* Bill Caldwell also termed him "one of the classiest, nicest men in Maine." (See also "Snort.")

Sumner Sewall   Maine Governor 1941 to 1945, he finished third in the Republican primary for U.S. Senate in 1948, receiving 17.7% of the vote. Sewall was the grandson of Bath's Arthur Sewall, William Jennings Bryan's Vice Presidential running mate in 1896.

Sex Sells   Advertising slogan which does not seem to apply to Maine politics since World War II.

Ray Shaddis   Led the first effort to shut down Maine Yankee in 1980. He failed during the very week Maine's first moose hunt in this century opened. "Hell, few can say 'I bagged a Shaddis on Tuesday and a moose on Thursday.' It was a good week." Still, Shaddis got his revenge and sense of accomplishment when in 1997, he was named to the board overseeing the decommissioning of Maine Yankee!

Shadow, short for **Shadow Staffer**   A staff person who follows an elected official or candidate around with great reverence and seldom speaks. "He's got two shadows with him this time."

Shameless Hirelings   Clear cutting ban proponents' name for Citizens for a Healthy Forest and Economy. (See also "CHFE.")

Samuel 'Sam' Shapiro   Former Maine State Treasurer. Term limited out in 1996. Widely admired in both parties and giver of many gifts. Was forced to abandon his personal PAC after getting lots of criticism in 1994.

Share   The percentage of all households in a given TV market which are watching a particular program regardless of whether or not all television sets are turned on.

Elwin Sharpe   Lost the Republican primary for the 2nd CD in 1958, receiving 34.1% of the vote.

Philip Sharpe   Democratic nominee for Congress from the 3rd CD in 1952, Sharpe lost the general election after receiving 23.8% of the vote.

Michael 'Mike' Shea   President of Shea Media in Boston, a prominent Democratic media firm. Did the ads for Duke Dutremble for Congress in 1994 and Joe Brennan for U.S. Senate in 1996.

She'll Fish   Downeast Maine saying for "It'll work." "Are you crazy? Have Collins do a welfare spot with three weeks to go?" "Don't worry, she'll fish."

Robert 'Bob' Shepherd   Former press secretary for Senator Ed Muskie. Did not advise the senator to go to New Hampshire and cry in the snow. Great political storyteller with a fine sense of humor.

Barbara Sherman   Major fund-raiser for George Mitchell, "lent" to the Brennan campaigns in 1990 and 1994 and for party fund-raising specials such as "The $100,000 Presidential Visit Fundraiser," July 31, 1994.

She's No Olympia Snowe   1996 statement about Susan Collins attributed to Virginia Murphy, chair of Maine's Democratic Party. Ms. Murphy, of course, also said of Olympia Snowe in 1994, "She's no Margaret Chase Smith," but so it goes on the campaign trail where it's hard for party flacks to get new material.

Shit from Shinola   Short for "he/she doesn't know shit from Shinola." Consultant-speak for "He or she doesn't know anything." "Lawn signs? He doesn't know shit from Shinola."

Shit Load   Rural Maine term for 'a lot.' "There is a shit load of votes to get in Lewiston but it's hard to get them."

Shit Storm   GOB term for something bad happening. Very bad fallout on the campaign trail. "There's going to be a real shit storm over this."

Shoot   A film or video session in which the raw footage of the candidate or the authority figure is shot.

Shoot the Messenger   Candidate inclination to blame the pollster for bad numbers. Or as Shakespeare put it in *Henry IV*, Part I: "The first bringer of unwelcome news hath but a losing office." "I love the way he tried to shoot the messenger when we had him dropping six points back. He liked our numbers when he was ahead by ten."

Short War   A campaign—usually a ballot measure—running the last two or three weeks of the election cycle. "We didn't have money enough for anything but a short war." (See also "Long War.")

Showtime   A big moment in the campaign when the spotlight is on the candidate, big time. "Come on, Linwood, it's showtime. Don't hold anything back."

Elden H. 'Denny' Shute   Republican candidate for Congress in Maine's 2nd CD. Received 44% of the vote in the 1968 general election against Bill Hathaway. Maine TV and radio broadcaster. An early, strong environmental force to buy and preserve the Bigelow Mountain Preserve. Later a reverend.

Sierra Club   With 2,400 members (1996), this environmental organization is one of Maine's more vocal groups. It played a role in stopping the Sears Island cargo port project by being the first to file a lawsuit against it, and in 1996 it convinced the national Sierra Club to spend several hundred thousand dollars in the forestry referendum during the last weekend, holding the forest compact to 48% of the vote instead of the 50.1% needed for passage.

Sighting   An unexpected view of an opposing candidate which causes great excitement—and often hope—in the camp of his or her opponent. To someone outside politics or even a casual observer of the political scene, it is difficult to imagine how these sightings could have any effect at all, but in the often Alice in Wonderland, hothouse, overstressed, sleep-deprived campaign headquarters, such an impact is very possible, indeed understandable as the sighting is regarded as a magic portent of things to come.

To illustrate: In 1992, some on the campaign staff of Pat McGowan were excited to the point of near mania by a report that Olympia Snowe had been seen in an airport with her hair down. "It's a sighting, it's a sighting, her hair is down to her shoulders, she's losing her power, she's losing her power." In 1994, late in the campaign, a staffer for the Brennan for Governor campaign was seen in Bangor, alighting from the campaign Winnebago and carefully positioning a footstool on the tarmac so that Joe Brennan could step down gracefully onto the parking lot. King-for-Governor staff roared their approval and delight. "It's a sighting, it's a sighting, Joe is playing Louis XIV and now he needs a Keeper of the Royal Footstool just to get out of the car. We're going to win this thing."

The Silent Candidate   Press characterization of Senator Margaret Chase Smith during her 1960 race against Lucia Cormier who was dynamic, very articulate, and a top-notch debater. Smith made sure that the debates in that campaign were few and far between. In fact there was only one.

Silent Coup   The removal of a campaign staffer from a position without the staffer realizing her or she is being shifted to an innocuous new position. "Get him out of the press room and into the pucker brush. It's a silent coup so tell him it's a promotion."

Herbert T. Silsby   Republican candidate for Congress in the 2nd CD, received 37% of the vote in the 1964 primary, losing to Ken MacLeod.

Harold Silverman   Republican state representative, then Independent State Senator from Calais. Ran against Olympia Snowe in 1980 as a Democrat, getting 21% of the vote.

Daniel 'Dan' Simpson   Gannett Statehouse reporter in the 1970's and early 1980's. According to other reporters, he had excellent sources and knew how to use them.

Roy U. Sinclair   Republican candidate for Congress in Maine's 2nd District. Received 43% of the vote in the Republican primary.

Sing's   Former Chinese restaurant in Augusta and site of many political luncheons. One of the most famous political lunches of all time was that of Senator Richard Pierce (R-Waterville), who, as chairman of Cohen for Senate, held a luncheon which ran from 11:30 A.M. to 7 P.M. in what is believed to be a Maine state record for such an event. Many illustrious consultants were unable to hang in there for the entire affair.

Sisterhood Is Powerful   (1) Male consultant's ironic explanation for anything that goes wrong on the campaign trail that can be traced to, or blamed on, a woman. "Sure the policy paper was all screwed up; sisterhood is powerful."

Sisterhood Is Powerful   (2) Male consultant lament when women in politics combine for any purpose. "Two women Senators? Watch out; sisterhood is powerful."

Skeletons in My Closet   Chapter from Bill Clarke's book, *It's Time to Take Our Country Back*, in which he detailed his sins and mistakes in order to preempt his opposition and reporters from doing so! Clarke, a Taxpayers Party candidate for the U.S. Senate in 1996, deserves inclusion in this lexicon for being the only candidate in recent Maine political history to call down napalm on his own position—long before there were any enemies in sight.

Skewed   To have polling results which are inaccurate. Sometimes this is done on purpose to give one candidate an edge. Sometimes it is done accidentally because the newspaper or other organization does not know how to do an objective poll properly. "Susan Collins was done in partially in 1994 by that skewed *Portland Press Herald* poll which didn't have any party identification with the candidates' names so it looked like she had been going backwards during the summer."

Skewed Coverage   Reporting which shows the reporter's bias. Most reporters have a definite point of view which comes through in their stories which are supposed to be objective. "That is such skewed coverage, he might as well be a flak for McKernan." (See also "Flak.")

Skull-Through   Polling term for thinking about a questionnaire and how it will be received by the public and what information it will produce. "When it came to saving Maine Yankee, the skull-through sessions were critical for framing the subsequent debate."

Skunky Beer   A commercial or campaign tactic which doesn't work out. "We all liked the ad but it turned out to be skunky beer."

The Slasher   Tom Daffron's name for Charles Cragin, Republican nominee for governor in 1982 and point man for various Republican candidates such as Bill Cohen. Cragin was very loyal to those candidates and served them well. "Slasher was a pit bull before pit bulls were cool; he did a lot to help us."

Slim and None   Zero chance. "I would say the chances of Joe choosing Ken Curtis as U.S. Senator are between slim and none."

Slime   Any personal attacks by one's opponent. "She's just resorting to slime to try to drag me down to her level."

Small Mouth Bass   Charles S. Bass, one-time fieldman for William S. Cohen, administrative assistant to Congressman Emery, and subsequently (1994 to present) a Congressman from New Hampshire.

Small Rolodex   Usually derogatory comment about a political reporter who only has, or only uses, a small number of sources. "He's the worst of the small Rolodexes."

Smear Strategy   To take a fair and legitimate criticism of a candidate or a candidate's position and claim that this is a "smear." "From 1948 on, Margaret Chase Smith used the smear strategy to perfection."

Smear Tactics   To attack one candidate's credibility by resorting to guilt by association or by using false or misleading charges that you know to be false.

The Smiling Man   Steve Campbell's 1997 name for Steve Forbes.

Jack L. Smith   Democratic candidate for the U.S. Senate in 1972, getting 9% of the primary vote. In 1966, he ran for the Senate as well, getting 16% in the primary won by Elmer Violette.

Margaret Chase Smith   First woman in the nation elected to the U.S. Senate entirely on her own right. Running for her husband's old Congressional seat in 1940, she won four elections in six months. She was then easily re-elected to Congress in 1942, 1944, and 1946. In 1948, she beat three men in the Republican primary for senator, and then won the general election with 72% of the vote. In 1960, she received 54% of the vote against Lucia Cormier. In 1966, she got 59% of the vote against Elmer Violette. From Skowhegan, she defeated Bob Monks in the 1972 primary with 66% of the vote but then lost in the general election (47%) to Bill Hathaway after turning back $40,000 to the Republican Senatorial committee in October of 1972, saying she didn't need it! Despite her final (and only) defeat, she remains one of the Titans of Maine post-war politics. (See also "I'm Great, I Know It" and "The Titans.")

Stewart Smith   Democratic candidate for Congress in Maine's 2nd CD. Lost in the 1974 primary to Mark Gartley, garnering 33% of the vote.

Smith and Haroff   Washington media firm which got its start with Congressman John Rhodes of Arizona and made its Maine name with Senator William S. Cohen. Subsequently did the political ads for Congresswoman Snowe, Governor McKernan, and Senator Snowe. Also did the media for Linwood Palmer for governor and Bob Monks for U.S. Senate.

Smith Brothers   In other parts of America, refers to cough drops but always George (direct mail) and Gordon (doctor's dollars) in Maine.

Smitty   As in "Good Old Smitty." George Smith, executive director of Sportsman's Alliance of Maine (SAM), political consultant, and direct mail specialist for 20 years. Campaign manager for Dave Emery's successful 1974 upset victory over Congressman Peter Kyros. From that point on, he has remained one of Maine's major political players, involved in many important referenda and candidate elections. He is widely credited for bringing SAM to the height of political influence and for helping to elect such diverse candidates as John Baldacci and Angus King. Even the liberal *Maine Times* is fascinated with his ability to keep many balls in the air without losing his own. See their February 21, 1996, issue "SAM I Am." "You need to pack the hearing? Call Smitty."

Smoke and Mirrors   Any campaign with more style than substance. To try to create an illusion with few resources. "Boy, we'll have to get by with smoke and mirrors on this one."

Snort   Insider nickname for Senator Joe Sewall, president of the James W. Sewall Company (established 1880), member (1967–1982) and President of the Maine Senate (1975–1982). Known for his love of fishing on the Upsalquitch, an Atlantic salmon paradise. One of the last of the gentlemen legislators who looked upon public service as an obligation one owes to society as opposed to finding out how much society can owe to the legislators. Joe Sewall invited worthy friends and foes to fish the Upsalquitch with him. "Many were called but few were chosen."

The Snow King   Les Otten, owner of Sunday River ski resort and supporter of various candidates for Congress and the U.S. Senate. Passed up a chance to run for the Senate himself in 1996 when he bought 6 more mountains instead.

Snow White and the Seven Dwarfs   (1) Senator Joseph McCarthy's term for Senator Margaret Chase Smith and the senators who supported her Declaration of Conscience speech in 1950. Actually there were only 6 other senators, but who's counting after all those years!

Snow White and the Seven Dwarfs   (2) Any primary situation with one major player and a number of insignificant players. "He's a great guy, but strictly one of the dwarfs going nowhere." With party fragmentation in Maine, it is now possible to have a Snow White and 4 or 5 dwarfs in a general election!

Olympia Snowe   State Senator (R-Auburn), elected to Congress in 1978, beating Mark Gartley with 60% of the vote, re-elected in 1980 with 78% of the vote, re-elected in 1982 with 66% of the vote, re-elected in 1984 with 75% of the vote, re-elected in 1986 with 77% of the vote, in 1988 with 66% of the vote, in 1990 with 51% and 1992 with 49%, and elected to the U.S. Senate in 1994 with 60% of the vote. Although she had a couple of close calls in 1990 and 1992, Olympia Snowe remains the most successful warrior in Maine politics since 1946, with 9 wins and 0 losses in major races. (See also "Queen of the Hill.")

So How Do You Really Feel?   Consultant sarcasm for a situation in a campaign when a strategy is trashed. "You say it sucks. So how do you really feel?"

Soap Opera News   TV news which keeps political coverage to a minimum and human interest stories to the maximum. Goes against the old newspaper adage that "life is life and death is death."

Soccer Moms   Women with children and who work in the home, an excellent target group for daytime advertising. Sometimes unnecessarily limited to suburban housewives. "She's still weak with the soccer moms; give them a good dose of that education spot and we'll get their attention again."

Social Moderate   Republican code name for liberals. "She's conservative on fiscal stuff and defense. On the other stuff she's a social moderate."

Socialist in Tweeds   Mary Adams's name for Governor Angus King during the forestry debate in 1996.

Soft Data   Individual comments accumulated by polling. By looking at the soft data in the context of the numbers, it is often possible to get a very vivid portrait of an issue. "The soft data shows why they are coming our way in the referendum."

Soft Money   Political funds which do not count against a candidate's or party's total, usually being spent by an interest group such as the AFL/CIO. Soft money played a major role in only one Maine race during the period under review, that of the Longley/Allen 1996 1st District House race, in which the national AFL/CIO spent nearly a million in attack ads on Longley that ran for a year before the election. Insiders believe it was decisive in determining the outcome of that race. "Soft money is as big a pain as PAC money; even bigger if you think how loose the record-keeping is for it."

Some College   The most difficult group to predict in Maine politics, "some college" refers to an educational category beyond high school but without a college degree. Went for Reagan in 1984 and for Bush in 1988 but for Clinton in 1992. Perhaps this category shows the accuracy of the statement "A little knowledge is a dangerous thing."

Some People Say . . .   Standard polling technique to give respondents different propositions to decide upon. "Some people say that abortion is wrong, other people say it is a necessary evil, while still others say it is a fine, acceptable medical procedure. Which view comes closest to your own?"

Somebody Has to Do It   Ed Muskie's remark when asked why he was running as a Democrat in 1946 for the Maine House. Quoted in Theo Lippman and Donald Hansen, *Muskie*. "Well, if I lived down South I'd probably be a Republican. Somebody has to do it."

SOS   Save Our Schools, an organization devoted to stopping the amalgamation of Maine schools into School Administration Districts led by Mary Adams of Garland in the 1970's. Mary later (1994) ran for governor and finished sixth in the 8-way Republican primary.

Sound Bite   TV phrase for short, pithy clip. The secret to success in political TV is to give great sound bites on the issues you know are popular and to give long-winded, abstract answers which can't be used on TV on the issues you know are unpopular. "Give them a sound bite they can't use; the numbers are all against us, chief." Sound bites by candidates should never be considered thoughtful policy pronouncements.

Sounds Like a Plan   A good idea, often an obvious good idea, which comes from someone else. "That sounds like a plan, Charlie."

Sourceless and Senseless   Unkind reference to TV reporters who seldom do any background research on anything political. (See also "Talking Heads.")

The Space Alien   Al Diamon's name for Congressman Jim Longley. In fairness to young Jim, several reporters for the *New York Times* have stated categorically to this author that in the Republican freshman class of 1994, "He was pretty moderate and pretty rational." Being called "a moderate," in fact, may be a curse in some circles but it is applauded in others.

David 'Dave' Sparks   Effective and likeable campaign manager for Olympia Snowe for Congress in 1978. Went to Washington to work for the Edie Mahe Company.

The Speaker   Aka "The Earl of Eagle Lake," Rep. John Martin (D-Eagle Lake). Once the single most powerful politician in Maine as Speaker of the Maine House from 1975 to 1994, he was ousted as Speaker in 1994 by an unholy alliance of liberal Democrats, conservative Republicans and term-limit advocates. He currently resides in Eagle Lake where his name is still held in awe. John Martin is not, however, without plans for the future.

Spec Creative   Advertising lingo for a situation where a client wants an unhired consultant to come in and pitch the account by doing creative things for no money, and then if the client really likes them and the agency, both are hired; but if the client likes the creative but not the agency, the client keeps only the creative. "Why agencies do spec creative is beyond me. They should refuse. Why give something away for nothing?"

Jerrold B. 'Jerry' Speers   Republican State Senator from Winthrop. Ran for governor in 1978, getting 13% in the Republican primary. Secretary of the Maine Senate (1967–1971) before becoming a Senator himself (1973–1979); he wound up as State Treasurer (1979–1981) and then became an official in Reagan's Treasury Department in Washington.

Ronald 'Ron' Speers   Father of Jerry, won the Republican nomination for Congress in Maine's 1st District with 60% in 1970, subsequently losing to Peter Kyros and getting 40% of the vote. Well known in consultant circles for having introduced the Smiths, Gordon, George, and Edie, to Maine politics. Only Department of Inland Fisheries and Wildlife commissioner known to have sought higher office. He is famous with insiders for having spent so much time during his campaign making posters and lawn signs in his garage.

Richard 'Dick' Spencer   Democratic Representative from Standish who ran a losing campaign against John Quinn in the 1978 Democratic primary for Congress, getting 25% of the vote, then made money backing Tom's of Maine natural health care products. Lost again in 1994 to Ann Rand when he ran for the State Senate position on Portland's peninsula. After that defeat, Dick decided to run for the U.S. Senate against Joe Brennan. He also lost that race, getting 12% of the vote. (See also "Pumpkin Man.")

Spew Numbers   To go public with polling numbers, putting them in the newspapers or on TV and radio. "I've never understood why otherwise perfectly sane clients insist on spewing numbers so everybody ends up knowing what they know."

Spin   As in "to spin," to put your interpretation on some political action of your candidate or opposition. Sometimes goes to extremes as in "She won the Nobel Prize for Peace but that really will hurt her in the long run." Reverse spinning is giving the reporters who dislike you the opposite spin on what you really want them to write, counting on their cantankerous natures to put in the reverse spin in their story. "I spun him so many ways I ended up confusing myself."

Spin Doctor   Someone who is good at spinning. Given the variety of electronic and print media, spin doctors have become a modern necessity in political campaigns. Spin doctors are especially important for fast-breaking stories when interpretation has to occur within minutes. This is a calling for which "many are called but few are chosen."

To Spin or to Prophesize   The truly awesome ethical versus self-preservation dilemma faced by all pundits who are partisans. Should they spin for their candidate, their party or their cause, or should they say what they really think will happen in order to save their reputation as pundits? "God, it was tough. I knew he was going down, but I didn't want to go down with him even though I didn't want to look disloyal. To spin or to prophesize? That's always a tough call that last weekend."

Spoon-Fed Job   When one candidate or cause gets a reporter to buy a story hook, line and sinker. "Once Day got the spoon-fed job from Bobby on the Monks poll, he ran with it and there was no way you could convince him Monks was actually in third place."

Squeeze the Undecideds   As an election winds down, there are still a number of voters who say they are undecided in a particular race. Some of these will actually vote, some will not, so part of the polling art is to squeeze the undecideds in the most realistic fashion, eliminating those least likely to vote so as to see who are the real undecideds among the voting cohort. One technique is to eliminate anyone who is undecided about three or more races. "Squeeze the undecideds; we've only got 2,000 GRPs left and we can't hit everybody." (See also "GRPs.")

Robert 'Bob' Squier   President Clinton's media expert during the Presidential campaign of 1996. Also close to Vice President Al Gore and many other major Democratic politicians. Did the media for Senator Ed Muskie in 1970 when he ran against Neil Bishop as a tune-up for Muskie's 1972 Presidential campaign.

Russell M. Squire   Only Maine politician to beat Ed Muskie. Won the 1947 mayoralty race in Waterville by 400 votes while Muskie was still in the Maine House. Waterville, although a Democratic city had—and has—a long tradition of ticket splitting and for choosing Republican mayors from time to time, including Cy Joly in the early 1960's, Don Marden in 1967 and Paul La Verdiere in 1977.

Squirrels   Consultant-speak for the fringes of the Republican right and the Democratic left. "Thank God in this state the squirrels cancel each other out and the center holds." (See also "The Center Holds.")

Staff   People who work for a candidate or elected official and are on the regular payroll. Also, a good indication said candidate or elected official (or their spouses) has gotten a swelled head from being in the public limelight. Any such person who is overheard to say "It's so difficult to get good staff now," has crossed that line.

Staff Test   The best litmus test for whether or not a candidate or elected official is doing well is whether or not they would be elected or re-elected if only their staff voted. "Governor, right now you have a draw in the staff test. Try to treat them a little nicer and get with it."

Stand-Up Guy/Gal   A consultant who goes down with a losing political ship and makes no excuses. "Bob Tyrer is a stand-up guy; he didn't abandon Emery in '82."

Starting Friction Is Greater Than Sliding Friction   Term from high school physics which in politics is often translated as "Big Mo." "It's taken a while to get her name identification up, but as I told you, starting friction is greater than sliding friction." (See also "Big Mo.")

A Statewide   An important campaign for a statewide office such as governor or Senator. "I've got two statewides and a Congressional this year."

Stay on Message   Keep focused on the theme or message which works for you as a candidate or for your cause. "Jim Erwin always had a hard time staying on message when he got attacked."

Oretis 'Rett' Stearns Head of Porteous who was unable to get the Maine Legislature to eliminate Maine's blue laws, but then singlehandedly pushed through the Sunday Sales referendum in 1990 and changed Maine's shopping patterns.

Marshall Stern   Former Muskie staffer and major fund-raiser for Democratic candidates and causes. For many years, a major player until his untimely death in a car crash. Was close to George Mitchell.

Ray W. Stetson   Three-time Republican primary loser in the 1st Congressional District, Stetson lost races in 1948, '50, and '54, garnering 9.7%, 19.3%, and 6.2% of the vote, respectively.

Greg 'Zen Master' Stevens   President of Greg Stevens and Company (now Stevens, Reed, Curchio and Company) whose very effective TV commercials helped turn a close Republican primary lead into a smashing victory for Susan Collins in 1996. A national player who developed perhaps the single most humorous political commercial of the 1980's (if you are a Republican), that of Mike Dukakis riding around in a tank, which made Dukakis look like *Mad* magazine protagonist Alfred E. Neuman. Began in Maine politics as a fieldman for Bill Cohen, became Olympia Snowe's administrative assistant and eventually worked with Roger Ailes. Major national player.

Stick a Fork in Him/Her, He's/She's Done   Finished, done. "Stick a fork in her, she's done. The Congressional race is over."

Arthur Stilphin   Longtime Democratic activist, especially in 1st District politics, charter Brennanista. Was Public Safety Commissioner in Brennan's cabinet, 1979–1982. Campaign manager for Joe Brennan in 1996, perhaps closing out an era.

Stonewall   To refuse to admit something. "He's not very good at stonewalling; this is going to backfire. If a candidate can't stonewall and do it right, he's better off coming clean right away."

Straight Shot   A good political situation, one you should win. "For Muskie, it would have been a crap shoot against Cohen but a straight shot against Monks." (See also "Crap Shoot.")

Straits of Florida   In the days of pirates and privateers, the Straits of Florida represented a wonderful opportunity to hijack the treasure fleets of Spain as they headed home. Refers to a situation in politics where you are able to win with resolute action. "We didn't get into the Straits of

Florida until early November but when we got there, by God, we knew what to do."

Strategic Marketing Services (SMS) Portland polling firm which is a division of Pan Atlantic Consulting. SMS seldom does work for political candidates but often releases political match-ups and referendum question results to the press. Insiders love to see these releases because candidates and causes then insist on having their own updated polling information to prove or disprove the findings of SMS. (See also "Pan Atlantic Consulting.")

Street People In politics, street people are specialists who work the streets doing door-to-door canvassing, putting up lawn signs, and bringing people to the polls on election day.

Stress Familiar Thoughts Best advice ever given to new candidates with primaries; attributed to Horace "Hoddy" Hildreth Jr. who ran for Congress in 1968. Refers to making party regulars feel at home by sounding like one of them. "Don't sound too 'new,' stress familiar thoughts."

Stroke To flatter, praise, give attention to. "Look at him stroke those civilians. You'd think election day was tomorrow."

Structure In polling, the structure of opinion refers to who holds that opinion and where they are located. "Gun control isn't just a rural issue in Maine; its structure is much more widespread. It goes right up the Franklin arterial."

Robert S. Stuart Republican candidate for Congress in 1970, getting 19% of the vote in the Republican primary.

Studmuffin Political term for handsome, virile male candidate who can exhibit a softer, caring side. "Ken Curtis is a studmuffin. So is John Reed."

The Stuffed Animal Room The west end of the first floor of the Maine Statehouse where a tribute to large dead fish and mammals from Maine is on permanent exhibit. Also a Democratic term for the Republican Legislative Caucus.

Stumps Don't Lie   Anti-clear cutting bumper strip seen during the referendum on forest practices in 1996.

Sucking Hind Tit   GOB slang for coming in last, not doing well. "After those commercials the poor guy is still sucking hind tit." On Maine farms apparently some pigs don't get as much nourishment as others if they only get to suck on the sow's hind tit.

Sucking the Numbers   Shorthand version of "sucking the numbers off a credit card," meaning an act or statement of extreme sychophantism. "Get that disgusting maggot away from the governor; he's been sucking the numbers all night long."

Suede on Suede   Congresswoman Olympia Snowe, based on her appeal to Yuppie women in the 1st Congressional District. "I told you she'd do great on the Gold Coast; she's suede on suede." (See also "The Gold Coast.")

Sufficient Unto the Day   Short for Matthew 6:34, "Sufficient unto the day is the evil thereof." Words to soothe rattled candidates who tend to worry about things they are going to have to do next month or next year if at all. Getting a candidate to focus on the campaign one day at a time is often one of the toughest jobs for any consultant or campaign manager.

Suits   Washington-based political operatives held in disdain by Maine political operatives. "Did you see what the suits did to Brennan's campaign? Typical. They didn't even listen to Joe. Those guys still don't get it."

Charles 'Charlie' Summers   Republican candidate for Congress in 1994, received 25% of the vote in the First District primary. Now staffer for Senator Olympia Snowe.

Sun Journal   Formerly know as the *Lewiston Sun Journal* but now becoming a more regional paper with expanded coverage into Oxford and Franklin Counties. Circulation around 40,000. Many insiders believe it has the most balanced team of political reporters of any paper in the state.

Super Susan   Nickname coined by Davis Rawson, reporter, and then editor for Waterville's *Morning Sentinel* and Augusta's *Kennebec Journal* for Susan Collins when she ran for the U.S. Senate in 1996. Rawson believed that Collins would be the Republican candidate with the best chance to defeat Democrat Joe Brennan.

Surrogate   A stand-in for a candidate or office holder. The selection and use of surrogates is really an art form in politics. There are so many invitations to so many appearances and debates that it is very important to use the candidate only for those which are critical. Sending a surrogate to forums which are useless or stacked in favor of one's opponent relieves pressure on the candidate. There is a world of difference, however, between a surrogate for a candidate and a surrogate who thinks he or she is the candidate. "Look at that jerk; he thinks he's the surrogate Senator. We're not going to send that loose cannon out for us again." (See also "Loose Cannon.")

La Survivance   Long-term nationalistic campaign among Franco Americans to maintain their language, culture and religion. Supported by French newspapers, societies and many of the Catholic churches and their parochial schools. Believed that a "loss of language meant a loss of faith, and a loss of faith meant a loss of identity." Movement gradually faded in the 1960's as more and more Franco Americans became truly assimilated into Maine society.

Elizabeth 'Betsy' Sweet   Campaign manager for Tom Andrews in the 1990 Congressional primary and longtime political activist working on a variety of campaigns including the ERA referendum of 1984.

Sweet Thing   Harry the Horse's name for any female of the human species. Actually any female of the higher primates. (See also "Horse.")

Swisher's #1 Brother   George Mitchell. George's brother John, known as "Swisher," was a basketball star and assistant coach at Colby College. In 1994, George was given a special basketball jersey which said "Swisher's #1 Brother" on it.

T

Use your talents

while you

still have them.

DR. DAVID L. GLUSKER

The Tailor's Son　Less-than-affectionate term for Senator Muskie. Attributed to Jane Muskie in *The Boys on the Bus* who, when asked to sew a button on his suit coat, replied, "You're the tailor's son; sew the button back on yourself."

Take a Powder　From the old expression meaning to take a headache powder and not go to an event. Now tends to mean a more purposeful rejection of an event. "I told her to take a powder on the Yarmouth Clam Festival. Too many yuppies and not enough real people."

Take-No-Prisoners Style　A candidate who is harsh and unrelenting in his or her criticism is said to have a take-no-prisoners style. "Usually, the Maine electorate does not respond favorably to a take-no-prisoners style."

Take the Bite   To win the battle of sound bites. Getting a pithy one-liner in ahead of your opponent. "Susan Collins won the debate but Jonathan Carter took the bite."

Take the Hot Hand   Hot-tar construction term for burning your hand but not dropping the tar bucket. If you drop the tar bucket to save your hand, you burn the rest of your body. In Maine politics it means taking short-term heat for longer-term gain. "Take the hot hand on Medicare and keep moving. Nobody will remember that one vote."

Edward D. 'Rab' Talberth   Political reporter, Gannett Newspapers (preceded Peter Damborg), important in 1946–1952 period.

Gerald Talbot   First African American to serve in the Maine House where he served from 1973 to 1979, and Democratic activist from Portland.

Talking Heads   Political slang for TV reporters and newscasters who are regarded as easy to spin because of their lack of knowledge of the basics of Maine politics. (See also "Sourceless and Senseless.")

Talle and Mala   Charles and Marlene Petersen, longtime Republican activists and focus group participants who function as Republican bellweather voters for the Portland area. Insiders also know them as some of the first troops Bill Cohen ever commanded as he started his first day's walk across the state from Gilead, Maine.

Tamp Down   To suppress your opponents' activities by smothering them with generated calls and letters. "BIW did a masterful job of tamping down when they went for those tax breaks."

Wakine G. 'Walking Tanoose' Tanous   Three-term Republican State Senator from Millinocket. Ran for governor in 1974, finishing 3rd in the Republican primary with 19% of the vote.

Tapeworm In   To get inside a campaign at a low level and then move up to get more and more control. "No way we are going to hire him. He just wants to tapeworm in and he'll make all of our lives miserable."

Lance 'Tap' Tapley   For many years Chair of Common Cause in Maine. He led the successful 1976 referendum initiative to save Bigelow Mountain from development and that referendum started the modern spurt of referenda so dear to the heart of Maine political consultants. Tapley was also an early campaign manager for Dick Barringer in 1994.

Swift Tarbell   Republican representative from Bangor. Famous in insider folklore for having been thrown out of the Maine House by Speaker John Martin for being a young whipper snapper. A bulldog on reapportionment as well. "Watching Swift and Eddie dividing up Bangor during redistricting was worth the price of admission, those two guys traded blocks back and forth like they were trading cards."

Target Audience   The portion of the electorate targeted for a TV or radio buy. "Our target audience with Lobster Boy was the male bonding crowd." (See also "Lobster Boy.")

The Tarrance Group   Washington-based Republican polling firm. Did David Emery in 1982.

Tax Gadfly   Al Diamon's name for Mary Adams who, he declared, "ran in '94 without anybody noticing."

Teach It Flat or Teach It Round   As in, "Is the world flat or round?" Consultant-speak for being able to work with a conservative or a liberal candidate. "It makes no difference to me; if I like the guy I can teach it flat or teach it round."

Telegraph the Punch   Phrase from an earlier era when people still communicated by telegraphs. Means to show what you are going to do in your campaign before you should, "to tip your hand." "It was incredible, on primary night, Joe was talking about AK-47's, telegraphing the punch for all to see."

Tell Me about It   Don't tell me about it, I know it already. "Muskie will be tough to beat? Tell me about it."

Term Limits   A plot by big states with many representatives in Washington to limit the power of small states, like Maine, by making sure they have a turnover in representation and never achieve any real influence in Congress. Ruled unconstitutional for U.S. Senate and Congressional officers by the U.S. Supreme Court in 1996.

Terminal   A candidate whose campaign is irrevocably doomed. "He's so terminal everybody else could drop out of the race and he'd still lose."

Testimonial Ad   An ad in which an ordinary person or a famous one endorses a candidate or cause. Usually such ads try to find good things about the person or cause endorsed. Some of these ads are bigger challenges than others.

That's a Wrap   An expression from film and TV commercial making. Its political meaning is usually "It's over, let's move on." "Come on, Governor, that's a wrap, the car is waiting."

That's All She Wrote   Nothing else, finished. "At this point, he cannot get back the Francos. That's all she wrote."

That's Washington on the Line   Consultant-speak for "I have another, more important call." "That's a great idea, but I have Washington on the line. I'll get back to you."

There Are Eleven Bostons, Many Londons, But Only One Skowhegan   Slogan of Margaret Chase Smith for her hometown newspaper, the *Skowhegan Independent Reporter*, when she worked for its advertising and circulation departments.

There's No There There   Consultant-speak—usually with no thanks to Gertrude Stein—for a very poor campaign, a less than influential interest group or a dumb candidate. "I tried all I could but frankly, there's no there there."

Think about It   Campaign slogan for Jim Longley for Governor in 1974. Developed by Jack Havey of Ad Media, the slogan is credited with focusing late deciding voters on Longley as the Independent alternative, leading to his victory.

Think about It: Vote Green   Not-so-original campaign slogan used by the Green party during the 1994 gubernatorial race in which their candidate, Jonathan Carter, received almost 6% of the vote. Jack Havey of Ad Media was not their consultant of record.

The Third Floor   The third floor of the Maine Statehouse where the houses of the Legislature sit. By tradition, and because of concerns for personal safety, the governor rarely goes to the third floor, except to give a speech after all the members of the Legislature are sitting down.

This Dog Won't Hunt   A plan which won't work. "Sure it sounds like a good idea, but I'm telling you, this dog won't hunt."

Cedric H. Thomas   Republican candidate for Congress in 1966, gathered 7% of the vote in the 1st District primary.

Thou Shalt Not Speak Ill of Fellow Republicans   The Eleventh Commandment according to Dr. Gaylord Parkinson.

Thousand Vote Candidate   Davis Rawson's somewhat premature epithet for Andrew Adam. Adam actually got 48,000 votes in the 1990 gubernatorial battle, thereby costing Joe Brennan the election by digging into his prospective margins in such key Democratic districts as Lewiston.

Three-Time Loser   Candidates who have lost three or more major races in recent Maine political history. Most people miss the point that these people are not "losers" but winners because they have stayed around long enough to run for office that much. With contested primaries, it takes a lot of staying power to run and lose three times. These include Republicans Jim Erwin and Bob Monks, and Democrat Joe Brennan. Also Plato ("Two Great Names, One Great Man") Truman who ran as a Republican, a Democrat and an Independent.

Throw-Up   A big fight on the campaign trail, usually among supporters of the same candidate. "We had another throw-up with the media guys again. I can't believe the footage they want to use."

Ticket Splitters   Voters who vote for Republicans and Democrats and Independents, often in the same election. Ticket splitters are often the target of TV commercials for candidates trying to enlarge their base.

James 'Jim' Tierney   Maine Attorney General and a longtime Democratic party activist who paid his dues. Ran for governor in 1986, getting 30% of the vote after winning the Democratic primary. Subsequently finished second to Tom Andrews in the 1990 Democratic primary for Congress in the 1st District, getting 33% of the vote. Now a major player in national legal circles and a regular analyst on Court TV. Great political storyteller with a good sense of humor.

Jim Tierney Lite   Al Diamon's name for Democrat Dave Perkins when he ran unsuccessfully for Cumberland County District Attorney in 1990 against Stephanie Anderson.

Tight Screen   The polling techniques used to narrow down participation in interviews to particular segments of the electorate. "Sure, we only have 43 in that sample, but we used a very tight screen. We had them say yes to three questions about electoral participation or we didn't talk with them."

Karin Tilberg   Audubon Society leader whose passionaate defense of the "sacred wetlands" (i.e., the drainage ditches beside the highway) turned public sentiment against widening the Maine Turnpike in 1991. Also a leading advocate of campaign finance reform.

Time Delay   The period between the time a TV commercial airs and the time it registers in the tracking polls. "Wow, the time delay on that baby was only 2 nights. We've got a winner."

Time-Limit Constraints   Advertising and political research term to cover the limits of certain methodologies. For example, if you are doing mall intercepts and coming up to people at random and speaking to a parent with small children and one of them has to go to the bathroom—badly. This is called a "time-limit constraint." "The problem with mall intercepts are those damn time-limit constraints; no matter how you try to filter, you end up with a lot of them." (See also "Mall Intercepts.")

Time Speeded Up by Events   Any campaign situation where real time, i.e., 24 hours in a day, is speeded up by something your opponent does. "Damn it, she's up on TV; we'll have to move the street people activity up a week; time's been speeded up by events."

Tin Cup   Consultant-speak for fund-raising activities. "I won't carry a tin cup. It's not what I do. It's revolting to have to ask those cheapies for money."

Tin Ear   Consultant-speak for a candidate who won't take good advice. "She's got a tin ear. I've showed her four ways to win and she rejects all four of them. She wants to do it on some stupid issue."

Tit in a Wringer   GOB name for a bad, hurtful situation, often of one's own making. "Ted got his tit in a wringer when he failed to file his election reports. He thought nobody would notice." First popularized by Nixon Attorney General John Mitchell with regard to Katherine Graham of the *Washington Post* when the Watergate story first broke. Mrs. Graham may have had the last laugh, but the phrase does have a GOB sound to it.

The Titans   Refers to the four towering figures in Maine politics since World War II: Senators Margaret Chase Smith, Edmund S. Muskie, George Mitchell, and William S. Cohen. Interestingly enough, Cohen is unique among the four for never having lost an election and for never having been behind in any election in which he ran.

Bonnie Titcomb   Candidate for Congress in 1994, received 23.9% of the vote in the 1st District Democratic primary. Finished second to Duke Dutremble. An EMILY's list favorite.

TNC   The Nature Conservancy. Maine's largest (12,000) and the most influential environmental group when it comes to saving land because of its non-confrontational approach to preserving the environment. The group most responsible for the passage of the landmark $35 million Land for Maine's Future Bond in 1987. Kent Wommack and Mason Morfit of Maine's The Nature Conservancy have probably done more to advance the cause of preserving Maine's priceless natural heritage than any other duo in recent Maine history. They remain major players in that important interface where politics meets the environment. Seldom get the recognition they deserve because of their non-confrontational style.

Toast   A finished or doomed candidate. "Longley made a pretty good final run at Allen but by the last weekend, he was toast."

The Toddster   Todd Webster, Bowdoin and George Washington University graduate from Yarmouth, Maine, and press secretary for Joe Brennan in his 1996 run for the U.S. Senate. Now works for Geddings Communications in Washington. "I saw the Toddster's hand in the press release about negative advertising. He learned a lot on the Duke campaign." (See also "*The* Duke.")

TOMA   Top-of-mind awareness. Polling expression for questions which seek respondents reaction to a candidate or cause without giving them any background, not even party affiliation. "He scored very poorly on the TOMAs but when you got to the informed ballot, he took off. I think he has a lot of true upside potential." (See also "Informed Ballot.")

Too Good to Check   A story which a reporter wants to write even if it turns out to be untrue. Many times reporters get rumors and decide to write a story about the rumor rather than checking out whether the rumor is right or not. "That damn scorp, it's another too-good-to-check story and he's running with it." (See also "Scorp.")

Jeff Toorish   A political reporter for WMTW television, Jeff is often billed as a political insider by that station. He probably comes as close as any TV reporter. He is knowledgeable and not afraid to ask tough questions of political figures. Now executive director of the Maine Pulp and Paper Association.

Top Crony   Davis Rawson's name for Davey Redmond, Joe Brennan's chief of staff as governor and administrative assistant in Congress. Insiders continue to wonder why all other major office holders in Maine have "friends" while Joe Brennan is thought to have "cronies."

Toss-Up   Any contest perceived to be close in terms of possible outcome. Incumbents always face the dilemma of trying to making their positions seem secure while getting their supporters and money people to act as if the race was a toss-up. Challengers often work their entire campaigns just trying to get the press and the money people to act as if they were in a toss-up race.

Toto, We're Not in Bangor Anymore   Felicia Knight to herself after she was savaged in a Davis Rawson column for looking like "a leftover Halloween Elvira" as she moderated a Congressional campaign debate between candidates Joe Brennan and Ted O'Meara. Felicia went on to become one of the best moderators on TV. Her extremely professional handling of Bob Monks, John Hathaway and Susan Collins in the 1996 Republican primary debate is regarded by insiders as a classic.

Tough As Any Man and Twice As Smart   Complimentary phrase for female candidate who plays politics with the boys without seeking special treatment for her sex. Opposite of "Affirmative Action Babe." "Janet Mills is as tough as any man and twice as smart."

Tracker   A single cut of a tracking poll. "That last tracker is garbage; we're not 10 points behind."

Tracking   Nightly or weekly polling numbers which show the direction of a campaign. "How's your tracking? We have him dropping 20 points in less than a week."

Traction   Ability of a candidate or campaign story to hold the attention of the media. "That Leary story sure had traction. They were talking about it 10 days after he broke it."

Barbara Trafton   Along with her husband, Richard, Barbara has been an important Democratic activist in Auburn and beyond. They have both had strategic and fund-raising impact on a number of situations. Barbara also served as campaign chair for the Maine Turnpike widening effort in 1991.

Willis E. Trafton   Republican nominee for Governor in 1956, Trafton lost the general election with 40.8% of the vote. Father and father-in-law to longtime Democratic activists Richard and Barbara Trafton.

The Train Is Leaving the Station   A candidate is going to win and you'd better endorse her or him now. "Look, I could use your help but the train is leaving the station." Often if the candidate has to speak like this, the train is stalled in the station.

Transmits Better Than Receives   Candidates who are more interested in themselves than in the voters and their concerns. "She transmits better than she receives, if she receives at all."

Trash   To speak badly of another consultant after he or she had gotten an account you wanted. "Did you hear they trashed us right after the pitch."

Tree-huggers   Kind GOB name for the Green Party.

Steven 'Steve' Tremblay   Head of Alpha One in South Portland and an important behind-the-scenes player on referenda (Turnpike Widening) and bond (Adaptive Loan Equipment Bond) campaigns as well as candidates (King for governor). Very knowledgeable on disability issues.

Triage Central   Political consultant office or party center alive with activity when a major candidate drops out and there is a mad scramble for new positions. "Sorry, Sue, we've got three for Congress already. How about the State Senate?" (See also "Musical Chairs.")

Triangulation   Term attributed to consultant Dick Morris, meaning to steal ideas from your opponent while criticizing some version of those ideas as extremist and thus moving yourself into the middle of the political spectrum and hence victory. "Few Maine political figures have the moxie to try triangulation, but it does work." (See also "Moxie.")

Howard Trotsky   Republican State Senator from Bangor who led the fight to stop log drives on the Kennebec River.

William 'Billy' Troubh   Former mayor of Portland, attorney, and good friend of Joe Brennan. Troubh is the man that Brennan should have appointed to the U.S. Senate a decade earlier, if he wanted to get there himself. Also ran for Congress in the 1st District Democratic primary of 1994, losing to "Duke" Dutremble, and finishing fourth in a 4-person race with 19% of the vote (See also *"The* Duke.") Now Commissioner of the AA Eastern Baseball League.

True Believer   Any staffer or civilian who really believes in the goodness of a candidate and the badness of his or her opponent. This is a phrase of praise coming from the candidate, but a phrase of derision coming from a political consultant.

True Gin   From Ernest Hemingway, "the real deal," "the true story," "the heart of the matter," "what really happened." "I still don't know where that scorp got it, but it's the true gin."

Plato Truman   Once a State Senator (1965–1966) and then a perennial candidate from Biddeford. Ran for First District Congress in 1982, (getting 3% in the Democratic primary) and for the U.S. Senate in 1976 (getting 16% of the vote in the Republican primary). Ran for governor as Democrat in 1970, garnering 36% of the vote against Ken Curtis and for Congress against Peter Kyros in 1968, getting 16% of the vote. Subsequently ran for U.S. Senate in 1966, getting 38% in the Democratic primary. Later, in 1994, he ran for the U.S. Senate as an Independent, getting 3% of the vote. (See also "Two Great Names, One Great Man.")

To Trust Is Good, Not to Trust Is Better   Consultant motto, especially where candidate promises of payments are concerned.

The Tsarina   Republican name for Hillary Rodham Clinton for her perceived power over the President and her social and economic agenda. "I don't mind him, he's really a GOB at heart, but I don't want 4 more years of the Tsarina." (See also "GOB.")

Tube   To send something down to defeat. "She sure tubed that initiative. It's lost."

Tundra City   Davis Rawson's name for Presque Isle. Davis had the courage to call it publicly what many Southern and weak political actors call it privately. Of course, it is not tundra city during either July or August.

Stanley 'Stan' Tupper   Three-term Republican congressman (1961–1967) who refused to support Barry Goldwater when he became the party's nominee for President in 1964. This earned Stan pariah status with conservatives in Maine, but made him a staple on the political panel circuit for the next 3 decades. His electoral record puts him among the top aces in Maine political history since 1946. Re-elected with 50.1% of the vote in 1964, narrowly beating Ken Curtis. Won the Republican primary for Congress in Maine's old 2nd District in 1960 with 57% of the vote and with 53% of the vote in the general election. An independent voice for moderate Republicanism and currently one of the more interesting pundits on the Maine political scene. A real gentleman.

Our Turf/Their Turf   In ballot measures, the issues on which you can win ("our turf") as contrasted with the issues on which the other side can win ("their turf"). "In Maine Yankee I, our turf was economics. Their turf was health and safety. If we talked about radiation and health and safety, even our own supporters went against us."

Turkey   A poor candidate. "What a turkey, he can't even give the speech I wrote."

Turn-out Driven   Election results affected by those who turn out to vote. Perhaps one of the most overrated variables in American politics and certainly in the Maine version. Actually in most instances those who don't vote would have voted almost exactly like those who did. One notable exception which proves the rule was Dale McCormick's better-than-expected showing in the Democratic 1st District Congressional primary in 1996. Had all registered Democrats voted, Tom Allen would have gotten 55% of the vote instead of the 52% he actually got. The difference can be attributed to McCormick's truly outstanding get-out-the-vote effort on election day. "The 1996 Democratic Congressional primary was turn-out driven, no question about it. Allen was lucky to hang on."

Twilight Zone   Description by Frank Coffin as to his status before beginning active campaigning for Congress in 1956. "I am not a Congressman; nor am I a 'private person,' I am in the twilight zone of a political candidacy, where one bids farewell to his pipe, slippers, hearth, and home and begins the endless task of trying to cross a hundred thousand thresholds and persuade a majority of the people that he is the man for the job."

Twin Towers   Jock McKernan's name for Senators Ed Muskie and Margaret Chase Smith.

Two-Car Funeral   Lowest common denominator for organizational ability on a campaign where you are often forced to make due. "He couldn't organize a two-car funeral; we can't use him in the field, maybe he can stuff envelopes."

Two Great Names, One Great Man   Campaign slogan of Plato Truman, perennial Democratic/Republican/Independent candidate. (See also "Plato Truman.")

Two Step   Name for the process by which a supporter goes from one candidate to undecided and then from undecided to a second candidate. Few voters switch directly, especially in a general election. "In 1994, it was a classic two step. Those Democrats went from Brennan to undecided to Collins, especially in the Bangor DMA. You could see it happening over a 10-day period."

Two Tie Clasps   Political insider term for a candidate who could use some political coaching. "You see, Dave, I never let my candidates wear one tie clasp, let alone the two you are using."

Twofer   Two for one. What any citizen of Maine gets when he or she votes and only half of the registered voters do the same.

Typhoid Mary   Consultant whose clients give up and who pull out or who don't even enter a particular race after talking about it. Note, this is not a consultant whose candidates run and lose, because a candidate who runs and loses is much more valuable to the political consultant than a would-be client who doesn't run. "In 1996, he was Typhoid Mary. Three probable clients fell by the wayside, and we'd already turned their opponents down."

Tyrannosaurus Rex   John Day's name for Bill Clinton, "a new species" who has "mastered the modern political campaign and elevated it to something akin to performance art."

Robert 'Bob' Tyrer   Press secretary and then administrative assistant to Senator William S. Cohen and longtime political operative in Maine. Great spinner of inside information and likable to boot. Loyally went to Maine from Senator Cohen's office to help out on Dave Emery's Senate campaign in 1982 against George Mitchell and Susan Collins's Senate campaign in 1996 against Joe Brennan. Bright, hardworking and a real spinmeister. A major player. Now serves as Cohen's chief of staff at the Pentagon.

U

Ultra Liberal   What Republicans call Democrats they want to push to the edge of the voting spectrum. "Tom Andrews is an ultra liberal."

An Unconstitutional Solution in Search of a Nonexistent Problem Governor King's description of the ban on same-sex marriages in Maine.

Undecideds   Short for "Undecided Voters," those voters who have not made up their mind about a candidate or ballot measure race. While the goal of all campaigns is to get the maximum number of these voters, the closer one gets to the election, the less likely it is that all voters who say they are undecided will actually vote.

Under Water   Behind, not likely to catch up. "It's a terrible cycle for me, I've got 2 candidates under water and only one referendum above."

Underdog   What you want your candidate to be thought of once a race begins. What you never want your candidate to be thought of before a race begins so you can keep other candidates out of that race. What scorps love in their hearts but not in their stories. "No Senator, you've got it wrong. I know you're really up by 8 points, but you're the 'underdog.' It's all a matter of positioning."

Unholy Alliance   A strange marriage of convenience between 2 political operatives normally on opposing sides. "Watching Mary and Jonathan respond when you called their joint opposition to the Forest Compact an unholy alliance was worth the price of admission."

Unintegrated Strata   Political science term for people who live in the great state of Maine, but who are unregistered to vote. "Don't every try to get petitions signed in the Maine Mall; two-thirds of the people you get are from the unintegrated strata."

Union Households   Excellent demographic group for predictive purposes. Especially when polling mill towns, the union household members as opposed to union members themselves often give a good indication of switches in political sentiment.

Unopposed Storytelling   Having negative commercials on the air while your opponent is not on television. "We had 2 weeks of unopposed storytelling, it was glorious. We picked up 10 points."

Untainted   A candidate who is not preceded by some flunky introducing him or her badly or awkwardly. "I like it when a candidate goes in untainted; you can set your own agenda and frame your own past."

Thomas Urquart   Director of the Maine Audubon Society, the most important environmental authority figure in Maine politics.

Useful Idiot   From Lenin, someone on the other side who helps your cause without meaning to. "Did you see him on TV, he made all our points for us. He's a useful idiot if I ever saw one."

User   Technically, any political operative who uses other people for her or his own ends; i.e., every politician (and consultant!).

Usual Suspects   People on the letterhead of campaigns and candidates. Republican letterheads, for example, have lobstermen and farmers and small business people. Democrats have identifiable labor people and organizations and women's groups. "Round up the usual suspects, we have a mailing to get out."

Their Usual Suspects   The other side's letterhead. "Nothing new, it's their usual suspects."

V

The spoils of victory will be freedom.

I'll give it to my son.

MARY ADAMS

V-Day: Voting Day, Volunteer Day and Victory Day for the Smith-for Senate Volunteers   Margaret Chase Smith's battle cry during the June, 1948 Republican Senatorial primary when she faced the sitting governor, Horace Hildreth, the former governor, Sumner Sewall, and Albion Beverage. She crushed all three.

Lew 'Lew Vaf' Vafiades   Major force in the Bangor area for Bill Cohen, Olympia Snowe, and Jock McKernan and statewide supporter for moderate Republican candidates. Self-effacing and modest, he had a major impact on the course of Maine politics. A longtime player. Super guy.

William 'Bill' Vail   Popular and self-effacing commissioner of Department of Fish and Wildlife under McKernan. Began with the Department as a game warden and came up through the ranks to become commissioner. Risigned in protest over the Administration's proposal to use dedicated fish and wildlife moneys to help balance the General Fund budget.

Involved in a number of referenda supporting sportsmen and women's issues. A player. Chaired the Coaliltion for Maine Citizen for Forest and Economy, formed to promote the Forestry Compact which won a 3-way race in 1996, getting 47% of the vote.

The Valley   The St. John Valley, home of most of the Franco Americans north of Waterville. Known for its beautiful, stylish women and somewhat dour men, the Valley usually votes Democrat and as such is often avoided by Republican candidates, except when they are in the area for the Potato Blossom Festival. But Republicans who spend a lot of time there, such as Bill Cohen or Olympia Snowe, get a warm welcome.

Vanity Candidate   A candidate having no chance of winning but who is willing to spend a lot of his or her own money to pretend he or she is in a real race. "Ben Fernandez ran for President as a vanity candidate, and the voters responded accordingly."

George Varney   Finished second in the Republican primary for governor in 1948, receiving 28.7% of the vote.

William Dawes Veazie   Finished third in the Republican primary for the 1st CD in 1956, receiving 9.5% of the vote.

Robinson Verrill   Finished third in the Republican primary for governor in 1948, receiving 12% of the vote, a partner in the law firm of Verrill, Dana.

Verrill, Dana   Prominent Republican law firm from Portland and Augusta which, in the past, often functioned as the Republican State Committee.

Viable Candidate   This term is very broad when used by consultants. It can mean "She has a good chance of winning" or it can mean "He has a fair chance of raising enough money to pay at least my consulting bills." It is broader still when used by candidates themselves. "If I can get 5% of the vote by Labor Day, I'm a viable candidate."

Elmer Violette   Respected Democratic State Senator (D-Van Buren) who ran against Bill Cohen in 1972, winning the Democratic primary with 78% of the vote after losing the general election with 45% of the vote. Later he became a Maine Supreme Court justice. His campaign manager, Neil Rolde (D-York), later ran against Senator Bill Cohen in 1990, spending over $1 million of his own money and getting 39% of the vote. Previously Elmer ran against Margaret Smith in 1966 and got 41% of the vote in the general election after having gotten 45% of the vote to win the Democratic primary that year. Father of Turnpike Authority executive director Paul Violette. Classy guy.

Virgin   Any candidate who has not run for political office. Virginity is considered a very valuable commodity in politics. "He's a virgin, thank God; we can break him in right."

Visibility   Recognition of a candidate or cause. "She has very high visibility but a lot of people don't like her. You need more than visibility to win in Maine."

Visuals   TV pictures of your candidate no matter how generated. "We can't lose the battle of the visuals, get him on the 5:30 news, they have plenty of open time."

VO   Voice over. In television a very important ingredient. Voice overs are critical when the candidate has a weak or whiny voice. "The VO saved us in that spot; he sounded so whiny on his own."

Voice of God   An expensive, out-of-state voice used in commercials. "They beat us to the voice of God. We had to go to L.A. to try to come up with a counter."

Volatility   In polling, this refers to how rapidly an opinion can be changed. "The elected PUC referendum was one of the most volatile issues in recent Maine history. It was popular with over 70% of the electorate when it started and dropped to 40% in a matter of weeks."

Vote As You Shoot   Rallying cry of the sportsmen and women. Taken from the Grant for President (1868) theme "Vote As You Shoot," referring to the veterans of the Civil War who were fighting for a Republican government against the Democratic and states' rights Confederates. Much of Republican domination of 19th century Maine politics stems from this sentiment.

Vote for Yourself   Campaign slogan of Wakine Tanous when he ran for governor in the 1978 Republican primary.

Vote Green; Elect a Republican   Davis Rawson's slogan for the Green Party after they helped elect Olympia Snowe in 1992 by siphoning off votes from Democrat Pat McGowan.

Voting with Their Feet   To go and vote. "The elderly usually vote with their feet. You can count on them."

Voting with Their Rear Ends   Ralph Nader's explanation of what non-voters are really doing when they stay home and fail to vote. "They don't like either candidate so they vote with their rear ends." After harping for decades about full disclosure, Nader ran for President in 1996 and refused to disclose his finances. The press let him get away with it without a whimper, another reason many scorps are held in about as high regard as most politicians.

Vox Pop   Short for vox populi, voice of the people. "When the vox pop speaks, consultants, if not candidates, listen."

Vox Populi, Vox Humbug   William Tecumseh Sherman's statement often used by *Portland Press Herald* columnist Jim Brunelle to rail against referendum politics which he doesn't like. Jim seems to object to citizens being able to rather easily (he's right about that) get ballot measures to the public in Maine. "Democracy is a messy business, so *vox populi, vox humbug* is the price of a ticket of admission."

Vulture   Another consultant name for a member of the press corps. "Here come the vultures; they've seen the new poll numbers. They think you're road kill." (See also "Scorps" and "Road Kill.")

W

Politics is the science of how who gets

what, when and why.

HAROLD LASSWELL

Wacky Tobaccy   Marijuana. Once urged as a possible alternative to potatoes as a major crop for Aroostook County. Governor Angus King stopped the use of helicopters for surveillance of suspected marijuana growers in 1995. Governor King authorized the state police to use the helicopters again in 1996.

Waffle   To give an answer which is neither a yes or a no. Can be positive or negative depending on the saliency of the question. "She's so good at waffling they never catch her." (See also "Fudge.")

The Walk   Bill Cohen's 600-mile 1972 mile walk across the state from Gilead to Ft. Kent, a tactic which was subsequently used by Emery, Snowe, and McKernan, and which changed the public perceptions of Maine Republicans for the next two decades.

Walking Around Money   Also known as "Street Money." In many states, this refers to the sometimes legal, sometimes illegal (depending upon the state) practice of handing out money on election day for voting or for getting people to vote. In Maine, it tends to have a less specific meaning; usually it refers to some petty cash used to enable a field person to take a local pol—or the field person's buddies—out to lunch. "Most Maine campaigns are short on walking around money since TV usually takes it all."

Walk On   A candidate who turns up out of the blue without prior experience in running for political office. "Angus King is the most successful walk on of the last decade. Jim Longley, Sr. was the best example of the previous era."

Adam Walsh   Lost the Democratic primary in the 1st CD in 1958, receiving 36.5% of the vote. A key player on some of Knute Rocknes's Notre Dame football teams and later, a Bowdoin coach.

Kent 'The Old Dawg' Ward   Longtime political reporter and columnist for the *Bangor Daily News,* famous with insiders and other scorps for recycling his great political moments. Also a much appreciated tower of strength against political correctness. Kent is beloved by many Eastern Maine readers and pickup truck drivers. His good-natured wit and ability to laugh at himself endears him to most factions on the Maine political scene. "I swear to you, Kent is using that Connally stuff again. I think it's the 11th time he's used it."

Richard 'Rick" Warren   Publisher of the *Bangor Daily News.* Loves Republican candidates and conservative Independents. Likes to use his influence in political races.

Warriors   Candidates who have proven themselves in electoral battles. "It may be surprising, but the top warriors of the last half century in Maine are Snowe, Cohen, Muskie and McKernan." (See the chapter, "The Warriors.")

Wash   (1) A TV flight which doesn't lead to any net gain to your candidate or cause. "It's a wash. We just spent $60K for a wash."

Wash   (2) A campaign strategy which calls for a tie in one part of the state, or with one demographic group, but counts on winning big in some other part or with some other group. "Give me a wash north of Augusta and we'll win the Turnpike Widening referendum."

Bonnie Washuk   Solid political reporter for the *Sun Journal*. Spinnable. Good sense of balance and takes political information with a grain of salt unless verifiable. According to numerous insiders, the Lewiston papers now have one of the best and most balanced political reporting teams of any of the daily newspapers.

The Way   A religious group in Maine during the 1970's, believed to be headquartered in Litchfield. Supported the 1978 candidacy of Hayes Gahagan when he ran for the U.S. Senate. Not much has been heard of the movement politically since Hayes got 7% of the vote.

We Cannot Escape History   Abraham Lincoln's famous quote, often used by consultants to bemoan the candidate's past. "What can we do? We cannot escape history; the jerk did that ten years ago."

We Need a Senator Who Is Young   For the record, neither Bob Monks nor Bill Hathaway in 1972 said this first. It was Joe McCarthy surrogate Robert Jones during his 1954 primary challenge to Margaret Chase Smith. He was 34, she was 56 at the time. She was 74 when Monks and Hathaway ran against her.

William 'Bill' Webster   Very important and unheralded innovator in Maine's political culture. Campaign manager who brought modern political campaigning techniques such as the use of computers to Maine in 1972 on behalf of Robert Monks when Monks ran for the U.S. Senate against Margaret Chase Smith bringing Bill up from Boston. Bill decided that he liked Maine and stayed on, having brought Maine politics into the modern era. As such, he had a major impact on the course of its politics. Insiders credit him with many of the innovations—such as the use of computer-generated letters, scientific scheduling and targeting segmentation—now taken for granted in Maine political campaigns. Webster also organized and directed the successful 1972 effort to eliminate the Big Box, a seminal event in Maine political history. (See also "Big Box.")

Wedge Issue   Any issue which enables a candidate to gain support at his or her opponent's expense. An issue which separates one candidate from another. "Olympia used Loring and gun control as wedge issues against Tom Andrews, and she ended up crushing him."

This Week in New England   Channel 8's public affairs program on Sundays at 12:30 P.M. This program is loved by insiders. Its relatively low viewership makes it ideal for the test running of candidates, causes and spokespeople.

Gordon Weil   Press secretary for George McGovern in 1972, worked with Joe Brennan on his successful 1978 gubernatorial campaign. Now a selectman in Harpswell, Maine. Also author of an interesting book on the 1972 presidential campaign of George McGovern, *Long Shot*.

We'll Never Get Them   A surprisingly important insight which political consultants often bring to the table. Civilians would be amazed at how much campaign time is taken up by thinking about getting support from people who already oppose your candidate or cause. Campaigns are always won by turning out one's own supporters and by getting the undecided rather than by trying to get those opposed to you. "The right wing? We'll never get them."

We're in Good Shape   Peter Burr's phrase which had nothing to do with how well a candidate or cause is doing but how much polling data is flowing in. "I got the overnights; we're in good shape for the weekend."

We're Looking at Our Own Polling Data   Bob Woodward recounting Ken Duberstein's comment when told by Senator Warren Rudman that Dole would beat General Colin Powell in the New Hampshire Republican primary and asked if Duberstein would like to see the Dole polling numbers. The Colin Powell for President polling in New Hampshire was done by Dr. Demento, who projected that Powell would beat Dole handily, getting at least 38% of the vote.

West Wing   Political portion of the White House. "Lynn Nofziger was supposed to come to the Republican state convention, but the West Wing needed him that day."

Wet Dream   A great consulting situation where the consultant has lots of control and makes lots of money. "Tons of money and very little supervision. I tell you it's a wet dream."

Whack Him First   Consultant advice to go negative first. "I tell you, Duke, you need to whack him first."

Whack Them Both   Consultant advice to go negative on everyone. "If you're going to do it, do it to both of them."

What Did He Know and When Did He Know It?   Senator Howard Baker's reference to President Richard Nixon concerning Watergate. Now a staple among insiders who, putting the most cynical spin on *everything*, hitch their observation to the phrase. "The private eye? What did he know and when did he know it?"

What Is Woman's Place? Everywhere   Margaret Chase Smith's much publicized speech during the 1948 Republican primary for U.S. Senate. A feminist without underscoring it, Senator Smith proved she could take on the big boys and win at their game.

What Ever Happened to Local Control?   A voter interest group concerned with issues of local control, generally active on a number of referenda in the 1980's. "We need some bodies at that hearing, call up and get 'What Ever Happened to Local Control?' Busy."

Whatever   No difference, no consequence. "May has organized Etna and Carmel? Whatever."

Where Are the New People?   Astute candidate lament when, giving a number of speeches during the day, sees mostly his or her entourage and staff people in the audience. "Jack Wyman was always asking, "Where are the new people?"

Whisper Numbers   Polling numbers believed to be the real ones, despite what politicians say. "Monks told the Sun King he had 35%. Day thinks the whisper number is really 28%."

White Boys   Sarcastic reference to most male players on the Maine political scene. Usually a Democratic epithet. "Those white boys don't know their asses from their elbows but they get all the money." Can also apply to males who are either not sympathetic enough on women's issues, or too sympathetic, as in "He's a pathetic white boy."

White Tail   White tail deer, the totem animal of the GOBs in Maine. How the GOBs rate the health of the north woods. "I don't care what the politicians say; the only thing that counts is the number of white tails." (See also "GOBs.")

The Whole Ball of Wax   The entire ballgame. "That negative spot in 1994 was the whole ball of wax for Longley. He won because of it. Before he went on the air, he was losing, yet he won by 2%. Seems pretty clear to me."

Wholesale Politics   Getting votes in big bunches, usually with TV or other electronic means. "Give me wholesale politics any day, it's so much easier on the candidate." Referendum politics are almost always wholesale in nature.

Whores for Numbers   Pollsters. "They don't really care about this campaign; they're just whores for numbers."

Who Struck John?   Constant campaign lament. Candidate campaigns are particularly prone to backstabbing and ongoing feuds leading to midnight calls to the candidate, formation of factions and ongoing splits among supporters and consultants. Insiders use this generic term to describe it. "I get so tired of who struck John? Can't we have one meeting and concentrate on just our opponent?

Who's the Client?   Who is going to pay our bills? Also used by candidates when they want to get their way over the advice of their consultants. "I won't use that spot. Who's the client anyway?"

Whose Ox Is Being Gored?   Whose fee schedule will be cut if there is a strategy change, i.e., from TV to field operations or vice versa. "Sure, it looks like a good plan but whose ox is being gored? You're cutting my portion of the budget."

Why Give Up a Dictatorship for a Democracy   Insider response to the question: "Why did John Martin never run for higher offices such as Congressman or Senator?"

Why Me, Oh Lord?   Consultant's lament when a candidate does a stupid, damaging thing which threatens his or her chances for victory and the consultant's chance for a bonus or even being paid his or her existing bills. "He did what? Why me, oh Lord?"

Why Not?   Why not get involved in politics and have some fun and do your civic duty at the same time?

James Russell Wiggins   Revered longtime editor and publisher of the *Ellsworth American.* His editorials are always of high quality and make you think, even if you disagreed with their thrust.

Patricia 'Patsy' Wiggins   Pleasant and affable host of Maine Public Television's "Maine Watch." Even when she asks politicians tough questions, she seems very nice. Retiring in the fall of 1997.

The Wild, Wild East   The psychological dimension of Maine which explains why we think we are on the frontier and why some of us want to kill coyotes and deer and others of us want to bring back wolves, why some of us—those that have been here the longest—want to spear and eat dolphins and why others of us want to release big lobsters into the Gulf of Maine, why some of us want to stop the cutting of trees and why others want to increase the cutting and why so many people from so many places—from Japan to Ethiopia—come and stand at the trout pool in L.L. Bean's and have a mystical experience.

Will Rogers Never Met Him/Her   Harsh judgment of a candidate or political player, ironic inversion of the saying attributed to Will Rogers: "I never met a man I didn't like."

Christopher Williams Staff writer for the *Sun Journal Sunday*. Good in-depth political reporting. One of the better reporters for long background pieces. Spinnable.

Roger Williams Advertising Portland-based firm led by Roger Williams and includes Jane Williams and Betty Angel. Has a lot of political advertising experience (Charles Cragin, Jim Longley Jr. and Dave Emery). Did a masterful job in winning the $35 million bond issue for public lands which had been defeated earlier. Dan Davidson provided a public relations dimension for the firm during the 1980's.

Wing and a Prayer A campaign with no game plan. "There is no game plan and it shows; they're flying on a wing and a prayer."

Win, Lose or Draw I'm done; I'm out of here no matter what.

Winner Almost anybody who gets involved in politics.

Charles 'Chuck' Winner Came to Maine in 1980 with his Los Angeles-based political consulting firm, Winner/Wagner, and won the Save Maine Yankee I effort. Bright, decisive and and delight to work with, Chuck forever changed the way ballot measure campaigns are conducted in Maine. Insiders know him for having "The smile of an angel, the teeth of a shark." Taught many consultants how to structure a contract and retain control over a ballot measure operation.

Withdrawal The intense pain, longing and feeling of emptiness experienced by a political junkie when an election cycle is over. The only known antidote is to get involved in another election.

Eldwin A. Wixson Finished fourth in the Republican primary for Congress in the 2nd CD in 1948, receiving 3.6% of the vote.

Women in the Home Most important swing group for television. Contrasted with "Men" and "Women Outside the Home," women in the home are easy to target with cheaper TV and are hence a very desirable segment in any candidate or ballot measure campaign. Men inside the home and men outside the home tend to vote the same, but not women.

Wonder Woman (1) Joy O'Brien, Democratic activist and Secretary of the Maine Senate for 13 of the last 15 years.

Wonder Woman (2) Barbara Billings, vice president of the Patten Corporation, who personally came to Maine and charmed the appropriate legislators into doing the Donnell Pond deal, which enabled Patten Corporation to continue working in Maine long enough to sell off its inventory of land in Maine. Patten now operates in Florida and Texas.

Wonder Woman (3) Edie Smith, Republican activist and political consultant known for her grass-roots organizational skills. Now executive director of the Maine Funeral Directors' Association.

Wonder Woman (4) Pat Eltman, Democratic activist and right-hand woman for Speaker John Martin. Perhaps the most effective party organizer in the Democratic party during the period under review. Also renowned among northern Maine GOBs for having shot a moose. (See also "The Speaker.")

Wonder Women Joy O'Brien and Pat Eltman, Democratic activists renowned for their organizational and get-out-the-vote skills. Largely credited by insiders with keeping the Maine Legislature Democratic for so many election cycles.

Wonderbar Chief political hangout and eatery in Biddeford, owned and operated by the politically important Droggitis family. Although a political clubhouse of prominent Democrats such as the Dutrembles, the Wonderbar always welcomed the likes of Dave Emery and Bill Cohen. A favorite stop of Ed Muskie, even before his son Steve married Alexis Droggitis! A lot of political history occurred here. For example, it was the site of a meeting between Bob Jones and Senator Joe McCarthy when the latter came to Maine to get Jones to run against Senator Margaret Chase Smith in 1954.

Robert 'Bob' Woodbury   Chancellor of the University of Maine who ran in the Democratic primary for governor in 1994, getting 8% of the vote.

Wooden Ballot Box   A potent symbol from a kinder, gentler era. In many Maine towns, wooden ballot boxes are still used, and when the nice white-haired lady pulls back the top and lets you put in your paper ballot it is possible—just possible—to imagine that your individual vote still does make a difference.

Mark Woodward   Previous editor of the editorial page of the *Bangor Daily News*. Insiders expected, and usually got, endorsements of Republicans and occasional conservative Independents and Democrats such as John Baldacci, but Woodward had a reputation for being relatively openminded and fair and someone who honored off-the-record conversations. In 1997, he briefly became communications director for Senator Susan Collins, later returning to the BDN as managing editor.

Word on the Street   Consultan ploy for getting the attention of the client. "The word on the street, Congressman, is that you are completely out of touch." Often the "word on the street" is the word inside the consultant's head.

Work the Refs   Call up reporters who are not favoring you cause or candidate and yell at them in a nice way. They won't change that particular story but they will probably bend things a little the next time around to even things out. Many reporters actually like to think of themselves as "balanced." "That was a terrible story, it's time to work the refs."

Worst Campaign Money Could Buy   Republican insider epithet for Bob Monks's ill-starred campaign for the Republican nomination for the U.S. Senate in 1996.

Wounded   A candidate who is hurt in the polls and therefore in the minds of the scorps. "Fred Nutter looked at me like I had terminal cancer. I'm not that wounded, am I?"

Wyatt Earp   A premier gunslinger. "I think she's the real Wyatt Earp of this cycle."

Jasper S. 'Jack' Wyman   Democrat House member (1977–1980) but later conservative Republican candidate and head of the Christian Civic League. Ran for the U.S. Senate as a Republican in 1988 and received almost 19% of the vote against George Mitchell. Ran for governor in 1994, finishing third with 17% of the vote. Probably deserves some of the barbs tossed his way but still, his presence on the Maine political scene made it more interesting and colorful, and virtually no one else during the period under review actually ever tried to bring Pro-Life and Pro-Choice factions together. Now working in Connecticut for Chuck Colson's Prison Ministry and serving on the local school board. A very engaging guy

Y

You can't beat

somebody

with nobody.

CAMPAIGN ADAGE

Yank and Bank   BNAS aviator slang for pulling back on the stick and moving to the right or the left. In Maine politics, it means a high-speed turn by a politician. "As soon as that NOW crowd got after her, she yanked and banked and before they knew it, she was gone." (See also "BNAS.")

Yankee Primary   A truly ugly attempt to bring together 6 states which have spent 200 years trying to stay apart. Presidential primaries in 5 of the 6 New England states labeled as one. First held in 1996 on "Junior Tuesday" to distinguish it from the next week's "Super Tuesday." (See also "Junior Tuesday.")

The Yard   The Kittery Naval Shipyard (if one lives in Maine) or the Portsmouth Naval Shipyard (if one lives in New Hampshire). Term is generally used to refer to the workers at the submarine repair facility as in

"You can tell a guy from the Yard, you just can't tell him much." The single largest political interest group in York County is made up of the Yard families and relatives who tend to vote pro-defense, pro-labor, and pro-incumbent, especially if the incumbent has gotten new contracts for the Yard. Politicians often encounter this group shopping in New Hampshire where they can avoid sales taxes. Even liberal candidates tend to favor submarines and frigates, although it hurts them inside when they do.

Year of the Elephant   1994, when the Republican Party took control of both the United States House and Senate for the first time in 40 years. (See also "Year of the Republican.")

Year of the Republican   1994, when the Republican party took control of both the United States House and Senate for the first time in 40 years. (See also "Year of the Elephant.")

Yellow Dog Vote   The bare minimum vote a Democrat or Republican Party-endorsed candidate will get just for showing up. For example, a yellow dog running as a Democrat would get 10%. Ten percent, however, is considered excellent for an Independent. For example, Andrew Adam running as an Independent in 1990 got 9%. The Green Party candidate for governor in 1994, Jonathan Carter, got almost 6%.

York County   Once a Democratic stronghold, it is now a behavioral Republican county, perhaps due to disillusionment with Democratic policies as a result of its getting much of its TV, and migration, from Boston, Massachusetts, and New Hampshire.

You Can Fool Some of the People All of the Time and All of the People Some of the Time—And Those Ain't Bad Odds   Consultant's credo.

You'll Never Work in this Town Again   Defeated candidate's threat to consultants. Utterly without merit or impact on future activities. (See "A Setting Sun Casteth Little Light.")

Christine Young   Important political reporter for the *Sun Journal,* and reporter for WMTW television. Has a deserved reputation for fairness, and her stories show a depth and understanding of the political process sometimes lacking in those of many other scorps.

Clifton H. 'Cliff' Young   Republican candidate for Congress. Received 21% of the vote against Bob Porteous in 1972.

Paul Young   Ran for governor in 1994, finishing fifth with 11% of the vote in the Republican primary and then ran for Congress against John Baldacci in 1996, receiving 23% of the vote. He has vowed to run again.

Young Turks   Democratic insider term for a cohort of young Democratic legislators such as Jack Cashman, Greg Nadeau, John Lisnik, Ed Kane, Dan Gwadosky and Paul Jacques who, because of the longevity and power of John Martin and Joe Brennan, did not run for the higher offices.

Yuppies   Any upscale voters who now influence elections in Maine, they voted for McKernan over Brennan in 1990, and for King over Collins and Brennan in 1994. Selected Tom Andrews over Dave Emery for Congress in 1990, and Olympia Snowe for Senate over Tom Andrews in 1994. Polling shorthand for upscale voters regardless of where they live.

Politics is not

a zero-sum game.

PROFESSOR C. P. POTHOLM

Paul F. 'Zorro' Zendzian   Democratic candidate for Congress in the Second District. Received 48% of the vote in the primary, losing to James P. Dunleavy in 1982.

Zero-Sum   Term from game theory meaning one actor wins everything and one loses everything. Politics sometimes appears to civilians as a zero-sum game but it seldom is. (See also "Mini-Max.")

Zinger   Smart, effective put-down of a candidate or a scorp. "I turned the tables on him; what a zinger I got off."

Stephen Zirnkilton   Got 26% of the vote in the 1994 Republican primary for Congress in Maine's 2nd CD, settling for that contest when Susan Collins decided to run for the Senate. Well known for doing many Hollywood voice overs.

ACES AND BASES

I am often asked by students what are the most salient features of Maine's political scene. Looking over the sweep of the last 50 years of Maine politics, I believe there are a number of trends and dynamics which are both important and relevant to a deeper and better understanding of election outcomes. In this section, I have chosen a half dozen to illustrate some of the more important practical aspects of Maine politics, many of which I had not had in focus when I began this study, and many of which are often overlooked by observers of the Maine political scene.

(1) Contrary to popular belief, in large measure the Maine electoral scene since World War II for Congress, U.S. Senate and governor has been dominated by Republican candidates. Republicans continue to have far more success in races for these offices than Democrats, Independents, Greens or Reform Party members.

(2) The Maine electorate, and indeed, even a plurality of Republican and Democratic primary voters, are more likely to be moderate than either conservative or liberal. Despite the print and electronic media attention often given the extreme elements in both political parties, in terms of Maine electoral outcomes, "the center holds."

(3) The Franco-American portion of the population, numbering 17–18% of the voting cohort—especially since 1972—has become the most important swing vote in the state. Franco Americans are the group which I have found most consistently determines the outcomes of both candidate and ballot measures in Maine.

(4) Independents, those not enrolled in a political party, number 39% of the total voter pool and actually are two different groups, one of which is very important to the political process, one of which is totally irrelevant. In reality, the election of Independent candidates to major office only oc-

curs when there is a de facto alliance between urban Franco Democrats, rural and small-town Republicans and the relevant unenrolled voters. Independents in and by themselves do not accomplish much unless there are massive defections from the Republicans and/or the Democrats.

(5) Women who work at home are another important, often unrecognized swing vote. They determine the outcome of many elections, both for candidates and ballot measures. Especially in ballot measure campaigns, they not only provide the margin for victory or defeat, they often telegraph statewide outcomes before the fact.

(6) Usually, geography qua geography does not play much of a part in determining election outcomes except in the most ironic sense of the dominance of candidates from northern Maine over those from southern Maine. It has been my experience that in terms of preparation for statewide races, coming from the much larger, much more rural northern 2nd CD is almost always better than coming from the southern 1st CD.

Let us look at each of these in turn:

The ongoing dominance of Republicans.

When I began this book, I actually had in the back of my mind a model of a very "balanced" Maine politics. For virtually all of my political life, I have operated with a model of roughly one-third Republicans, one-third Democrats and one-third Independents in the state. In point of fact, there are now more unenrolled "Independents" than either Republicans or Democrats, and Republican enrollments have been in steady proportional decline since World War II. But in terms of predicting election outcomes, the ⅓,⅓,⅓ model has worked very well, since the unenrolled actually vote in lower numbers than either Republicans or Democrats, and rural Republicans tend to vote in high enough numbers to offset any ongoing Democratic advantage.

I assumed that this numerical balance translated into electoral balance over time.

Also, being a college professor, I always try to make my lectures balanced and to give all sides in political debates an equal opportunity to make their case, so my sense of Maine politics also reflected this sense of balance and proportion.

Thus, although I knew that Republicans had dominated Maine politics until the mid-1950's, I had the impression that the two major parties had been fairly evenly matched since that time. And with the success of two Independent governors, Longley in 1974 and King in 1994, plus the surprising second place showing of Ross Perot in Maine's 2nd CD during the Presidential election of 1994, I had a sense of surging Independent voters now leading to a more balanced political set of outcomes.

Moreover, the generalized prestige of both Ed Muskie and George Mitchell and the seeming domination of the state Legislature by Democrats in general and John Martin in particular for much of the last two decades also served to give me a somewhat exaggerated impression of Democratic ascendancy and control in the context of the overall political system of Maine.

Yet nothing could be further from the truth.

For the last 50 years, Republicans have dominated the important electoral patterns of the state.

From World War II until the present, Republicans have won far more elections for Congress, the U.S. Senate and governor than have Democrats. While this was a more pronounced pattern in the earlier portion of the period under review, it remains true overall.

Looking at Republican vs. Democratic patterns since World War II by decade, these outcomes can be clearly seen. In the decade and a half from World War II (1946) until 1960, the Republicans won 31 of 38 contests for governor, Congress and the U.S. Senate for a very impressive winning percentage of 81.5%. Democrats were able to win only one out of five races. This dominance helps to underscore just how impressive was the impact of Ed Muskie on the political scene of Maine.

The Democratic upsurge following the successful run for governor by Ed Muskie in 1954 changed Maine politics dramatically. The Muskie "revolution" or "reformation" of the political dynamics began in 1954 but actually saw its fruition in the following decade. From 1954 until 1970, the Democrats won 18 out of 35 contests for a narrow winning percentage of 52% to 48% as Democratic gains in enrollment and the example and force of personality of Ed Muskie attracted or inspired many high-quality candidates such as Frank Coffin, Ken Curtis, Bill Hathaway and Peter Kyros.

Democrats recruited high-quality candidates, and their success attracted the interest of others.

This phenomenon of the Muskie revolution and the upsurge in Democratic enrollment which followed his success in 1954 has rightly been the center of much scholarly and media attention. Starting off with only 90,000 Democrats out of 480,000 registered voters, Ed Muskie made it possible for many other Democrats to have the hope that they could run good campaigns and not be swamped by Republican pluralities (and those pluralities shrunk year by year as older Republican voters died off and newer, younger voters were more likely to be Democrats). This Democratic revolution captured the popular and scholarly imaginations for much of the last 20 years, as well it should have.

But a historical overview is needed to put the Muskie revolution in perspective. Only during the immediate period following the Muskie revolution did Democrats in Maine win a majority of elections for any period. The emphasis on the Muskie revolution has thus far obscured an even more profound trend in Maine politics, one which has been much overlooked and under-studied until the present day. For however important the Muskie reformation of Maine politics in the late 1950's and early 1960's is, it was matched by an equally important "counter-reformation" or "counter-revolution" begun by Bill Cohen in 1972. This electoral shift led to a return to a most pronounced pattern of Republican success.

While a lot has been written about Bill Cohen and his personal achievements, virtually all observers have missed the extent to which his victory in 1972 for Congress, followed by his near race against Ed Muskie during 1975 and his subsequent victory over Bill Hathaway for the U.S. Senate in 1978, completely rejuvenated the Republican Party candidate cohort. By showing how a modern campaign waged by a young, energetic candidate could overcome rising Democratic enrollments (Democrats actually passed Republicans in enrollment by 1978) and diminishing Republican control of the political system, Bill Cohen became a role model for Republicans who wanted to win in the 1970's, 1980's and 1990's.

By his example, Cohen set in motion profound political dynamics which restored Republicans to their position of electoral dominance in terms of major races. Party stalwarts such as Ted Curtis, who played important roles in the 1960's would argue, and I think correctly, that the very success of Cohen's independent brand of campaigning reduced the importance of the Republican Party qua party and ended up divorcing Republican legislative fortunes from those of the major candidates. As the Cohen Independent campaigning mentality expanded, the GOP state committee's power declined precipitously, to the loss of party discipline, loyalty and ultimately elections to the Legislature.

I believe that this is one reason observers of the Maine political scene missed the importance and impact of the Cohen counter-reformation. Another was because Ed Muskie's victory in 1954 was followed by other Democratic successes *and* was accompanied by a big upsurge in Democratic enrollment. There was nothing comparable in terms of Republican enrollment following Cohen's breakthrough election in 1972.

Muskie, far more than Cohen, was a party builder. Cohen led by example and by establishing a campaign pattern, not by building up the Republican Party at the grassroots level. He was not a "party person" either by temperament or by ideology.

In this regard, Cohen was thus very much in the tradition of Margaret Chase Smith, whose "independence" appealed to voters across the political spectrum and who did not depend on the Republican Party apparatus for her electoral success. But for observers of the Maine political scene, there was a more discernible connection between Muskie and increased Democratic enrollments than between Cohen and the increased Republican success at the ballot box.

Moreover, as Olympia Snowe suggests, the Cohen revolution was not just one of style or electoral emphasis. It was accompanied by an outreach effort which went beyond the campaign setting. Prior to Cohen's election in 1972, members of Congress in Maine usually had a single district office for constituent service with the Washington office doing most of the case work. Even Senators Smith and Muskie only had one or two district offices. The credit for using district offices in an outreach effort probably should go to Peter Kyros, who had an office in Portland and a part-time one in Rockland, while Muskie had a single office in Waterville at the time. But it was Cohen and his staff who turned the idea into an art form.

After 1972, Cohen opened district offices in Bangor, Presque Isle and Lewiston and staffed them with local people. And he introduced the practice of "citizen's hours," in which he would go out to various towns and hold office hours for anyone who wished to drop by. Federal office holders rarely went out into the countryside and asked for people to come forward with their problems on a regularly scheduled basis.

This combination of a tripling of offices and greatly expanded opportunities to see the Congressman in person set in motion significant changes in the style of constituent activity in Maine. During the 1975 "pseudo election," for example, Muskie opened a number of offices of his own to counter the perceived threat of Cohen running against him in 1976. For Snowe, this change in outreach emphasis was key to the way Republicans (and soon thereafter Democrats) conducted their business all across Maine. She is also correct that this style has now become such a universal pattern (with staffers often substituting for the office holders during office hours) that we forget there was a time when nobody conducted business that way!

In any case, from 1971 until 1980, the Republicans captured ten out of fifteen contests (with Jim Longley taking one contest for governor as an Independent) for a winning percentage of 66.6%, as the Cohen example attracted a series of young, attractive, moderate Republican candidates— candidates who swept aside and held off older, more conservative elements within their primaries. Dave Emery, Olympia Snowe and Jock McKernan all moved up from the Legislature. All walked across their districts or the state and all were victorious. On the Democratic side, only Joe Brennan emerged as a formidable Democratic newcomer who won enough victories (five) to set a discernible pattern.

In fact, if we broaden the time frame somewhat and look at the period from 1972 following the Cohen counter-revolution until 1996, we find the Republicans actually enjoyed a 25–14 edge, with Independents winning two races (Longley Sr. and Angus King, both for governor). This 61% to 34% to 5% edge for Republicans shows just how profound was the Cohen counter-revolution.

Perhaps Joe Brennan's success as a two-term governor and then as a Congressman for two terms gives something of a Democratic sheen to the next decade but on examination, the next period of Maine political life was still dominated by Republicans as well. In the period from 1981 until 1996, for example, Republicans actually enjoyed considerable dominance, winning fifteen out of twenty-six contests for a decade-winning percentage of 57.6%. Independents (Angus King for governor) took one contest of 3.8% and the Democrats ten contests or 38%.

With Brennan defeated twice in runs for the governorship and the retirement of Muskie, Mitchell and Cohen, the political hierarchies shifted
considerably until by 1996, Republicans controlled both Senate seats,
Democrats both Congressional seats and the governorship was held by an
Independent, again reinforcing the popular perception of a Maine balanced by the success of both parties.

It should be noted that the election of two Independent governors,
Longley Sr. in 1974 and King in 1994, puts Maine in a unique position
nationally and their individual efforts to achieve the governorship should
serve as examples of the triumph of individual will over party politics.

But looked at in true historical perspective, Republican domination of
the major political outcomes of the post-war period in Maine remains considerable.

Of the 95 major elections held since 1946, the Republicans have won
61, or 64%, while the Democrats have won 32, or 34%, and Independents
have won 2, or 2%.

This nearly 2–1 advantage enjoyed by Republicans makes it the most
prominent theme of the post–World War II era to date.

The Republican dominance of the major elective offices in the state is
all the more surprising since it occurred against the backdrop of a mirror
image of Democratic success in the Legislature.

For the last 25 years, Democratic dominance of that arena has been
most pronounced. Beginning in January, 1975 and continuing more or less
uninterrupted (except for the 1979–1980 session and part of 1996), Democrats have controlled the Legislature and with it, the important offices
controlled by that body. We often forget that Maine is unique among the
50 states for giving its Legislature the power to select statewide offices of
Secretary of State, Attorney General, Treasurer of State and State Auditor,
as well as the more widely legislative-selected President of the Senate and
Speaker of the House.

As Paul Mills has so incisively pointed out, since January 1975, the
Democrats have occupied no less than 85% of those positions. Yet despite
the high profile given to those offices such as Attorney General and Secretary of State, few Democrats have been able to move up from them to
higher elected office. Although Ken Curtis moved up from Secretary of
State earlier, since 1975 only Joe Brennan, who was Attorney General
from 1975 until 1979, has been able to use one of the state offices as a

successful springboard to higher office. Many others, such as Leighton Cooney, Bill Diamond, Jim Tierney and Duke Dutremble tried and failed, and others, such as Senate President Pray and Speaker John Martin, didn't try.

For many hard-core Democratic activists then, it may have been that the Legislature (and perhaps the governorship) were simply far more important than the other offices such as U.S. Senator or Congressman. Certainly John Martin's Speakership both required and stimulated Democratic control of that body, and party chairs and activists of the 1970's and 1980's such a Tony Buxton, Severin Beliveau, Barry Hobbins and Rod Quinn put in as major effort to constantly recruit good candidates and make sure the party apparatus backed up their campaigns.

In any case, Maine political history since World War II shows a quite amazing bifurcation of control, with Republicans continuing to dominate the selection of major elected offices, such as those for Congress, governor and U.S. Senate and the Democrats (especially during the last 25 years) dominating the Legislature and the positions it appoints. The reasons for this frank dualism of our Maine political heritage lie beyond the scope of this book but should be explored in the future.

How to explain the continuing Republican dominance of the major elected offices?

Some patterns may help to explain the numerical success of the Republican party in the post-war period especially within the context of the Muskie revolution as the primary challenge to Republican power during this period.

I believe that a very important part of the explanation of Republican resurgence as well as their continued domination can be seen by looking at the biggest winners in Maine politics, the "aces." In the lexicon portion of this work, I defined an "ace" in Maine politics as someone who had won at least five major races (for Congress, U.S. Senate or governor) without a loss. Conceptually, the "ace" designation goes a long way to helping us understand Republican supremacy in the post-war period.

Republican domination of the post-war period has been due in large part from having many more aces than the Democrats. The Republicans have simply had significantly more big winners than have the Democrats. Individual Republicans have won more races, more consistently. This fact has received very little media or even political insider attention but is of considerable importance to our understanding of political patterns in post-war Maine politics. Bear in mind that these ace records are from the post–World War II era to the present (1946–1996) and do not cover the victories and losses before that period. Margaret Chase Smith, for example, had a number of victories prior to 1946.

Take Olympia Snowe, for example. Maine's senior Senator is the foremost winner among all the aces of post-war politics. She remains undefeated at 9 wins and 0 losses. She has never had primary opposition and she has won all of her general elections. She is the premier ace in the period under review and must now be considered the standard against which all post-war political figures must be judged in terms of electoral success.

Initially coming from Maine's northern 2nd CD and being somewhat in the national shadow of Bill Cohen, Snowe never enjoyed much media attention and editorial interest from the Portland TV and print markets. Moreover, her narrow victories over Pat McGowan in 1990 and 1992 obscured a truly outstanding electoral achievement and gave hard-core Democrats a somewhat mistaken view of her vulnerability. Her crushing defeat of Tom Andrews in the U.S. Senate race of 1994 changed that perception and firmly established her as a major electoral player, even though many news accounts focused on the poor campaign run by her opponent Andrews rather than on the truly superb campaign she and her campaign team put together.

Of all 228 candidates who have run for higher Maine office since World War II, Olympia Snowe is the most successful!

Bill Cohen turns out to be the second leading ace, with a winning record of 7 and 0. Cohen had one primary victory and six general election victories. As we have noted, his impact by example has been considerable, showing that a young, energetic Republican could contest Democrats at all levels and in all arenas and emerge successful, indeed changing the very perceptions of the Maine Republican Party.

In terms of long-term significance, Cohen's counter-revolution by example is second only to Ed Muskie's 1954 revolution in importance for the political system of post–World War II Maine politics and for the subsequent outcomes in Maine political history. The Cohen counter-revolution blunted and in many ways reversed the pattern which Muskie had begun and prevented Democrats from further capitalizing on the growing numbers and attractive candidates.

Cohen's potency as a candidate is unrivaled in Maine 20th-century politics, for he was never defeated, never behind in any race and never seriously threatened after his primary victory in 1972. His example of how to run a modern campaign as a Republican and his self-positioning on the issues spectrum was of enormous significance for the next 25 years of Maine politics.

Next on the list of Maine aces comes Ed Muskie with six general election victories and no primary challenges. He began the reformation of Maine politics and those he propelled (by example and by assistance) were very important to the politics of the state. His impact on the political system of Maine remains the most profound of any player or candidate during the period under review.

Although he once lost a local race for mayor of Waterville, he is the only major Democratic ace undefeated in major races. He remains one of the true Titans in Maine politics, not only for his national standing and impact but for the sheer number of his victories without a loss in the postwar period.

But tied with Muskie on the ace list is Jock McKernan. With six victories and no defeats, including two primaries and four general elections, McKernan is thus the third most successful of all the undefeated political figures who ran for major office since World War II. McKernan suffered from considerable bad press and voter esteem as the national economy eroded the Maine economy during his second term, and his fractious struggles with the Legislature dimmed his luster as a political figure somewhat, so that this down drag has obscured his electoral place in history.

As an electoral vote getter and winner, however, he is in the elite of Maine political figures. This is especially true when one thinks of the fact that of all the people who contested Maine's major offices, his record is the third best. Third best out of 228! That is quite an accomplishment, an accomplishment for which he today receives almost no credit. In fact, even among political insiders, McKernan's ballot success is dramatically underappreciated.

Next on the list of top undefeated aces in Maine political history since World War II come two more Republicans, Stan Tupper, who retired undefeated at 5 and 0, including two primaries and three general elections, and Charles Nelson was undefeated as well, with four general election victories and one primary victory for a total of five.

So, of the total of six undefeated Maine political warriors, aces who won at least five major contests without losing one, five out of six were Republicans, and 83% of the undefeated aces since World War II were Republicans. I would argue that it is not by chance that the Republicans have the most undefeated aces and that the pattern of their individual successes help us to understand Republican domination of the political system over five decades.

Next, when we take a look at those warriors who lost at least one major race (virtually all their last), we again see a pattern of Republican majority, even though it is less pronounced than in the undefeated ace category.

Republican Robert "Bob" Hale won five primaries and six general elections, losing only one general election in 1958 to James Oliver for a record of 11 and 1. He leads all aces with but a single loss.

From 1946–1972, Margaret Chase Smith (whose overall electoral successes straddled World War II) was 9 and 1, with four primary victories and five general election victories and one general election loss to Bill Hathaway in 1972. Her entire political career, going back to 1940 thus includes 15 wins and only one loss, a modern Maine record. Except for her loss to Bill Hathaway, she won all her victories by large margins. These included very hotly contested primaries when she was starting out (both for Congress and then for the U.S. Senate), and finishing up her winning streak by crushing Bob Monks in the 1972 Republican primary.

Indeed, I would argue that the ease of her victory in that primary may well have lulled her into a false sense of security with regard to the fall general election, a false sense of security which Bill Hathaway exploited to significant advantage.

Democrat Peter Kyros was also 9 and 1, having a primary challenge every time he won, winning five of those and winning four of the five general elections he contested, losing only to Dave Emery in 1974. Kyros dropped from the Maine political scene after the recount of 1975, but he needs to emerge here as a historical electoral winner of the first rank.

Democrat Bill Hathaway had an impressive record as well. His 7 and 2 record, winning two primaries and five general elections, losing two general elections (one in 1962 to Cliff McIntire and then to Bill Cohen for the U.S. Senate in 1978) gives him a winning percentage of 77%.

Two more Republicans had outstanding electoral records as well:

Cliff McIntire was 7 and 1, winning seven general elections and losing only one general election in 1964 to Ed Muskie.

Fred Payne was 6 and 1 since World War II, winning three primaries and three general elections, losing only one general election, that in 1958 to Ed Muskie.

Democratic Ken Curtis rounds out our list of aces with a single loss as he was 5 and 1 with an early loss in the 1964 general election to Stan Tupper.

So not only did more Republicans have more victories in both primaries and general elections, Republicans had more of the undefeated aces and more of the aces who had only one loss. When putting the post-war period in perspective, we have to conclude that one very important element was the effectiveness of the individual Republican efforts. There are too many examples of success for the pattern to be sheer coincidence. This in no way should detract from the importance of the party qua party in the 1950's and 1960's but in the more fluid and competitive environment of the 1970's and beyond, individual Republicans simply had to depend more on themselves than on the shrinking party apparatus.

By comparison, even important national Democratic figures such as George Mitchell had rather modest electoral success in Maine's political history, with three wins (two generals and one primary) and one loss in the general (to Jim Longley in 1974). Mitchell does hold the highest winning percentage (81%) in any single modern election for his victory over Jasper Wyman in 1988.

How to explain this very important sub-theme in Maine politics, the far more impressive track record of Republican undefeated and once defeated aces? How to account for this phenomenon? I believe the answer lies in the extent to which these successful Republican candidates actually mirror the Maine electorate even as they do not precisely fit the portrait of national Republicans.

The moderate nature of successful Maine candidates.

Earlier, I said that much had to do with the early Republican success and then what I termed the Cohen counter-revolution. Cohen's 1972 victory and the tactical and strategic patterns it established for those who followed—Emery, Snowe, McKernan and Collins—have been largely over-looked by observers of the Maine political scene. To George Smith, Dave Emery's campaign manager in 1974 (and Bill Cohen's driver and field man during the 1972 election) goes much of the credit for translating the successful tactics to another candidate.

Both Olympia Snowe and Jock McKernan, while running their own campaigns and developing their own strategies and tactics, also made walking across their districts a central focus of their campaigns. Their energetic, youthful style looked much more like Cohen's than those of earlier Republican candidates.

Yet while Cohen's campaigns became the models for subsequent successful Republican candidates, in and of themselves they do not obviously explain the success of Republican candidates before 1972. I believe there is another strand to Cohen's and subsequent Republican successes and that is their ideological perspective, i.e., "moderate Republican with independent stances on national issues." For all their new tactics and strategic sense, for all their excellent use of modern political techniques, Cohen, Emery, Snowe and McKernan remained very much in the mold of Margaret Chase Smith and Stan Tupper.

Tupper and Smith were to have a famous and long-running feud which sometimes obscures the features of their commonalty. Ironically, however, Tupper and Smith actually had much more in common than they did with more conservative Republicans from all the decades under review (and perhaps, from the perspective of distance, more in common with one another than they would have thought). They both fought bruising battles with their party's right wing and both stood apart from the national Republican leadership on many key issues of the day.

Going back to 1940, but especially since 1972, it has been a general pattern in virtually all Republican primaries that the more moderate, less or least conservative, candidate has won. With the notable exception of Linda Bean versus Tony Payne in 1992 and perhaps Jim Erwin over Harry Richardson and Wakine Tanous in 1974, *in Maine, the more moderate candidates have usually won their Republican primaries.*

Smith beat Hildreth and Sewall in 1948 and Tupper beat Sinclair in 1960 and Garland in 1962. Cohen beat Green in 1972; Emery beat McCormick in 1990; McKernan beat Lowery in 1982 and Leighton in 1986;

Collins beat Wyman, Adams, Lipman and Webster in 1994 and Hathaway in 1996 (I would put Monks with Collins in terms of "moderation").

In fact, I believe that one of the major reasons for Republican success during the last 40 years has been the penchant of Republican primary voters for picking the more (or most) moderate of candidates, those with the least ideological baggage. These candidates have then gone on to be very successful in the general elections, leading to the conclusion that the Republican Party primary dynamics have been very important in producing the kind of candidate who was to go on to win many more elections than that primary. Snowe and McKernan, for example, were always, apart and separate, moderate candidates with moderate stances on most public issues.

Quite simply, in Maine electoral politics during the period under review, "the center holds." The electorate of Maine has, since World War II, liked "moderates" or at least perceived moderates from both parties. If Republican successful general election candidates have tended to be moderate both in terms of their primary opponents and on the broader political spectrum of general election politics, so too have those Democrats who have been successful. Given the ever-declining Republican party registrations during the period under review, the success of Republicans during this era had to come with the nomination of candidates who would appeal to the broad middle, the center of Maine politics in the general elections.

Not only is the general electorate more moderate than is often recognized, so too is the Democratic party. I believe that one of the great myths of Maine politics is that a majority of Democratic voters are "liberal."

Especially when it comes to the 1st District, pundits, reporters and even party workers are fond of saying how liberal Democratic primary voters are. Of course many are, and certainly there are liberal candidates in the Democratic party, but, on balance, taking the law of large numbers within the Democratic Party—especially the Democratic party in general elections—the truth is rather different. The 50,000 Democrats who vote in the 1st CD primary are often regarded as "liberal," when in fact I believe they are simply "more liberal." Usually, the less liberal candidate wins in the Democratic primaries. Note for example, Joe Brennan's long stretch of primary victories and the way Tom Allen (who by Republican litmus tests is liberal) narrowly defeated the even more liberal Dale Mc-Cormick in 1996.

In some relative sense, Democratic primary voters are more "liberal" than their Republican counterparts, at least on some issues, but a majority of Democratic primary voters self-define themselves as either "moderates" or "conservatives" rather than "liberals." That is, when you ask Democratic voters how they would characterize themselves, a plurality call themselves "moderate" and a majority designate themselves as "moderate" or "conservative." It works out roughly to 20% conservative, 42% moderate and 38% liberal/progressive.

Of course, a "conservative" Democrat is not necessarily the same as a "conservative" Republican, but in the context of Maine party politics, conservative and moderate Democratic voters almost always carry the day.

Without understanding this background, it is not possible to understand the longevity and popularity of Joe Brennan. Although Brennan lost the last three major general election races he entered (governor in 1990, governor in 1994 and U.S. Senate in 1996), he has always won his party's nomination handily, often getting more than a majority in crowded fields. And he has almost always been the more moderate, even the more "conservative" of those candidates.

Democratic primary voters, like their Republican counterparts, normally choose the more moderate candidates over more liberal ones within the context of their primaries. For example, they chose George Mitchell for governor over Peter Kelley in 1974, and in 1996 chose Tom Allen over Dale McCormick for Congress in the First CD. In 1994 they chose Duke Dutremble over Bonnie Titcomb, Bill Troubh and Bill Diamond. And in the Second CD, in 1994 they chose John Baldacci over Janet Mills, Jim Howaniec, Jean Hay, Shawn Hallisey, Mary Cathcart and Jim Mitchell.

This is not to say that liberal voters aren't important to the outcome of Democratic primaries. They are, especially in the 1st District primaries. They often provide the most ardent grass-roots workers. They often have a big impact on conventions. But they are not the epicenter of the Democratic Party, even though outsiders and reporters often say that they are. They do not usually determine the outcome of those primaries even though some Democratic candidates believe they do after they have been through the primary vetting process!

Take, for example, the case of Tom Andrews. Tom Andrews was the most liberal candidate in the 1990 Democratic primary for Congress. And his success within the Democratic Party is often credited to his liberal credentials. Much is also made of his organization (which undoubtedly was a deciding factor in his earlier state Senate races). Grass-roots activity in Maine can add 1 to 2% at most on a statewide basis in either a primary or a general election. Grass roots activity in the 1st CD Democratic primary can add perhaps a bit more, perhaps up to 3%.

In 1996, for example, Tom Allen would have beaten Dale McCormick by about 6% in his 1st CD primary but her effective grass-roots organization made up half the difference between them. This is not an insignificant factor when one is in a close race, but it is not the most important determinant of electoral outcomes.

For grass-roots activity—by liberals or by anybody else, including conservatives in the Republican primaries—really has very definite limits and relatively low limits in a Congressional or gubernatorial general election. It is almost never the independent variable some believe. Tom Andrews won the 1992 Congressional primary because he was more energetic and a better campaigner, controlled the free media much better and had the best TV of any of the candidates. I would argue that he won not because he was the most liberal, but because he ran the most effective campaign. Certainly his TV commercials were both outstanding and effective, bordering on the deceptive in terms of portraying him as both a friend of business and a moderate!

When he ran against Olympia Snowe for the U.S. Senate in 1994, however, his liberal stance hurt him (as did his stand against Loring Air Force Base and for gun control). Not only did he have a liberal voting record in Congress, his opponent made skillful use of that record. Held to the light of vivid campaign analysis (i.e., the glare of the 30-second commercial), Andrews was simply too liberal for a statewide race against a formidable candidate, if that candidate knew what he or she was doing and could match Andrews in terms of energy and quality of her television. And since it is impossible to organize the state in any meaningful way using grass-roots organization, Andrews could not—and I believe did not expect to—win by going that route.

Of more importance to the outcome, I believe, was the fact that Andrews and his supporters were simply not ready for this particular race and were completely unprepared to run on a statewide basis when Senator George Mitchell and President Bill Clinton insisted that he do so.

By contrast, Olympia Snowe was. She had been waiting for a chance to run statewide since 1982, when Dave Emery ran against George Mitchell and lost. In 1994, Olympia Snowe ran a textbook campaign, keeping Andrews off balance, moving into his 1st CD with impunity and using very effective TV to define him. Her campaign in 1994 became a classic in how to beat a potentially powerful rival in a number of ways at the same time.

To sum up, liberal Democrats and conservative Republicans often dominate their respective state committees. Liberal Democrats and conservative Republicans often dominate news coverage of their party conventions. Liberal Democrats and conservative Republicans often determine the party platforms. Liberal Democrats and conservative Republicans can always get good coverage at their press conferences. Liberal Democrats and conservative Republicans can always obtain considerable visibility attacking more moderate office holders of their own party.

What the last 50 years of Maine politics show, however, is that in the law of large numbers, liberal Democrats and conservative Republicans do not win many elections, even in their own primaries when, challenged by strong moderates. In fact, neither group is much of an independent variable in forming general electoral coalitions. Maine voters simply prefer moderate Democrats and moderate Republicans, "moderate" often meaning liberal on social issues and conservative on national defense and spending issues.

If liberal Democrats and conservative Republicans are not the epicenters of Maine politics and do not determine the outcome of most major races (including primaries), who does?

I believe the Franco-American voters are the most important swing cohort, not only in statewide general elections across the state, but within the Democratic Party as well.

The emergence of Franco Americans as the key swing voting group in practical Maine politics.

Voters of Franco-American heritage make up approximately 17–18% of the electorate. A majority are registered as Democrats but, in my experience, a majority of those are ticket splitters if approached in the right way. They will vote for a Republican or Independent candidate more readily than will other Democrats. Since 1972, they have emerged as the most important swing group in state practical politics, both in terms of candidate campaigns and ballot measures.

Why are Franco Americans in Maine so important to the political process?

First, although a majority of Franco Americans in many communities are registered as Democrats, in terms of basic personal ideology, many Franco Americans probably would have in fact become Republicans had not the mill and factory owners in Biddeford, Saco, Sanford, Brunswick, Lewiston, Auburn, Winslow and Waterville been Republicans when the waves of Franco-American immigration came to Maine at the end of the 19th century.

Many Franco Americans became Democrats because, initially, they could see no place for themselves in the Republican Party qua party and saw themselves as discriminated against and exploited by the mill and factory owners and the Republican political establishment. Not surprisingly, they often voted a straight Democratic ticket.

In fact, even though candidates such as Frank Coffin and Ed Muskie appealed to Independents and some Republican voters, huge Democratic enrollment margins among Franco-American communities were the real basis for the success of the Muskie revolution and the subsequent resurgence of Democratic candidates. This is because they were against what they perceived to be the wealthy Republican domination of economic—and social—life of the state.

Second, many Franco Americans, party affiliation aside, hold social and personal views which are quite "Republican" in character. In survey after survey that I have done, if you remove the party label, they choose values such as "smaller government," "less government intrusion," etc. which one associates with Republican rhetoric and views. And as many Franco Americans moved from factory worker positions to small business positions, their ideological perspective became more and more Republican and "Independent."

Democratic activists often miss this shift, as do mainstream Democratic candidates. One of the reasons Duke Dutremble did so poorly among Franco voters outside of Biddeford in his 1994 Congressional bid was that, rightly or wrongly, he was portrayed by his opponent as a "tax and spend," "big government" "liberal." Although a Franco American, he ran up against Franco-American aversion to big government and especially intrusive government and ran below a necessary winning Democratic percent-age in all the Franco-American communities except Biddeford, his hometown.

Third, Democratic politics in Maine since World War II have tended to rely on Franco-American support without always returning that support. Put even more baldly, outside the Maine legislative arena where John Martin usually watched over their interests, the Democratic establishment has generally taken the Franco Americans for granted.

Thus, those Republican candidates such as Bill Cohen and Olympia Snowe, who campaign vigorously among and for Franco Americans, have been richly rewarded. After the removal of the "Big Box" voting method in 1972, Franco Americans could no longer be taken for granted by Democrats except at their peril. Observers of the Maine political scene often miss this fact when looking at voting statistics because it is a matter of degree rather than kind.

As I have written elsewhere, over the past 25 years the Franco-American vote has been the most important category of ticket splitters in the state of Maine.

Bill Cohen, David Emery, Olympia Snowe and Jock McKernan were all elected by making substantial inroads into the Franco community. Remember, Republican candidates did not have to carry such Democratic strongholds as Androscoggin County, they only had to cut down their margin of loss there. For example, prior to Bill Cohen's successful run for Congress in 1972, Republican candidates normally came out of the Androscoggin Valley 20–25,000 votes behind. He cut the margin to 8,000 in his first race and actually carried the Androscoggin Valley in some subsequent races. His 1976 victory over Leighton Cooney marked the first time since 1926 that a Republican had carried the city of Lewiston in a major general election.

This pattern has prevailed in practical politics ever since, and 22 years later, when Olympia Snowe moved south to contest the U.S. Senate race with Tom Andrews, her appeal to Franco Americans in the 1st CD, when combined with her overwhelming support in Lewiston and Auburn in the 2nd, sealed his fate.

And it is not by chance that both Independent governors in recent Maine history, James Longley in 1974 and Angus King in 1994, were elected by statewide coalitions of urban Francos and rural and small-town

Republicans. Jim Longley Sr. carried Lewiston and cut down George Mitchell's margins in other Franco areas in 1974 and became governor. Twenty years later, Angus King carried Lewiston and other Franco areas against Joe Brennan in 1994 and became governor. In both cases, the Republican candidates could not get their usual traction in the Franco areas, thus giving the Independents a chance to make political hay at the expense of the Democratic base and the Republican swing voters.

I believe Lewiston is one of the most critical barometers of electoral success across the 2nd District and the entire state, and always one of the most important battlegrounds for successful Republican candidates.

For example, in 1954, Ed Muskie got 78% of that city's vote, compared with 22% for the Republican candidate Burt Cross, and won the governorship. Margaret Smith, however, got 10% more (32%) than Cross and beat her Democratic opponent Paul Fullam for the U.S. Senate statewide.

In 1970, Republicans lost all three contests running up margins of only 12% (Neil Bishop for U.S. Senate), 22% (Jim Erwin for governor) and 10% (Maynard Connors for Congress) as the Democratic winners received 88% (Ed Muskie), 77% (Ken Curtis) and 89% (Bill Hathaway).

In 1972, however, Bill Cohen got 29% of the vote in Lewiston for Congress as he won district-wide against a Franco-American candidate, Elmer Violette. Margaret Chase Smith received 23% of the vote for Senate, losing statewide to Bill Hathaway. But when Cohen ran against Hathaway for the U.S. Senate six years later in 1978, he received 40% of the Lewiston vote in a four-way race, keeping Hathaway to only 50% in Lewiston. Hayes Gahagan got 8%, John Jannace 1.7% and Plato Truman 5%. Cohen won statewide with 58% of the vote.

In 1982, Dave Emery was able to get only 22% of the Lewiston vote as he lost the U.S. Senate race to George Mitchell who got 77% of the vote. But that same year, Olympia Snowe was actually carrying Lewiston 50.2% to 49.8% for James Dunleavy. Naturally, she won a smashing victory district-wide 67% to 33%.

In 1986, Olympia Snowe took Lewiston with 61% of the vote as she crushed Richard Charette statewide, 77% to 23%. Jock McKernan did just well enough in a four-way Lewiston contest, getting 26% of the vote to defeat Jim Tierney (44.5%), John Menario (19%) and Sherry Huber (10%) statewide for the governorship. One look at the exit polls on election day in Lewiston confirmed that Jim Tierney from nearby Lisbon Falls was doomed.

In 1990, Neil Rolde, the Democratic candidate, received 51% of the vote in Lewiston, but Cohen got 49%. By contrast, Olympia Snowe lost Lewiston 62% to 38% as Pat McGowan nearly upset her. But it was still her strong showing in Lewiston which kept her in Congress.

In 1994, Olympia Snowe received 47% of the vote in Lewiston on the way to her impressive victory over Tom Andrews who only got 48% of the vote in Lewiston. Angus King received 43% of the vote to 42% for Joe Brennan, while Susan Collins received only 10% and Jonathan Carter 4%. Democrat John Baldacci, however, took Lewiston with 58% of the vote to 22% for Republican Rick Bennett (while two Independents got the rest), as Baldacci carried the 2nd CD handily.

This brings us to one of the more interesting paradoxes of the long and important career of Joe Brennan.

Joe Brennan played a vital role in truly integrating ethnic voters (Franco and Irish) into the political coalitions of the 1970's and 1980's. But although Franco Americans got a great deal of political patronage from the ascendancy of John Martin as Speaker of the House and within the legislative context, Franco politicians have always had to struggle within the broader statewide Democratic Party where the Irish hold on the central core of the party, especially for the major nominations for Congress, governor and U.S. Senate, is much more pronounced. We often forget that 17–18% of the electorate of the state is Irish American because that population is more scattered around the state than is the Franco-American cohort.

The Democratic Party has seldom put Franco-American candidates forward for the most important elected positions in the state, leaving important Franco politicians to feel left out or taken for granted. Of course the same charge could be even more easily made against the Republicans. But during the period under review, Francos did not expect Republicans to push their candidacies, so their disappointment was most often targeted toward Democratic leaders, especially Irish. Francos did expect the Democrats to do so. When they didn't, Republican candidates often found fertile grounds for gaining Franco support in community after community.

Part of this is due to the fact that each of the Franco-American communities—such as Sanford, Saco, Biddeford, Westbrook, Brunswick, Waterville, Lewiston, Auburn and the St. John Valley—has its own local political leadership. Some of these are constantly being rewarded by Democrats if they are part of the political establishment. But there are always some who are not. These factions are often willing to make short-term alliances of convenience with Republican candidates, not just for presumed patronage but to be able to consider themselves as insiders in a winning campaign. There are always personal and ideological as well as patronage divisions within the Franco cities.

Smarter Republican candidates such as Cohen, Emery, Snowe and McKernan have always made sure that local Franco leaders subsequently got enough attention to make them believe their support was important as well as worthwhile.

In this context, we need to examine the paradox of Joe Brennan and the Franco-American voter. No group has been more important to keeping Joe Brennan successful within the Democratic Party for such a long time than the Francos. Every time Joe Brennan has run for office in a Democratic primary, he has had very considerable support from Democratic Franco voters.

Even as late as 1996, after Brennan's two heartbreaking defeats for governor when both Tom Andrews and John Baldacci looked at the possibility of running against him in a Democratic primary both—but especially Andrews in the 1st CD—saw an overwhelming block of Franco-American voters for Brennan. Neither saw much upside potential for them in the primary, and in Baldacci's case at least, he was not ready to make the leap of faith necessary to run statewide so soon after his emergence on the 2nd District scene. In any case, both backed away and Brennan crushed his primary opponents in 1996, Sean Faircloth and Richard Spencer.

Brennan has always won his primaries with massive Franco-American support. But he has then won or lost his general elections by his ability or inability to hold on to this cohort of Franco-American primary voters and go beyond them to the more independent and Republican-leaning Francos in the general election. When he won close or potentially close races (as in 1978 and 1986), it has been because he held enough Francos to do the job. But when he lost (as in 1990 and 1994), it has been because he did not.

Again, just looking at vote totals can be deceptive. Joe Brennan carried Lewiston 2–1 in 1990 against Jock McKernan. But he needed to carry

Lewiston by a margin of 2½ to 1 to have enough Franco votes to stave off defeat in that particular race. He did not get them.

In this case, neither did Jock McKernan get as many as he wanted, as 13% of the vote in Lewiston went to an unknown Independent candidate, Andrew Adam, who ended up getting 9% of the vote statewide, helping to deny Brennan the election.

And in 1994 when Brennan lost to Angus King for governor, it was King who actually carried Lewiston, with 43% of the vote to Joe Brennan's 42.5%.

When I think of Maine politics and who counts for successful outcomes, I immediately think of the Francos. For me, to paraphrase Archimedes, "Give me the Francos and I will lift the world."

The unenrolled voter category in Maine, the so-called Independent voter cohort, is actually two different groups, and these play an ambiguous role in Maine politics.

Much political myth-making about Maine politics revolves around this "Independent" voter. With 29% of the voting age population registered as Republicans and 32% registered as Democrats, that leaves 39% or the largest group as unenrolled. Common usage terms them "Independents." So it is only natural that commentators look to this group as being most important. And, in some candidate elections, it is.

There also is a lot of truth to the notion that the Maine voter is "independent" in the sense that while Maine voters as a whole generally do not like the label "conservative" or "liberal" on their candidates, they do like the label "independent." Margaret Chase Smith created an entire political persona out of it and Ed Muskie followed suit. Maine voters came to love the "independent" nature of Bill Cohen and now expect that officeholders, especially senators, will be "independent." Senator Susan Collins, for example, got off to a tremendous start in Washington as of 1997, including an admiring piece in the *New York Times Magazine,* based on her "independent" stance on campaign finance reform.

But in terms of voting blocs as opposed to perceptions, the reality is somewhat different. There is another dimension to the role of the unenrolled voter. In fact, more than half of the unenrolled voters simply do not vote and are hence an "unintegrated stratum" of potential voters rather than actual voters. They are not so much Independents as they are disengaged from the political center.

That leaves less than half of the Independents to be concerned about in general elections. This portion is important, of course, and tends to occupy the middle of the voting spectrum in terms of ideology. They look an awful lot like moderate Republicans or moderate Democrats rather than the much smaller extremely conservative minority within the Republican primary voter pool or the much smaller extremely liberal minority within the Democratic primary voter pool. Perhaps the best way to think about those "Independents" in Maine who do vote would be as "Republicans" or "Democrats" who never got around to enrolling in a party.

This group thus tends to reinforce the selection of moderates by both parties. "Moderate" Republicans and "moderate" Democrats simply do better in general elections than very conservative or very liberal candidates because their messages are automatically more receptive to those Independents who normally vote in the fall general elections.

Interestingly enough, it has been my experience that while Independent voters are more likely than either Republicans or Democrats to vote for Independent candidates, in order for an Independent candidate to win a general election in Maine, there has to be a massive defection from one party and minor, but crucial, defections from the other. Independents in and by themselves do not accomplish much without this corresponding political devolution within one or both parties during a particular election.

In 1974, for example, there was a massive defection from Republicans in support of the candidacy of Jim Longley Sr., with Jim Erwin, the Republican nominee finishing a distant third. But enough urban Francos also abandoned the Democratic nominee, George Mitchell, especially in Longley's home town of Lewiston, to give him the victory.

I always like to go to Lewiston on Election Day because it almost always gives me a sense of how things are going to turn out. I remember racing up there in 1974, expecting to learn that Mitchell was going to win, Longley coming in second and Erwin third. Mitchell's campaign had organized the biggest get-out-the-vote effort I have ever witnessed in Maine.

But as soon as I hit Lisbon Street, I got a sense the Democrats were making a terrible, terrible mistake. They were carting hundreds of voters to the polls, all right, but those voters were not voting for Mitchell, they were going for Longley. I remember running into frantic Democratic workers who, like me, had figured out what was happening but couldn't figure out how to shut off the bubble machine. Longley was to be Maine's next governor and the Democratic apparatus was powerless to stop it. Instead, they were actually helping to ensure it.

In 1994, there was again a similar massive defection from Republicans who abandoned their nominee Susan Collins and went to Independent Angus King. As in other elections, the fate of the Democratic nominee, Joe Brennan, was ultimately sealed by King's outstanding showing in Franco Democratic areas such as Lewiston. Independents are, of course, important to Independents who want to win elections but they cannot accomplish this on their own.

The 39% of the Maine electorate who are the unenrolled "Independents" thus play a most ambiguous role in the politics of the state. Generalizations about them are best examined in the context of specific elections, but on balance, in the world of insider, practical politics, they are not really as dependable as other specific segments of Maine's demographic and psychographic makeups. In fact, I find media preoccupation and fascination with this group to be often misplaced and almost always overdone.

Women who work in the home are often predictive and actual outcome determinators.

By contrast, women who work in the home are very important tactically, strategically and in terms of media targeting. Women in the home represent one of the most important determinants of electoral outcome in Maine, and this is true for ballot measure campaigns as well as for candidate campaigns. I always look to them right after I look to Francos for help in passing anything on a statewide basis.

Before we look at this critical group, I would like to point out some interesting aspects of some other groups which are less important for strategic purposes.

One of the most important aspects of polling is the process of segmentation, that is, breaking the electorate into smaller, more manageable groups based on demographics (population categories such as age or income) or psychographics (lifestyle patterns). Every pollster probably has his or her favorite (hence "most important" category), as polling firms routinely put in questions about party affiliation, age, income, education, religion, etc.

Over the years, I've developed some reactions to the value of certain groups. Those 18–25-year-olds, for example, are unfortunately of little consequence in Maine politics because they vote in such small numbers. This has always irritated someone like me who pushed hard for the 18-year-old vote. Those 55 +, however, have never disappointed me in terms of turnout! They turn out in fair weather and foul, for good candidates and bad, for important referenda and less important bond issues.

One of the most interesting "new" categories—one of hardly any interest 20 years ago—which I have noted is the educational grouping, "some college." Maine voters have a definite profile when you look at them by the following education categories: grade school education (mostly correlated with older voters), high school education (still the largest group in Maine), college education (usually fairly balanced by party affiliation) and those with "some college." This group, with high school diplomas and some education—even a single course—beyond high school are most fascinating.

Some might be quick to label them a group for which "a little knowledge is a dangerous thing" because they are so erratic. They are, in fact, the hardest educational group to predict its positioning, as it often seems to hold contradictory issue positions. But it is often a very good "flash" group to put one onto short-term trends.

For example, this was the group which most clearly and earliest indicated the upcoming success of Ronald Reagan and it "called the turn" against Michael Dukakis (along with Francos) even when he was ahead by 17% over George Bush. But because it is so unpredicatable—it liked Maine Yankee in 1980, but not the Maine Turnpike in 1991—it is fascinating but difficult around which to build a successful election. It is simply a dependable predictor of outcomes in Maine even though the group can be interesting to watch. It is also impossible to organize or reach through segmentation.

Over the years, I have come to depend more and more on the category of "women who work at home," both to tell me how an election is going to come out and, in an operational sense, who to target for conversion purposes.

With more and more women entering the work force outside the home, those women who continue to work in the home have become one of the most important swing votes in Maine politics. They are also one of the most overlooked.

This group currently makes up 25% of the voting population and remains even more important in terms of swing voters. Women who work at home are not always as focused on news programs as women outside the home and men. They are often the last to make up their minds on issues or the last to change their minds if they are already for or against something unless you bring your candidate and your messages to them early. Women in the home often take their political cues at different times of the day from other groups and are usually swayed by different messages and especially by different authority figures. Most importantly, they can be reached by daytime TV, which is so much cheaper than prime-time TV or news adjacencies.

Thanks to exit polling, I know just how important women in the home are, both for candidates and for causes.

As a group, they are almost overlooked by reporters and pundits alike, but they can often spell the margin of victory. For example, Democratic women in the home voted in large numbers for Duke Dutremble in the Democratic primary for Congress in Maine's 1st CD in 1994, helping to provide his margin of victory over his three opponents. In fact, exit polling showed that he received more votes from women in the home than any other candidate in that primary, including Bonnie Titcomb, Bill Troubh and Bill Diamond.

But in the general election of 1994, many Republican and Independent women in the home went for Dutremble's opponent James Longley Jr., in part because of their confusion over the abortion issue (many sububan women through he was pro-choice) enabling him to carve out a narrow and short-lived victory. Two years later, this same group largely abandoned Longely (and the Republican Contract for America), turning to Tom Allen, ensuring his victory. Longley would have been much more competitive had he not lost women in the home so early due to a massive AFL/CIO TV blitz.

For over 25 years, I have been paying women in the home special attention, both in terms of polling and campaign tactics and have always insisted that media firms target them early and often. Some Democratic activists such as Barry Hobbins noticed this pattern of TV buying as far back as the

Senate election of 1978, but few have imitated this emphasis. One exception would be the Congressional election of 1988, when Joe Sudby and Pat Eltman, campaign managers for Joe Brennan, adopted a similar strategy. Concerned over Joe Brennan's near loss to Rolli Ives, and fearing the Republican Ted O'Meara might come as close, they heavily targeted suburban women with daytime TV and won handily.

The closeness of the 1994 race for governor was also due in part to King's initial failure to attract large number of women in the home. Brennan had a lead with this group and overall until the final week of the campaign, but it was a last weekend defection of Brennan women in the home to Collins which helped tip the balance.

Here is one of the great ironies of that race. The Brennan campaign leaked a "poll" which supposedly showed Collins coming on and pedaled it to the *Bangor Daily News*. It thought that a surge for Collins would come from those Republicans who were now for King. The *Bangor Daily News*, which had already endorsed Collins, endorsed her again, and featured the poll as evidence she was coming on and could win. She did come on a bit the last weekend, but the women in the home who flocked to her banner the last weekend came not from King but from Brennan. Democratic women, especially blue collar, women in the home in the 2nd District decided she did have a chance and therefore their vote would not be wasted. Exit polling again picked up both this shift and the crucial role played by women in the home.

Olympia Snowe was the only Republican candidate that year who did not suffer from a gender gap with women as she made a major effort to target women in the home, especially those in the Portland DMA.

On balance, I have always found women in the home to be a most valuable building block for any winning coalition, second only to Francos in importance. On more than one occasion, they have saved my candidate or cause. In the Sunday Sales referendum, for example, they held firm even as other groups were defecting as that race got closer and closer.

In 1996, women in the home kept the Forest Compact under 50%. Interestingly enough, women in the home were initially unmoved by all the TV commercials which featured the Maine Audubon Society, and only went to a small plurality for the Compact when ads featuring Governor King came on TV. But in the last weekend, 3% of the total vote and 7% of women in the home switched their vote from supporting the Forest Compact to opposing it when the Sierra Club jumped in with a massive TV blitz accenting spraying and its implied danger to children. The Compact won the three-way race but ended up with 47% of the vote instead of 50% and thus required a run-off in 1997.

Because women who work at home are so important to the outcome of so many races and because they can reached by "special means" (i.e., less costly daytime TV), I have found them to be critical variables in most political situations but especially in ballot measures and referenda contests.

As I say to my students, "Give me the Francos and the women in the home and I will win nine out of ten ballot measures."

Geography is not as much of a major determinant of outcomes except in the ironic sense that the political landscape has generally been dominated by politicians from northern Maine.

One of the great ironies of political discourse in Maine politics is the extent to which pundits and others talk about two Maines, a north and a south. Of course there are differences and distances (Fort Kent is as far away from where I am writing as is New York City), and northern, rural and Republican legislators often complain about domination by those from the south.

And yes, some politicians try to exploit the differences.

Yet, John Martin's long shadow over the Legislature comes from the north, not the south. Even more important for the political phenomenon we are looking at, the dominant political figures have more often come from the north than the south.

While Joe Brennan was from Portland, many statewide office holders came from north and west of Augusta. Margaret Chase Smith came from Skowhegan. Ed Muskie came from Rumford and Waterville. Bill Cohen and Jock McKernan were from Bangor, George Mitchell from Waterville, Dave Emery was from Rockland, Olympia Snowe from Auburn, Susan Collins is from Caribou.

Beyond that, one of the most interesting patterns I have observed is the extent to which coming from the 2nd Congressional District is an independent variable. In fact, I think there is a proving ground and incubator of political success. Hathaway came from that killer CD, the largest CD east of the Mississippi. So did Cohen. So did Snowe. So did Collins. Coming down into the smaller, more compact, single TV market 1st CD is easier! Anyone who has not run for Congress in the 2nd CD will have a hard time appreciating just how difficult it is to get around.

For one thing, it takes a long time. You have to drive hour after hour. Even if you take a light plane, you need lots of time to get from Rumford to Calais or from Bar Harbor to Fort Kent. As Paul Hazelton so aptly put it a quarter of a century ago as he drove Ed Muskie from little town to little town: "No one can ever appreciate election politics if they haven't driven the candidate from Rumford to Jonesport to Wytopitlock in a single day to meet with a total of eight town committee people. That's truly retail politics." People are scattered all around the district, not concentrated. Yet they expect to meet the candidates.

There is also lot of diversity within the CD itself. For example, Aroostook County in and of itself is three different worlds. There is the Republican world of Houlton and the smaller towns to the south. There is the Democratic world of the St. John Valley and there is the swing world of Caribou-Presque Isle. The Bangor media market is one electronic world, the Presque Isle media market is another. Radio stations are scattered far and wide.

Those who start from the 2nd CD are much better off. Those who have become Congresspeople from the 2nd CD are more battle-tested by the terrain. They have already put in the time to get from place to place to place. They can then "go south" much easier; getting into the Portland media market is more expensive if you are buying TV time but it is much easier to get to the news outlets for personal appearances.

It is much harder for a candidate to go north. It is much harder to organize those towns. It takes a lot more out of you to go north than for your opponent to go south. I would always rather have a candidate who is running from the 2nd CD than the 1st CD.

It will be interesting to see if this pattern holds in the future. If I am correct, John Baldacci should have the best chance of being elected to the U.S. Senate or governor, at least a better chance than any of the candidates who are not already tested by the 2nd CD.

Advantage to "southern candidates"? No, when it comes to Maine politics, the north almost always has an advantage in electing its candidates.

Maine politics, the way life should be.

This paraphrase of Governor McKernan's paean to the state is where I would like to end this work. We are very fortunate to live in a state where the political system is clean, fair and very open.

I believe that on balance the American political system is clean, fair and open.

I know the Maine one is.

The Maine political system is so open to talent it is truly amazing. Take Margaret Chase Smith, with no college degree and no power base, making of herself one of the most powerful forces in Maine's political history and one of the most powerful women figures of the entire mid-20th century (1949–1973). Take Ed Muskie, starting out with a party base one-half the size of the other party and by force of will changing it completely and for the next 50 years. Take Bill Cohen, going from mayor of Bangor to Secretary of Defense by dint of hard work, independent thinking and personal courage.

But if you have read this book carefully, you know that these important political figures are only the beginning of the story. We concentrate on them but there are hundreds, even thousands of people who made it possible for them and others to run and win. If you care about politics or issues and you live in Maine, you can jump right in and influence things.

You do not need a lot of money to run for office in Maine. In fact, for every person who like Angus King has used his money successfully, numerous others—Dick Spencer, Linda Bean, Neil Rolde, Bob Monks, John Hathaway—have not done well. Essential name identification can be gotten other ways. You have to put in the time. You have to make the effort. You have to take time away from your family and other activities and make the sacrifices, but there is an openness to the Maine political scene to reward you if you do.

Both the Democratic and Republican Parties—to say nothing of the Greens and the Reform Parties—remain to this day very open to talent and hard work. Anyone who wants to get involved in Maine politics can be assured that there is a place for him, as a candidate and as an important supporter who can make a difference.

Think of the 238 people who ran for Congress, governor and U.S. Senate during the period under review. The vast, vast majority of them were citizen-politicians. They made their own way, took their ideas and carried them along. They made an impact on the political system. Think of the thousands who have helped elect them.

In my mind, there is no excuse for non-participation. This is a great time to get involved in Maine politics. There are many important things to do. Individuals can make an important statement and have a considerable impact on the political system even if they do not win primaries or general elections. They can impact the state by helping to pass ballot measures. They can impact the state by promoting causes. Individuals can literally create themselves.

Look at Jonathan Carter. Every time you see him on TV or at press conferences you can see just how much fun he is having. A few years ago, he was an obscure college professor with no following, no standing in the political structure and no money. He decided to run for Congress as a Green. He ran his own campaign and although he did not win, he did have an impact on the election, drawing enough Democratic votes to ensure that Olympia Snowe was re-elected and by getting 8.8% of the vote, enabling the Greens to run officially a candidate for governor in 1994.

In 1994, Carter ran for governor, this time getting only 6% of the vote statewide but helping to ensure that Angus King was elected governor by draining off Brennan votes in Portland, especially on Munjoy Hill, votes Brennan desperately needed to offset his poor showing in Lewiston. Carter actually got 10.6% in Portland overall and 14% in Munjoy Hill's 1-1 and 16% of Munjoy Hill's 1-2.

In 1996, Carter led the fight against clear-cutting and his ballot measure got 28%. Jonathan Carter, much to the chagrin of Democrats and others, simply made himself into a statewide figure, one who without being elected to anything has had considerable impact on the way the state elections have come out and setting an agenda for public debate. He entered politics on his own terms and he remains an activist both because he believes in his causes and because he gets enjoyment from his involvement. Nobody "groomed" him to play a political role. He jumped in and became an activist on his own. Love him or hate him, he's *sui generis*.

Or look at Mary Adams. What person ever got more enjoyment out of being in politics? A gadfly in the 1970's and 1980's, she worked with the "Freedom Fighters" and led the successful citizen-initiated referendum that repealed a controversial statewide property tax system in 1977. She is still going strong in the 1990's. Mary Adams ran for office in 1994, getting 8.7% of the vote in the Republican primary for governor and finishing sixth out of eight candidates but carrying the northern counties of Piscatiquis, Penobscot and Hancock.

Asked to lead the opposition to the Forest Compact of 1996 because of her considerable grass roots experience, she got tremendous public exposure for her ideas and appeared all across the state urging citizens to reject the Forest Compact. After the Compact got 47% of the vote in November, 1996, she formed Common Sense for Maine Forests and was off and running again, challenging Governor King and many in the forest products industry, this time in a most unusual non-alliance "alliance" making common purpose with Jonathan Carter to defeat the Compact.

Of course, she has been energized by her strong beliefs in local control, and her opposition to central state planning and her convictions give her strength to keep her going. But she obviously brings to politics a zest and enjoyment to her causes. When you see her on TV, she looks like she is having the time of her life, and politics is the reason. Remember, Mary Adams didn't wait to be asked by some party bigwig to get involved. She just saw a need and got involved and has stayed involved. Whether you agree or disagree with her positions, the political debate in Maine is richer for her activity and as a citizen activist, she shows what can be done.

After being fortunate enough to have been in Maine politics for 25 years, I feel even more strongly about the openness of the political system in this fine state. Remember the words of President Dwight D. Eisenhower, who said almost 50 years ago, "Politics ought to be the part-time profession of every citizen." Remember too the words of Thomas Jefferson: "The government is strongest of which every man feels himself a part." If you don't really participate, you can't really expect to be a part.

If you want to affect politics, get involved. Do something. You have no real excuses.

The political system of Maine is waiting for you. Maine politics is for everyone.

THE WARRIORS

....

Ad astra, per aspera.

(To the stars, through difficulties.)

....

Olympia Snowe (R) 9–0 (9G)	1.000
William Cohen (R) 7–0 (1P, 6G)	1.000
John McKernan (R) 6–0 (2P, 4G)	1.000
Edmund Muskie (D) 6–0 (6G)	1.000
Stanley Tupper (R) 5–0 (2P, 3G)	1.000
Charles Nelson (R) 5–0 (4G, 1P)	1.000
Frank Fellows (R) 3–0 (3G)	1.000
John Baldacci (D) 3–0 (1P, 2G)	1.000
Clinton Clauson (D) 2–0 (1P, 1G)	1.000
Angus King (I) 1–0 (1G)	1.000
James Longley Sr. (I) 1–0 (1G)	1.000
Robert Hale (R) 11–1 (Won 5P, 6G Lost 1G)	.916
Peter Kyros (D) 9–1 (Won 5P, 4G Lost 1G)	.900
Margaret Chase Smith (R) 9–1 (Won 4P, 5G Lost 1G)	.900
Clifford McIntire (R) 6–1 (Won 6G Lost 1G)	.857
Frederick Payne (R) 6–1 (Won 3P, 3G Lost 1G)	.857
Kenneth Curtis (D) 5–1 (Won 3P, 2G Lost 1G)	.833
William Hathaway (D) 7–2 (Won 2P, 5G Lost 2G)	.778
Thomas Andrews (D) 3–1 (Won 1P, 2G Lost 1G)	.750
Frank Coffin (D) 3–1 (Won 1P, 2G Lost 1G)	.750
Susan Collins (R) 3–1 (Won 2P,1G Lost 1G)	.750
George Mitchell (D) 3–1 (Won 1P, 2G Lost 1G)	.750
John Reed (R) 3–1 (Won 1P, 2G Lost 1G)	.750
David Emery (R) 5–2 (Won 1P, 4G Lost 2G)	.714

Joseph Brennan (D) 8–4 (Won 4P, 4G Lost 1P, 3G)	.667
Thomas Allen (D) 2–1 (Won 1P,1G Lost 1P)	.667
Burton Cross (R) 2–1 (Won 1P, 1G Lost 1G)	.667
James Longley Jr. (R) 2–1 (Won 1P, 1G Lost 1G)	.667
Horace Hildreth (R) 4–3 (Won 3P, 1G Lost 1P,2G)	.571
Frederick Barton (D) 1–1 (Won 1P Lost 1G)	.500
Richard Bennett (R) 1–1 (Won 1P Lost 1G)	.500
Owen Brewster (R) 1–1 (Won 1G Lost 1P)	.500
Richard Charette (D) 1–1 (Won 1P Lost 1G)	.500
John Donovan (D) 1–1 (Won 1P Lost 1G)	.500
James Dunleavy (D) 1–1 (Won 1P Lost 1G)	500
Dennis Dutremble (D) 1–1 (Won 1P Lost 1G)	.500
Markhan Gartley (D) 2–2 (Won 2P Lost 2G)	.500
Barry Hobbins (D) 1–1 (Won 1P Lost 1G)	.500
John Kerry (D) 1–1 (Won 1P Lost 1G)	.500
Louis Lausier (D) 1–1 (Won 1P Lost 1G)	.500
Kenneth MacLeod (R) 1–1 (Won 1P Lost 1G)	.500
John Maloney (D) 1–1 (Won 1P Lost 1G)	.500
Thomas Maynard (D,I) 1–1 (Won 1P, Lost 1G)	.500
James Oliver (D) 4–4 (Won 3P, 1G Lost 4G)	.500
Edward O'Meara (R) 1–1 (Won 1P Lost 1G)	.500
Linwood Palmer (R) 1–1 (Won 1P Lost 1G)	.500
L. Robert Porteous (R) 1–1 (Won 1P Lost 1G)	.500
John Quinn (D) 1–1 (Won 1P Lost 1G)	.500
James Reid (R) 1–1 (Won 1P Lost 1G)	.500
Ronald Speers (R) 1–1 (Won 1P Lost 1G)	.500
William Trafton (R) 1–1 (Won 1P Lost 1G)	.500
Elmer Violette (D) 2–2 (Won 2P Lost 2G)	.500
James Erwin (R) 2–3 (Won 2P Lost 1P, 2G)	.400
Peter Garland (R) 2–3 (Won 1P, 1G Lost 2P, 1G)	.400
Linda Bean/Bean-Jones (R) 1–2 (Won 1P Lost 1P, 1G)	.333
F. Davis Clark (D) 1–2 (Won 1P Lost 2G)	.333
Lucia Cormier (D) 1–2 (Won 1P Lost 2G)	.333
Charles Cragin (R) 1–2 (Won 1P Lost 1P, 1G)	.333
Maynard Dolloff (D) 1–2 (Won 1P Lost 1P, 1G)	.333
James McVicar (D) 1–2 (Won 1P Lost 2G)	.333
Robert Monks (R) 1–3 (Won 1P Lost 2P, 1G)	.333

James Tierney (D) 1–2 (Won 1P Lost 1P, 1G)   .333
Neil Bishop (R,I) 2–6 (Won 2P Lost 3P, 3G)   .250
Earl Grant (D) 1–3 (Won 1P Lost 1P, 2G)   .250
Roger Dube (D,True D) 1–4 (Won 1P Lost 2P, 2G)   .200
Leland Currier (D,I) 1–5 (Won 1P Lost 3P, 2G)   .166
Linda Abromson (D) 0–1 (1P)   .000
Andrew Adam (I) 0–1 (1G)   .000
Mary Adams (R) 0–1 (1P)   .000
Benjamin Arena (D) 0–1 (1G)   .000
David Ault (R) 0–1 (1P)   .000
Richard Barringer (D) 0–1 (1P)   .000
Clyde Bartlett (D) 0–1 (1P)   .000
Edward Beauchamp (D) 0–1 (1G)   .000
Severin Beliveau (D) 0–1 (1P)   .000
Georgette Berube (D) 0–1 (1P)   .000
Albion Beverage (R) 0–1 (1P)   .000
Gilbert Boucher (D) 0–1 (1P)   .000
Henry Boyker (I) 0–1 (1G)   .000
Ralph Brooks (R) 0–1 (1P)   .000
Chipman Bull (D) 0–1 (1G)   .000
David Bustin (D) 0–1 (1P)   .000
Pamela Cahill (R) 0–1 (1P)   .000
Richard Carey (D) 0–1 (1P)   .000
Donnell Carroll (D) 0–1 (1P)   .000
Everett Carson (D) 0–1 (1P)   .000
Mary Cathcart (D) 0–1 (1P)   .000
Dana Childs (D) 0–1 (1P)   .000
William Clarke (Tax) 0–1 (1G)   .000
John Coghill (D) 0–1 (1G)   .000
Maynard Connors (R) 0–1 (1G)   .000
Leighton Cooney (D) 0–1 (1G)   .000
Robert Cram (R) 0–1 (1P)   .000
George Curtis (R) 0–1 (1P)   .000
James Day (R) 0–1 (1P)   .000
Thomas Delahanty (D) 0–1 (1G)   .000
Henry Desmarais (D) 0–1 (1P)   .000
Richard Dubord (D) 0–1 (1P)   .000

Frank Dunton (R) 0–1 (1P) .000
Eben Elwell (D) 0–1 (1P) .000
Sean Faircloth (D) 0–1 (1P) .000
Charles Fitzgerald (I) 0–1 (1G) .000
John Fitzgerald (D) 0–1 (1G) .000
Howard Foley (R) 0–1 (1G) .000
Judith Foss (R) 0–1 (1P) .000
John Fortunato (D) 0–1 (1P) .000
Herman Frankland (I) 0–1 (1G) .000
Paul Fullam (D) 0–1 (1G) .000
Hayes Gahagan (I) 0–1 (1G) .000
Ernest Gallant (D) 0–1 (1P) .000
Eli Gaudet (D) 0–1 (1P) .000
James Glover (R) 0–1 (1P) .000
Albion Goodwin (D) 0–1 (1P) .000
Gerald Grady (D) 0–1 (1G) .000
David Graham (D) 0–1 (1P) .000
Calvin Grass (R) 0–1 (1P) .000
Hollis Greenlaw (R) 0–1 (1P) .000
Frederick Halla (R) 0–1 (1P) .000
Shawn Hallisey (D) 0–1 (1P) .000
Owen Hancock (D) 0–1 (1P) .000
Leith Hartman (Write-In) 0–1 (1G) .000
James Hathaway (R) 0–1 (1P) .000
Kenneth Hayes (D) 0–1 (1G) .000
James Henderson (D) 0–1 (1P) .000
James Howaniec (D) 0–1 (1P) .000
William Hughes (I) 0–1 (1G) .000
Leroy Hussey (R) 0–1 (1P) .000
H. Rollins Ives (R) 0–1 (1G) .000
John Jannace (I) 0–1 (1G) .000
Robert Jones (R) 0–1 (1P) .000
Jacqueline Kaye (I) 0–1 (1G) .000
John Keenan (D) 0–1 (1G) .000
Roland Kellam (D) 0–1 (1G) .000
Peter Kelley (D) 0–1 (1P) .000
Kevin Keogh (R) 0–1 (1P) .000

George Kittredge (R) 0–1 (1P) .000
Alexander LaFleur (R) 0–1 (1P) .000
Lloyd LaFountain (D) 0–1 (1P) .000
Oram Lawry (R) 0–1 (1P) .000
Stanley Leen (I) 0–1 (1G) .000
Porter Leighton (R) 0–1 (1P) .000
Jerald Leonard (D) 0–1 (1P) .000
Sumner Lipman (R) 0–1 (1P) .000
Ralph Lovell (R) 0–1 (1P) .000
Donald Lowery (D) 0–1 (1P) .000
Glenn MacNaughton (R) 0–1 (1P) .000
J. David Madigan (I) 0–1 (1G) .000
Louis Maisel (D) 0–1 (1P) .000
Guy Marcotte (D) 0–1 (1P) .000
Lewis Maxwell (D) 0–1 (1P) .000
J. Horace McClure (R) 0–1 (1P) .000
Dale McCormic (D) 0–1 (1P) .000
John McCormick (R) 0–1 (1P) .000
Peter McDonald (D) 0–1 (1G) .000
John Menario (I) 0–1 (1G) .000
Carlton Mendell (D) 0–1 (1P) .000
Gary Merrill (R) 0–1 (1P) .000
John Michael (I) 0–1 (1G) .000
Janet Mills (D) 0–1 (1P) .000
Jadine O'Brien (D) 0–1 (1P) .000
John O'Leary (D) 0–1 (1P) .000
Harold Pachios (D) 0–1 (1G) .000
Anthony Payne (R) 0–1 (1P) .000
James Perkins (R) 0–1 (1P) .000
Richard Pierce (R) 0–1 (1P) .000
John Purcell (R) 0–1 (1P) .000
Theodore Rand (R) 0–1 (1P) .000
Gunder Rasmussen (R) 0–1 (1P) .000
David Redmond (D) 0–1 (1P) .000
Carlton Reed (D) 0–1 (1P) .000
Bruce Reeves (D) 0–1 (1P) .000
John Rensenbrink (Green) 0–1 (1G) .000

Harrison Richardson (R) 0–1 (1P)	.000
John Rigazio (D) 0–1 (1P)	.000
David Roberts (D) 0–1 (1G)	.000
Frank Rodway (R) 0–1 (1P)	.000
Herman Sahagian (R) 0–1 (1P)	.000
Aldric Saucier (I) 0–1 (1G)	.000
Sumner Sewall (R) 0–1 (1P)	.000
Philip Sharpe (D) 0–1 (1G)	.000
Elden Shute (R) 0–1 (1G)	.000
Herbert Silsby (R) 0–1 (1P)	.000
Harold Silverman (D) 0–1 (1G)	.000
Roy Sinclair (R) 0–1 (1P)	.000
Stewart Smith (D) 0–1 (1P)	.000
Jerrold Speers (R) 0–1 (1P)	.000
Kenneth Stoddard (I) 0–1 (1G)	.000
Robert Stuart (R) 0–1 (1P)	.000
Charles Summers (R) 0–1 (1P)	.000
Wakine Tanous (R) 0–1 (1P)	.000
Bonnie Titcomb (D) 0–1 (1P)	.000
Cedric Thomas (R) 0–1 (1P)	.000
William Troubh (D) 0–1 (1P)	.000
George Varney (R) 0–1 (1P)	.000
William Veazie (R) 0–1 (1P)	.000
Robinson Verill (R) 0–1 (1P)	.000
Adam Walsh (D) 0–1 (1P)	.000
Charles Webster (R) 0–1 (1P)	.000
Frederick Whittaker (I) 0–1 (1G)	.000
Eldwin Wixson (R) 0–1 (1P)	.000
Robert Woodbury (D) 0–1 (1P)	.000
Clifton Young (R) 0–1 (1P)	.000
Paul Zendzian (D) 0–1 (1P)	.000
Stephen Zirnkilton (R) 0–1 (1P)	.000
Johnathan Carter (Green) 0–2 (2G)	.000
Philip Chapman (R) 0–2 (2P)	.000
A.M. Chiaravalloti (D) 0–2 (2P)	.000
Kenneth Colbath (D) 0–2 (2G)	.000
Ralph Conant (D) 0–2 (2P)	.000

Lucia Cormier (D) 0–2 (2G)	.000
G. William Diamond (D) 0–2 (2P)	.000
Roy Fernald (R) 0–2 (2P)	.000
Abbott Greene (R) 0–2 (2P)	.000
Jean Hay (D) 0–2 (2P)	.000
Sherry Huber (R,I) 0–2 (1P, 1G)	.000
Patrick McGowan (D) 0–2 (2G)	.000
Philip Merrill (D) 0–2 (2P)	.000
Elizabeth Mitchell (D) 0–2 (1P, 1G)	.000
James Mitchell (D) 0–2 (2P)	.000
Neil Rolde (D) 0–2 (1P, 1G)	.000
Elwin Sharpe (R,Write-In) 0–2 (2P)	.000
Jack Smith (D) 0–2 (2P)	.000
Richard Spencer (D) 0–2 (2P)	.000
Jasper Wyman (R) 0–2 (1P, 1G)	.000
Paul Young (R) 0–2 (1P, 1G)	.000
Ray Stetson (R) 0–3 (3P)	.000
Adrian Scolten (D) 0–4 (3P, 1G)	.000
Plato Truman (D, R, I) 0–7 (5P, 2G)	.000

General Election Winners and Losers

Olympia Snowe (R) 9–0	1.000
William Cohen (R) 6–0	1.000
Edmund Muskie (D) 6–0	1.000
John McKernan (R) 4–0	1.000
Charles Nelson (R) 4–0	1.000
Frank Fellows (R) 3–0	1.000
Stanley Tupper (R) 3–0	1.000
John Baldacci (D) 2–0	1.000
Thomas Allen (D) 1–0	1.000
Owen Brewster (R) 1–0	1.000
Clinton Clauson (D) 1–0	1.000
Angus King (I) 1–0	1.000
James Longley, Sr. (I) 1–0	1.000
Clifford McIntire (R) 6–1	.857
Robert Hale (R) 6–1	.857

Margaret Chase Smith (R) 5–1	.833
Peter Kyros (D) 4–1	.800
Frederick Payne (R) 3–1	.750
William Hathaway (D) 5–2	.714
Thomas Andrews (D) 2–1	.667
Frank Coffin (D) 2–1	.667
Ken Curtis (D) 2–1	.667
David Emery (R) 4–2	.667
George Mitchell (D) 2–1	.667
John Reed (R) 2–1	.667
Joseph Brennan (D) 4–3	.571
Susan Collins (R) 1–1	.500
Burton Cross (R) 1–1	.500
Peter Garland (R) 1–1	.500
James Longley, Jr. (R) 1–1	.500
Horace Hildreth (R) 1–2	.333
James Oliver (D) 1–4	.200
Andrew Adam (I) 0–1	.000
Benjamin Arena (D) 0–1	.000
Frederick Barton (D) 0–1	.000
Linda Bean (R) 0–1	.000
Edward Beauchamp (D) 0–1	.000
Richard Bennett (R) 0–1	.000
Henry Boyker (I) 0–1	.000
Chipman Bull (D) 0–1	.000
Richard Charette (D) 0–1	.000
William Clarke (Tax) 0–1	.000
John Coghill (D) 0–1	.000
Maynard Conners (R) 0–1	.000
Leighton Cooney (D) 0–1	.000
Charles Cragin (R) 0–1	.000
Thomas Delahanty (D) 0–1	.000
Maynard Dolloff (D) 0–1	.000
John Donovan (D) 0–1	.000
James Dunleavy (D) 0–1	.000
Dennis Dutremble (D) 0–1	.000
Charles Fitzgerald (I) 0–1	.000

John Fitzgerald (D) 0–1	.000
Howard Foley (R) 0–1	.000
Herman Frankland (I) 0–1	.000
Paul Fullam (D) 0–1	.000
Hayes Gahagan (I) 0–1	.000
Gerald Grady (D) 0–1	.000
Leith Hartman (Write-In) 0–1	.000
Kenneth Hayes (D) 0–1	.000
William Hughes (I) 0–1	.000
Barry Hobbins (D) 0–1	.000
Sherry Huber (R,I) 0–1	.000
H. Rollins Ives (R) 0–1	.000
John Jannace (I) 0–1	.000
Jacqueline Kaye (I) 0–1	.000
John Keenan (D) 0–1	.000
Roland Kellam (D) 0–1	.000
John Kerry (D) 0–1	.000
Louis Lausier (D) 0–1	.000
Stanley Leen (I) 0–1	.000
Kenneth MacLeod (R) 0–1	.000
J. David Madigan (I) 0–1	.000
John Maloney (D) 0–1	.000
Thomas Maynard (I) 0–1	.000
Peter McDonald (D) 0–1	.000
John Menario (I) 0–1	.000
John Michael (I) 0–1	.000
Elizabeth Mitchell (D) 0–1	.000
Robert Monks (R) 0–1	.000
Edward O'Meara (R) 0–1	.000
Harold Pachios (D) 0–1	.000
Linwood Palmer (R) 0–1	.000
L. Robert Porteous (R) 0–1	.000
John Quinn (D) 0–1	.000
James Reid (R) 0–1	.000
John Rensenbrink (Green) 0–1	.000
David Roberts (D) 0–1	.000
Neil Rolde (D) 0–1	.000

Aldric Saucier (I) 0–1	.000
Adrian Scolten (D) 0–1	.000
Philip Sharpe (D) 0–1	.000
Elden Shute (R) 0–1	.000
Harold Silverman (D) 0–1	.000
Ronald Speers (R) 0–1	.000
Kenneth Stoddard (I) 0–1	.000
James Tierney (D) 0–1	.000
William Trafton (R) 0–1	.000
Frederick Whittaker (I) 0–1	.000
Jasper Wyman (R) 0–1	.000
Lucia Cormier (D) 0–2	.000
Jonathan Carter (Green) 0–2	.000
F. Davis Clark (D) 0–2	.000
Kenneth Colbath (D) 0–2	.000
Leland Currier (D,I) 0–2	.000
Roger Dube (D,True D) 0–2	.000
James Erwin (R) 0–2	.000
Markhan Gartley (D) 0–2	.000
Earl Grant (D) 0–2	.000
Patrick McGowan (D) 0–2	.000
James McVicar (D) 0–2	.000
Plato Truman (I) 0–2	.000
Elmer Violette (D) 0–2	.000
Neil Bishop (R,I) 0–3	.000

ACKNOWLEDGMENTS

A very special thanks to those who, during the long process of thinking about politics and finally writing this book about Maine politics, contributed ideas, thoughts, reality checks, additions, corrections and even suggestions to eliminate material (strange as that may seem!). Many were inspiring with their knowledge of, and love for, Maine politics.

A special thanks also to all those who helped me learn about politics over the years and enabled me to form my portrait of political life and the various political subcultures. Among those who should be mentioned are:

Ken Curtis, Davey Redmond, Jonathan Carter, Joyce Searle-Tripp, Bob Millar, Fred Nutter, Pat McGowan, Tom Howard, Anna Lidman, Jack Linnell, John Cole, Carolyn Good, Jim Tierney, Umbreen Khalidi, Larry Benoit, Barbara Reinertsen, Peter Burr, Jim Betts, Sandra Potholm, Dan Levine, Anonymous I, Bob Tyrer, Amy Pritchard, Ben Katz, George Msibi, Barbara Kennelly, Lee Burnett, Allen Springer, Kathy Guerin, John Cleveland, Don Larrabee, Sobusa II, William Tolbert, Keith Brown, Makhosini Dlamini, Anonymous II, Jim Brunelle,

John Rensenbrink, Richard Morgan, Mason Morfit, Anonymous III, Dora Ann Mills, Bob Deis, Tom Allen, Don Bourassa, Roger Putnam, Dave Emery, Al Austin, Tony Corrado, Dick Ames, George Smith, Ursala Lapiere, George Mitchell, Dagmar Potholm Peterson, Florence Richardson, John Quinlan, Morris Boucher, Bill Cohen, Betty Angel, Joe Squillacote, Joe Cowie, Anonymous IV, Jay Hardy, Ed Muskie, George Campbell, Steve Campbell, M. C. Zerack, Margaret Chase Smith, Tom Davidson, Jim Bradley, Charlie Micoleau, Linda Hornbeck, Hal Pachios, Sandra Linehan, Peter Snowe, Jack Havey, Tom Hanrahan,

John Oliver, Steve Tremblay, Mert Henry, Phil Harriman, Dennis Austin, Dave Vail, Heather Potholm, Duke Dutremble, Liz Chapman, George Neavoll, Elaine Bickmore, Babe Dutremble, Angus King, Ted Curtis, Ken

McCloud, Stan Tupper, Jed Lyons, Tony Buxton, Eliot Richardson, Carey Mitchell, Severin Beliveau, Janet Mills, Dick Pierce, Kent Wommack, Julie L'Heureux, Mogan Wheeler, Greg Nadeau, Kay Rand, Sandy Maisel, Peter Mills, Tom Daffron, Al Dimon, Jane Williams, Dave Ring, John Christie, Toby Tighe, Sarah Cleaveland, Claire Quinlan, Dave Anderson, Jane Titcomb, Raymond Greenwood, Bob Porrelo, Barbara Bush, Marty Linsky, Jim Longley, Jr.,

Ezra Smith, Hatti Bickmore, John Woods, Brownie Carson, Linda Smith, Dave Dyer, Diane Dunn, Harry Richardson, John Howland, Harold Potholm, Carey Turoff, John Day, Anonymous V, Maria Fuentes, Zhou Zhu, Dale Ahern, Karin Day, Alex Gage, Art Pritchard, Andy Anderson, Bruce Eliot, Barry Hobbins, Joyce Brown, Nancy Johnson, Dave Kovenock, Evan Richert, Ken Krause, Karin Morley, Bob Dyke, Jill and Paul Franco, Erik Potholm, Paul Mills, Tom Andrews, Rich Bland, Bob Fisher, Pat Robinson, Dan Paradee, Neil Reisel, Ron Blaise, Olin Robison, Gary Bowne, Shep Lee, Jill Sendor, Cynthia Howland, Porter Leighton, George Erswell, Bill Young, Raj Sharma, Roy Greason, Skip Thurlow, Bonnie Grimm, Brian Clement, Carolyn Palombo Clement, Maya Ault, Sharon Forney,

Don Nicoll, Patty Ames, Olympia Snowe, Mal Leary, Ann Springer, Pat Eltman, Bob Loeb, Charles and Marlene Petersen, Peter Chalk, Dave Wright, John Baldacci, Lucille Burr, Marcia Weigle, Peter Choate, Art House, Ella Dagne Carlson, B. J. Johnson, Dave Kennedy, Bob Cott, Mary Adams, Karin Michaelson, Seth Kursman, Ann Ramsay, Nancy Clark, Dave Clough, Dale Hanington, Kathy Johnson, Carey Thurlow, Jeff Buttland, Bob Shepherd, Mary Mayhew, Judy Gleason, Wayne Brown, Dan Boxer, Peter O'Donnell, Pat Leask, Steve Clarkin, Bob Palombo, Roger Howell, Bruce Davis, Rob Williams, Dave Heller, Nancy Egan, Henrietta Page Crane, Chuck Kelley, Colin Powell, Tony Jackson, Charlie Moreshead, Jim Rioux, Harry Patten, Will Meacham, Dick Davies, Craig Cleaves, Amos Eno, Ed Youngblood, Chris Grennon, George Bernier, Wally Bunker, Alberta Gould, Bob Edwards,

Hal Gossilyn, Pat Peard, Alex Ray, Thalia Sklavonous, Ron Johnson, Wade Johnson, Jock McKernan, Mike Heath, Chuck Beitz, Karin Morley, Norm Temple, Rachel Bernier, Greg Douglas, Robin Lambert, Corey Johnson, Cam Niven, Dan Osgood, Greg Stevens, Sue Bridge, Stan Bennett, Wakine Tanous, Steve Ballard, Jack Benson, Will Robinson, Julie Parker McCahill, Gus Grant, Deb Quinlan, Bob Turner, Alan Brown, Georgette Berube, Gunner Hornbeck, Jim Erwin, Milly Monks, Doug Hodgkin, Holly Asselin, Pete Kovach, Marcel Bilodeau, Don Collins, Phil Merrill, Ariane Bailey, Joe Sewall, Mike Harkins, Lee Harrison, Ken Burrill, Bob Leason, Leslie Anderson, Roger Mallar, Dana Connors, Dave Huber, Christina Palombo, Duncan Stout, Lil Caron, Chris Duval, Carol Emery, Don Ring, Fred Steeper, Lynn Yanok,

Chuck Winner, Henretta Watson, Shirley Grace, Dennis Tompkins, Ed Dinan, Mark Gartley, Bill Webster, Bob Monks, Edie Smith, Lee Perry, Dan Payne, Frank Goodwin, Sam Collins, Otis Brown, Mort Morgan, Peter Kyros, John Hadden, Dick Barringer, Goose King, Dave Ott, Jim Harrington, Holly Rafkin, Dale Geary, Mike Hastings, "Sub" Ricker, Bonnie Washuk, Fran Malvadones, Dave Kerry, Fred Hill, Terry Meager, Ethan Wagner, Matt McWilliams, Sumner Ricker, Pat Collins, Harold Jones, Leslie Merrill, Jimmy Chute, Ev Petty, Kristin Dawn St. Peter, Pete Sims, Sandra Choate Faucher, Tex Ranger, Tex "Coop" Cooper, Laddy Widden, John Reed, Bill Whiteside, Paul Mandabach, Les Otten, Roger Williams,

Bill Hathaway, Carol Baudler, Walter Higgins, Feets Reagan, Charlie Cragin, Sherry Huber, Gordon Weil, Andrea Maker, Albie Yanok, Jamie Furth, Gordon Manuel, John Menario, Mark Lawrence, Jon Doyle, Jim Dodson, Gene McCarthy, Kay Widden, Jerry Plante, Dave Ault, Hoddy Hildreth, Bob Dole, Rett Stearns, V. Lance Tarrance, George Bush, Chris Lockwood, Glenda Ricker, Jean Yarbrough, Jacque McDermott, Ike Ricker, Steve Brown, Ginny Manuel, Walter Graff, Pete Callahan, Mary Small, Mary Herman, Clarke Canfield, John Holt, Dick Anderson,

Chuck Cianchette, Bruce Andrews, Jack Wyman, Manu Sabharwal, Charlie Bridge, Steve Clarkin, Scott Allen, Sherry Huber, Alan Caron, Ed Dinan, John Martin, Don Asselin, Tom Jones, Marty Hill, Lynda Kresge, Janet Martin, Caroline Brown, Sid Watson, Joshua T. Reitzes, Ed Pols, Bill Geohegan, Chris Church, Ernst Helmrich, Betty Riossi, Ann Milner, Nat Kendrick, Gerard Brault, Fran Quinn, Paul Hazelton, Eaton Leith, Dan Levine, Bill Whitesides, Nat Dane, Ann Miller, John Mederos, Tim Brown, Zeke McNeil, Pat Kemper, Nancy Perry, Dave Rawson, Leslie Madison, Judy Toranto, Cam Nevin, Martin McKenna, Marcia MacVane,

Neil Reisel, Bobbi Cavoanaugh, Mal Conary, Pat Cutillo, Ray Bordner, Annette Bonnanno, Phil Pasquale, Lousie Ballentine, Bob Mark, Bob

Menghi, Wally Kumpitsch, Pat Lenci, Marge Jennings, Fred Holt, Ken Hill, Judy Hoagland, Mike Barrett, Joe Gaffney, Barbara Gora, Antonette Vera, Larry Drew, Harlan Sturgis, Larry Scanlon, Butch Allen, John Troland, Joe Medeiros, Joe Heap, Maureen Looby, Mac MacDonald, Peter Makuck, Sabilia Palmer, Bob Rockholz, Eve McLoughlin,

Dorothy Page, Fidèle Mugavero, John Paganoni, Nancy Rice, Jeff Sheley, Joe San Juan, Bob Picazio, Henry Shay, Russ Harris, Carl Heintzleman, Malcolm Greenaway, Louise Lacy, Lewis Lake, Solomon Gordon, Diane Freeman, Judy Graham, Dick Groppelli, Gladys May, Nancy Sullivan, Mike Volgouse, Bill McNamara, Steve Botchis, Faith Damon, Jerry Davis, Jeane Faulkner, Bob Foley, John Balentine, Maura Sullivan, Bob Menghi, Marion Camillucci, JoAnn Cochrane, Mal Conary, Tom Farrell, Jeanette Filosi, John Flaherty,

Al Offstein, Jon Peterson, Rudy Ruedel, Charlie Smith, Trudie Sisson, Bill Rinoski, Roberta Ward, Betty Watson, Warren "Dog" Whitehouse, Gene Yuhas, Sharon Wright, Jean Ganoe, Tony Busca, Pete Benson, Wood Woodworth, Dick Stommer, Pricilla Wronowski, Judy Hartman, Laura Smith, Carol Rosene, Harriette Washton, Tom Henry, Loretta Britagna, Carol Villa, Steve Botschis and especially Chris Stearns.

I hope I didn't leave anyone out.

There really are a lot of outstanding people who truly care about their state and their country and the health of our political life and who enjoy the interplay which makes that subculture so interesting. And they know a lot about what really goes on behind the political headlines of the day. I appreciate all of their imput.

A special thanks also to all of my students, not just at Bowdoin but at Dartmouth and Vassar as well; their questions over the years have helped me immensely in understanding not only how politics works but also how it is perceived.

Finally, kudos should also go to the first-rate production and marketing team at Madison Books: Nancy Ulrich, Kerstin Vogdes, and Daphne Christie. My gratitude to Jed Lyons continues unabated.

INDEX

ABOUT THE AUTHOR

Christian P. Potholm is DeAlva Stanwood Alexander professor of government and legal studies at Bowdoin College where he teaches Understanding Maine Politics. He has also taught at Dartmouth and Vassar.

A Phi Beta Kappa graduate of Bowdoin, he is the author of a dozen books, including *Just Do It! Political Participation in the 1990's* and *American Politics: Dynamics of Choice and Directions of Change.* Professor Potholm has also worked on and behind the Maine political scene for three decades.

He was campaign manager for Bill Cohen in 1972 during his initial run for Congress and served as the consultant on consultants for Angus King in 1994. In between, his research firm, Command Research, tracked virtually every important political race in Maine, including both candidates and referenda. His inside knowledge of what has occurred in recent Maine political history is unsurpassed.

He was closely involved in the major campaigns that have impacted so many lives in recent Maine history, including Save Maine Yankee I and II in 1980 and 1982, the Elected PUC referendum of 1981, the Sunday Sales referendum of 1990, the 1983 Moose Hunt referendum, the 1996 and 1997 Forest Compact debates, the fights to widen the Maine Turnpike in 1991 and in 1997, the Gay Rights referendum of 1995, and the 1991 $35 Million Bond for Public Land Acquisition. In 1994 Citizens for Colin Powell chose him to poll in the New Hampshire primary.

For thirty years, he has spoken truth to power.